Prentice Hall
LITERATURE
Timeless Voices, Timeless Themes

Selection Support:
Skills Development
Workbook

D

COPPER LEVEL

Prentice
Hall

Upper Saddle River, New Jersey
Glenview, Illinois
Needham, Massachusetts

ISBN 0-13-054822-7

4 5 6 7 8 9 10   06 05 04 03

CONTENTS

UNIT 5: MYSTERIOUS WORLDS

UNIT 6: SHORT STORIES

UNIT 8: DRAMA

UNIT 9: POETRY

UNIT 10: THE ORAL TRADITION

Name _____ Date _____

"The Sound of Summer Running" by Ray Bradbury

Build Vocabulary

Using the Root: *meter*

Words that contain the root *meter* have something to do with measurement. A *barometer*, for example, is an instrument that measures changes in the pressure of the atmosphere.

A. Directions: Match each description in the left column with the correct word in the right column. Write the letter of the word on the line next to its description. Use the clues in parentheses for help.

_____ 1. an instrument that measures electric current

_____ 2. an instrument that measures the speed of the wind

_____ 3. an instrument that measures altitude

a. anemometer (found at a weather station)

b. altimeter (found in an airplane)

c. voltmeter (found in an electrician's toolbox)

Using the Word Bank

seized	suspended	loam	barometer
alien	limber	revelation	

B. Directions: Complete each sentence with a word from the Word Bank. Use each word only once.

1. We looked up at the model of the solar system that was _____ from the ceiling.

2. According to the _____, the air pressure had dropped only slightly since yesterday.

3. The little terrier had never seen a horse before, and he carefully studied the _____ creature before approaching it.

4. Because I had already guessed who the criminal was, the mystery story's ending did not come as a _____ to me.

5. These warm-up exercises are designed to help _____ the muscles and prevent injuries.

6. Just in time, Frannie _____ her little brother and prevented him from running into the street.

7. We admired the rich, fertile _____ in Mrs. Green's garden.

"The Sound of Summer Running" by Ray Bradbury

Build Spelling Skills: Words with *ie* and *ei*

Spelling Strategy A well-known rule states: "Use *i* before *e* except after *c* or when sounded as 'ay,' as in *neighbor* and *weigh*."

Examples of words that follow this rule include *believe*, *receive*, and *freight*. In *believe*, *i* comes before *e*. In *receive*, *e* comes before *i* because the two letters appear "after *c*." In *weigh*, *e* comes before *i* because the word is "sounded as 'ay.'"

Exceptions: The words *seized*, *either*, *leisure*, *weird*, *height*, and *protein* are exceptions to this rule. In all these words *e* comes before *i*, even though the letters do not follow *c* and are not sounded as "ay."

A. Practice: Choose the correctly spelled word to complete each sentence. Write the word on the line. Hint: The words below follow the i-before-e rule unless they are noted in the list of exceptions. You can use a dictionary to check your spellings.

1. We were invited to go camping, and we (siezed, seized) _____ the opportunity to enjoy the fresh mountain air.

2. I (recieved, received) _____ the package of supplies that you sent.

3. My (nieghbors, neighbors) _____, the Robinsons, enjoy birdwatching.

4. They go on field trips whenever they have some (liesure, leisure) _____ time.

5. This (peice, piece) _____ of cake is delicious.

6. I (believe, beleive) _____ that it is made with coconut.

7. The (frieght, freight) _____ company needs you to fill out this form.

8. Do you know the width, (hieght, height) _____, and (wieght, weight) _____ of the package?

B. Practice: Complete the paragraph by choosing the appropriate words from the box and writing them on the lines. Use each word once.

seized	perceive	conceives	believe

In "The Sound of Summer Running," Douglas _____ of a clever way to get a pair of Royal Crown Cream-Sponge Para Litefoot Tennis Shoes even though he doesn't have quite enough money to pay for them. He offers to run errands for Mr. Sanderson, the store owner, in order to make up for the dollar that he would owe for the shoes. First, however, Douglas must convince Mr. Sanderson to _____ in him and his plan. To do so, Douglas persuades Mr. Sanderson to try on a pair of the sneakers himself. With the help of Douglas's amazingly vivid descriptions, the middle-aged man is able to _____ the special qualities of the shoes and the reasons the boy wants them so badly. In fact, for a few moments, he is _____ with memories of what it is like to be Douglas's age and put on a brand new pair of sneakers.

"The Sound of Summer Running" by Ray Bradbury

Build Grammar Skills: Nouns

Look around. Name some of the sights that you see. The words that you will use are nouns. **Nouns** are words that name people, places, and things.

Now read the following sentences from Ray Bradbury's story. The nouns appear in italics.

Here *Douglas* stood, trapped on the dead *cement* and the red-*brick streets*, hardly able to move.

The *boy* looked down at his *feet* deep in the *rivers*, in the *fields* of *wheat*, in the *wind* that already was rushing him out of the *town*.

A. Practice: Identify the nouns in the following sentences. Write the nouns on the lines provided.

1. Douglas was coming back from a movie with his family.

   _____

2. The boy saw a fantastic pair of sneakers in a brightly lit window.

   _____

3. Douglas shared his thoughts and wishes with his father.

   _____

4. Douglas tried to describe how it felt to lace up a new pair of sneakers on one of the first days of summer and then go running through the neighborhood, feeling as if you could jump over fences, sidewalks, and dogs.

   _____

5. Mr. Spaulding advised his son to save up his money.

   _____

B. Writing Application: Write a sentence about each topic provided below, using the noun or nouns given. When you are finished, reread your sentences and underline any additional nouns that you used.

1. Write a sentence about the author, using the noun *Ray Bradbury*.

   _____

2. Write a sentence about the story's main character, using the nouns *Douglas* and *sneakers*.

   _____

3. Write a sentence about a hot day, using the nouns *sidewalk*, and *grass*.

   _____

4. Write a sentence about your favorite pair of shoes, using the nouns *shoes* and *feet*.

   _____

5. Write a sentence about "The Sound of Summer Running," using the nouns *story*, *sneakers*, *summer*, and *magic*.

   _____

"The Sound of Summer Running" by Ray Bradbury

Reading Strategy: Reading Fluently

Long, complicated sentences sometimes contain too much information to take in all at once. They can be difficult to read, especially aloud, and can be hard to figure out. In "The Sound of Summer Running," Ray Bradbury often uses long sentences to express Douglas's breathless excitement about new sneakers. To help you read these sentences fluently, and determine their meaning, you can use a simple strategy: **read phrase by phrase rather than word by word.** Study this example, in which Douglas tries to explain what a new pair of sneakers feels like when he first puts them on. Each time you see a *caret* (^), pause briefly.

> They felt ^ like it feels ^ sticking your feet ^ out of the hot covers ^ in wintertime ^ to let the cold wind ^ from the open window ^ blow on them suddenly ^ and you let them stay out ^ a long time ^ until you pull them back in ^ under the covers again ^ to feel them, ^ like packed snow.

The carets mark "word chunks" or phrases that are more easily understood when looked at alone. Then, once you determine the meaning of separate phrases, you will be able to read fluently and with understanding when the phrases are together again as a sentence. If you learn to break up long sentences in this way, you will find it a lot easier to understand them. There is no "right" size to a phrase; break the sentence down enough to make it easy to read clearly and smoothly. Though Bradbury sometimes runs phrases together for effect, in most long sentences, you will have punctuation marks, such as commas and semicolons, or conjunctions (connecting words such as *and* or *but*) to help you determine where pauses go. Breaking a sentence into phrases like this also more nearly matches how you speak, and therefore helps a listener understand the meaning if you are reading aloud.

A. Practice: Use carets (^) to mark phrases that are easier to read and more easily understood, so that the whole sentence below makes sense when you read the phrases joined together.

> Well, he felt sorry for boys who lived in California where they wore tennis shoes all year and
>
> never knew what it was to get winter off your feet, peel off the iron leather shoes all full of
>
> snow and rain and run barefoot for a day and then lace on the first new tennis shoes of the
>
> season, which was better than barefoot.

B. Practice: Read the following passage to yourself two or three times, pausing briefly at the end of each "word chunk." Then, when you think you understand the passage and can communicate its meaning to others, try reading it aloud as your teacher instructs. *Hint: In all but the last sentence, the punctuation will help you. Pause briefly at commas and end punctuation.* Feel free to mark the last sentence with carets if you wish.

> "Bang! I deliver your packages, pick up packages, bring you coffee, burn your trash, run to
>
> the post office, telegraph office, library! You'll see twelve of me in and out, in and out, every
>
> minute. Feel those shoes, Mr. Sanderson, *feel* how fast they'd take me? All those springs in-
>
> side? Feel how they kind of grab hold and can't let you alone and don't like you just *stand-*
>
> *ing there?*"

"The Sound of Summer Running" by Ray Bradbury

Literary Analysis: Characters' Motives

To understand the characters in a story, you must understand the **characters' motives**—the reasons for their actions and behavior. Early on in "The Sound of Summer Running," Ray Bradbury lets readers know about the factors that drive the behavior of the main character, Douglas Spaulding. Look at these excerpts from the story:

Late that night, going home from the show with his mother and father and his brother Tom, Douglas saw the tennis shoes in the bright store window. He glanced quickly away, but his ankles were seized, his feet suspended, then rushed. The earth spun; the shop awnings slammed their canvas wings overhead with the thrust of his body running. His mother and father and brother walked quietly on both sides of him. Douglas walked backward, watching the tennis shoes in the midnight window left behind.

"Dad!" He blurted it out. "Back there in that window, those Cream-Sponge Para Litefoot Shoes . . ."

His father didn't even turn. "Suppose you tell me why you need a new pair of sneakers. Can you do that?"

These passages, along with others in the story, clearly reveal the motive for Douglas's actions in the story: He wants the new sneakers.

A. DIRECTIONS: Read the following passage. Then explain what it reveals about Mr. Sanderson's motive or motives. Write your answer on the lines below.

The boy . . . spun about with a whisper and went off. The door stood empty. The sound of the tennis shoes faded in the jungle heat.

Mr. Sanderson stood in the sun-blazed door, listening. From a long time ago, when he dreamed as a boy, he remembered the sound. Beautiful creatures leaping under the sky, gone through brush, under trees, away, and only the soft echo their running left behind.

"Antelopes," said Mr. Sanderson. "Gazelles."

_____

_____

_____

B. DIRECTIONS: Motives cause characters to act in a certain way. Use the lines below to name two actions that result from the characters' motives. Identify at least one action that Douglas takes and at least one action that Mr. Sanderson takes.

Douglas:_____

_____

Mr. Sanderson: _____

_____

"Stray" by Cynthia Rylant

Build Vocabulary

Using the Suffix -ly

Writers add the suffix -ly to a word when they want the word to describe how or in what way an action happens. For example, in the sentence, "Dennis jumped up suddenly," the word *suddenly* means *in a sudden way.* It tells how, or in what way, Dennis jumped up. Words that end in the suffix -ly can bring a sentence to life by telling more about the action.

A. DIRECTIONS: Add -ly to the following words; then use the newly formed words to complete each sentence below. Each word will be used only once.

furious   sad   contented   quick

1. Josh finished the test more _____ than anyone else.

2. Jenny stared in silent terror as the huge dog barked_____ .

3. Jamie opened the cage door, but the bird sat and chirped_____ on its perch.

4. Alana stared _____ out the window, watching the raindrops fall.

Using the Word Bank

timidly	trudged	ignore	grudgingly	exhausted

B. DIRECTIONS: In each sentence, replace the word or words in italics with a word from the Word Bank. Write your words in the space provided.

1. He was told to share his candy, but he did it *unwillingly.* _____

2. The Scout troop had hiked for ten miles and felt *tired.* _____

3. If you *pay no attention to* the instructions, you will find it hard to put together the model

   plane. _____

4. The boy opened the door and peered *fearfully* inside, hoping that he had not come to the wrong house. _____

5. With a sigh, the man picked up the heavy suitcase and *walked with difficulty* down the long hallway toward the parking lot. _____

Recognizing Synonyms

C. DIRECTIONS: For each of the words in CAPITAL LETTERS, circle the letter of the word or phrase that is most nearly the same in meaning.

1. GRUDGINGLY
   a. happily
   b. resentfully
   c. pleasantly
   d. eagerly

2. EXHAUSTED
   a. grateful
   b. nervous
   c. weary
   d. hungry

3. TRUDGE
   a. march
   b. work
   c. wish
   d. run

Name _____ Date _____

"Stray" by Cynthia Rylant

Build Spelling Skills: Words That End in the "j" Sound

Spelling Strategy When a word, sounds like it ends with the letter *j*, it is actually spelled with the letters -*ge* as in *seige* or -*dge* as in *trudge*.

A. Practice: Fill in the blank in each sentence below with a word that ends with a "j" sound. The first sentence has been filled in as an example. You may use a dictionary to check your spelling.

1. It is better to forgive a friend than to hold a _____grudge_____.

2. Actors in the theater perform on a platform called a _____.

3. When people want to get across the river, they can walk across the _____.

4. Someone had torn out the last _____ of the book, so we never found out how it ended.

5. I grabbed a _____ to soak up the spilled water.

6. The driver stopped the car just before it went over the _____ of the cliff.

B. Practice: In the following paragraph, the missing words end with the "j" sound. Each one should be spelled with the letters *ge* at the end. Write each missing word in the space provided. The first space has been filled in as an example.

When Doris found the puppy, she did not know its _____age_____, but guessed

that it was about six months old. Mr. Lacey earned a _____ that was too

low to be able to afford a pet. Even though her parents said she could not keep the pup, Doris

hoped that they would _____ their minds. However, when Mr. Lacy saw

how the dogs were kept at the pound, with ten locked in each _____, he

took the puppy back home.

Challenge: In the story, Doris finds a puppy. The word *puppy*, as you know, means a young dog. Many special words for young animals, such as *puppy*, do not sound like the word for the adult animal. Examples of such words are *colt*, meaning "young horse," and *faun*, meaning "young deer." Other words for young animals, however, sound similar to the words for the adult animals; for example, *chick / chicken*, and *duckling / duck*. In the spaces provided, write the word for the young animal on the right that goes with the name of the adult animal on the left. You may have to use a dictionary to look up some of the young-animal words.

	Adult Animals	**Young Animals**
1. _____	swan	calf
2. _____	bird	fledgling
3. _____	goose	piglet
4. _____	elephant	gosling
5. _____	pig	cygnet

"Stray" by Cynthia Rylant

Build Grammar Skills: Compound Nouns

Some nouns (words naming people, places, or things) are made up of two or more words. These are called **compound nouns.** These nouns can be spelled as single words, as hyphenated words, or as two or more separate words.

Examples: **Single word:** cinderblock
Hyphenated word: ten-year-old
Two words: sweet potato

A. Practice: In each sentence below, underline the compound noun or nouns. Look for a single word, a hyphenated word, or two words.

1. Doris was holding a snow shovel when she first saw the puppy.

2. Mr. Lacey was cleaning his fingernails with his pocketknife.

3. The snow was keeping him home from his job at the warehouse.

4. The puppy was big for a six-month-old.

5. Mrs. Lacey looked into the room from the doorway.

B. Writing Application: Rewrite each sentence below, including a compound noun formed from the word *dog* plus the word in parentheses. If you are not sure whether a compound noun should be written as a single word or as separate words, use a dictionary to find out.

1. Doris gave her puppy a _____ as a treat. (biscuit)

_____

_____

2. She saved up to buy the puppy a _____ to wear. (collar)

_____

_____

3. She attached a _____ to the puppy's collar. (tag)

_____

_____

4. Doris's father built a _____ in the yard. (house)

_____

_____

5. The family thought the puppy might make a good _____, because it barked at an approaching stranger. (watch)

_____

_____

Name _____ Date _____

"Stray" by Cynthia Rylant

Reading Strategy: Distinguishing Shades of Meaning

Shades of meaning are the differences in ideas, images, or emotions created by different words that mean almost the same thing. For example, *whimper, sob,* and *weep* are all slightly different ways of expressing the word *cry.* But *whimper* implies many small, quiet cries. *Sob,* in contrast, suggests louder, more heartrending outbursts of sorrow. *Weep* suggests prolonged misery and abundant tears.

Writers use these shades of meaning to communicate more than just the facts. They search for terms that describe the exact sense of an experience. That is, they want readers to get a vivid picture of a situation and to understand the emotions and feelings that accompany it. Read this sentence from the short story "Stray."

> Icicles hung three feet or more from the eaves of houses, snowdrifts swallowed up automobiles and the birds were so fluffed up they looked comic.

The story's author wanted readers to understand the effect of the recent snowfall in the town where the Laceys live. She could have written that the snow was *deep,* or *heavy,* or that it was impossible for people to get around. Yet, by writing that snowdrifts *swallowed up* automobiles, she knew that readers would picture a monster that devoured everything in its path—exactly the shade of meaning she intended.

DIRECTIONS: For each item below, explain briefly why the word the writer used expresses the most accurate shade of meaning for each situation. The first one is done for you.

1. The puppy had been *abandoned.* Why does *abandoned* have a more accurate shade of meaning than *left behind?*

    An owner might forget and "leave behind" a lamp or a chair when moving away, but not a

    puppy. "Abandoned" suggests that the owner dumped or discarded the puppy on purpose

    without caring about what would happen to it.

2. Doris *trudged* through the deep snow that covered the yard. Why is *trudged* a more precise word than *walked?*

    _____

    _____

    _____

3. When Mr. Lacey takes the puppy to the pound, Doris dreams that she is *searching* for things lost. Why does *searching* express a more exact shade of meaning than *looking?*

    _____

    _____

    _____

4. Later that afternoon Doris wakes up *exhausted.* Why does *exhausted* express a more accurate shade of meaning than *tired?*

    _____

    _____

    _____

"Stray" by Cynthia Rylant

Literary Analysis: Surprise Ending

A **surprise ending** to a story startles readers because it is not the ending they would have predicted. For a surprise ending to be effective, the author must trick readers by making them expect the story to end differently. In "The Stray," the author starts giving misleading clues about the story's outcome from the moment Mr. Lacey first sees the puppy.

"I don't know where it came from," he said mildly, "but I know for sure where it's going."

Shortly afterward, readers discover that Mr. Lacey plans to take the puppy to the pound. Further clues build up the reader's belief that Doris will not be allowed to keep the dog. The author does not reveal the happy surprise until very late in the story.

DIRECTIONS: In the space provided, explain why each of the following clues from the story makes the reader expect the ending to be sad for Doris and her puppy, rather than happy.

1. When Mrs. Lacey sees the puppy for the first time, she says, "Where did *that* come from?"

   _____

   _____

2. Mrs. Lacey allows Doris to feed the puppy table scraps only because she "was sensitive about throwing out food."

   _____

   _____

   _____

3. Even after a week had gone by, Doris didn't name the dog.

   _____

   _____

4. At dinner, Doris says: "She's a good dog, isn't she?" and "She's not much trouble. I like her," and, finally, "I figure she's real smart. I could teach her things." Her parents remain silent.

   _____

   _____

   _____

5. When Doris gets hungry for dinner, she doesn't want to go into the kitchen or past the basement door.

   _____

   _____

   _____

6. When Doris enters the kitchen, neither of her parents speaks to her, at first.

   _____

   _____

"**Dust of Snow**" by Robert Frost
"**My Picture-Gallery**" by Walt Whitman
"**Saying Yes**" by Diana Chang

Build Vocabulary

Homophones

The words *rued* and *rude* are homophones. So are the words *to*, *two*, and *too*. **Homophones** are words that sound alike but have different meanings. These similar-sounding words often have different spellings.

A. DIRECTIONS: Choose the correct homophone from Column A to complete each sentence in Column B. Write the word on the line.

A

won
one

B

1. There is only _____ correct answer to this question.

2. Do you know who _____ the song-writing contest?

rain
reign

3. The _____ and sleet went on for days.

4. The _____ of King Louis XIV of France lasted for 72 years.

so
sew
sow

5. The time to _____ these seeds is after the last frost.

6. The skaters decided to _____ their own costumes.

7. I was _____ tired that I fell asleep instantly.

Using the Word Bank

suspended	tableaus	rued

B. DIRECTIONS: Answer each of the following questions to demonstrate your understanding of the Work Bank words. Circle the letter of your choice.

1. Which of the following situations might someone have rued?

   a. He or she won the lottery.   b. He or she hurt another person's feelings.

2. Which of the following is an example of a suspended object?

   a. a crystal chandlier hanging in a ballroom   b. an antenna attached to a roof

3. Which of the following could be called tableaus?

   a. pictures of people dining, strolling, and dancing   b. heavy pieces of furniture

C. DIRECTIONS: Circle the letter of word or phrase that is closest in meaning to the Word Bank word.

1. TABLEAUS a. tables b. ovals c. scenes d. jewels

2. SUSPENDED a. propped b. hung c. broken d. erased

Name _____ Date _____

"**Dust of Snow**" by Robert Frost
"**My Picture-Gallery**" by Walt Whitman
"**Saying Yes**" by Diana Chang

Build Spelling Skills: Adding Suffixes and Verb Tense Endings to Words Ending in *ue*

Spelling Strategy Whenever you add a suffix or verb-tense ending to words ending in *ue*, drop the *e* if the ending to be added starts with a vowel.

Examples: glue + -ed = glued   true + -er = truer   rue + -ed = rued

             glue + -ing = gluing   true + -est = truest   rue + -ing = ruing

A. Practice: Add the suffix indicated at the top of each column to the words at the left. Write the new words on the lines.

	-ed		*-ing*
cue	_____		_____
issue	_____		_____
argue	_____		_____
	-er		*-est*
blue	_____		_____

B. Practice: Complete the sentences by adding the indicated ending or suffix to each given word. Write the new words on the lines provided.

1. In "Dust of Snow," a crow (rescue +ed) _____ the speaker from his unhappy mood.

2. In "Say Yes," a series of questions is (cue + ing) _____ the speaker to reveal her thoughts about her heritage and identity.

3. In "My Picture-Gallery," Walt Whitman uses suprising images to create a (true + -er) _____ and more imaginative view of reality.

4. Poets sometimes enjoy (issue +ing) _____ challenges to their readers.

5. People have even (argue +ed) _____ about the meanings of poems.

Challenge: In "My Picture-Gallery," Whitman says that his gallery is full of "tableaus of life." The word *tableaus*, which means "dramatic scenes or pictures," comes from French. Another word that is French and whose ending has a similar spelling and pronunciation is *bureau*, meaning "a chest of drawers" or "a department or agency that performs a service."

On the lines below, write a sentence for the word *tableau*. Then write two sentences showing the two different meanings of *bureau*.

1. tableaus (pictures): _____

2. bureau (chest of drawers): _____

3. bureau (department or agency): _____

"Dust of Snow" by Robert Frost
"My Picture-Gallery" by Walt Whitman
"Saying Yes" by Diana Chang

Build Grammar Skills: Common and Proper Nouns

Nouns may be either common or proper. A **common noun** is a general name for any one of a group of people, places, or things. A **proper noun** names a particular person, place, or thing. A proper noun always begins with a capital letter. *Do not confuse a proper noun with a common noun that is capitalized because it is the first word of a sentence.*

Examples:	**Common Nouns**	**Proper Nouns**
	girl	Beth
	teacher	Mrs. Cramer
	state	Connecticut
	museum	Metropolitan Museum Art
	dog	Fido
	poem	"Dust of Snow"

A. Practice: In the sentences, underline common nouns once and proper nouns twice.

1. Diana Chang writes of a heritage with roots in both China and the United States.

2. She knows that she is an American but also knows that this is only part of her identity.

3. Her poem "Saying Yes" acknowledges both worlds.

4. The poet Walt Whitman grew up in Brooklyn, New York.

5. His first book, "Leaves of Grass," had a huge impact on poetry in America.

6. Robert Frost won the Pulitzer Prize for poetry four times.

B. Writing Application: Rewrite each sentence below. Correct any errors of capitalization, making certain that proper nouns are capitalized and common nouns are not.

1. Where is the Gallery of which walt whitman speaks in his poem?

_____

_____

2. Might robert frost have been a Lover of birds?

_____

_____

3. Having lived in new england for years, frost was well acquainted with Snow.

_____

_____

4. Perhaps the Poet was speaking of the Power of nature to change one's outlook.

_____

_____

5. A poet from louisiana or texas would probably have described a very different Scene.

_____

_____

"Dust of Snow" by Robert Frost
"My Picture-Gallery" by Walt Whitman
"Saying Yes" by Diana Chang

Reading Strategy: Rereading to Clarify

You may sometimes find it helpful to reread a phrase, sentence, or passage to clarify an author's meaning. Doing so can help you identify a significant detail or make connections between ideas.

Read and reread these opening lines from "Saying Yes."

"Are you Chinese?"
"Yes."

"American?"
"Yes."

"Really Chinese?"
"No. . . not quite."

"Really American?"
"Well, actually, you see . . ."

Did you note that the speaker is both Chinese and American the first time around? Did you realize that she is beginning to express the complexity of her personal identify as you reread? These are some of the ideas that may have occurred to you as you read and then reread.

DIRECTIONS: Answer the following questions, rereading as indicated.

1. Diana Chang ends her poem with the words "I'd rather say it / twice / yes." Reread the first four lines above. To what is the speaker saying "yes"? What do you think the deeper meaning of saying "yes" twice is?

   _____

   _____

2. Below is the opening line from "My Picture-Gallery." Consider your responses to the two statements within it. What do you picture when you read the first statement? How does your response to the second statement prepare you for the rest of the poem?

   In a little house keep I pictures suspended, it is not a fix'd house . . .

   _____

   _____

3. In the first half of "Dust of Snow," the speaker describes how a crow shook some snow onto him. In the second half, he describes how this action affected him. According to the speaker, the action

   Has given my heart / A change of mood / And saved some part / Of a day I had rued.

   Reread these lines several times. Then think about whether Frost's use of rhyme and rhythm is appropriate to the meaning of the poem. Why or why not?

   _____

   _____

Name _____ Date _____

"**Dust of Snow**" by Robert Frost
"**My Picture-Gallery**" by Walt Whitman
"**Saying Yes**" by Diana Chang

Literary Analysis: Images in Poetry

Poets use **images**, words that appeal to the senses, to vividly re-create scenes and experiences. For example, the image of a hemlock tree in Robert Frost's "Dust of Snow" helps you see and smell a fresh outdoor scene on a winter day. Through imagery, poets also help readers understand the messages they are trying to communicate. Each image has its own special meaning within the poem.

The chart below shows how the image of the hemlock tree adds to the overall meaning of "Dust of Snow." Use this chart to explore other images in Frost's poem and in Walt Whitman's "My Picture-Gallery."

DIRECTIONS: For each image, note the senses that are involved. Then write a sentence or two about how the image helps you understand the meaning of the poem. The first one has been done as an example.

"Dust of Snow"		
Image	**Senses**	**Meaning in Poem**
1. Hemlock tree	sight, smell	This image suggests crispness and cheerfulness. It also suggests that nature has a refreshing quality.
2. Crow shaking snow onto speaker		

"My Picture-Gallery"		
Image	**Senses**	**Meaning in Poem**
3. A little house in which pictures are suspended		
4. A little house that is "not fix'd," round, only a few inches across, and can hold unlimited "shows" and memories		

Name _____ Date _____

"Jeremiah's Song" by Walter Dean Myers

Build Vocabulary

Using the Prefix: *dis-*

The prefix *dis-* means "the opposite of." When the prefix *dis-* is added to the beginning of a word, the new word means the opposite of the base word. For example, someone with a pleasant personality can be described as *agreeable*. A person who is not pleasant is *disagreeable*.

A. DIRECTIONS: Add the prefix *dis-* to each of the words below and write a sentence that uses the new word in the space provided. The first word has been done as an example.

	New Word	**Sentence**
1. pleased	displeased	The displeased customer asked for his money back.
2. order	_____	_____
3. approve	_____	_____
4. obey	_____	_____
5. organized	_____	_____
6. like	_____	_____

Using Words from the Selection

The words *diagnosis* and *disinfect* are defined for you in the selection. Here are definitions of two other words from the selection.

condition a state of health or physical fitness
setback a stopping of progress; a reversal

B. DIRECTIONS: Fill in the blanks with the word that best completes the sentence.

1. Grandpa was not well, but the family hoped that his _____ would improve.

2. Dr. Crawford had already made his _____ of Grandpa's health.

3. Ellie used bleach to _____ Grandpa's room.

4. In spite of help from family and friends, Grandpa suffered a _____ in August.

Analogies

C. DIRECTIONS: Each item consists of a related pair of words in CAPITAL LETTERS, followed by four lettered pairs of words. Circle the letter of the pair that best expresses a relationship similar to the one expressed in the pair in capital letters.

1. DISINFECT : GERMS ::
   a. broken : toy
   b. jump : pounce
   c. douse : fire
   d. hour : minute

2. SETBACK : WORRIED ::
   a. progress : encouraged
   b. flu : virus
   c. question : answer
   d. happy : cheerful

16 Selection Support © Prentice-Hall, Inc.

"**Jeremiah's Song**" by Walter Dean Myers

Build Spelling Skills: Adding *dis-*

Spelling Strategy A prefix never changes the spelling of the word, even when the word begins with a vowel.

Examples: *dis- + qualified = disqualified*

   dis- + organized = disorganized

A. Practice: Add the prefix *dis* to each word. Write the new word on the line.

1. *dis- + appear*   _____

2. *dis- + similar*   _____

3. *dis- + like*   _____

4. *dis- + approve*   _____

5. *dis- + respect*   _____

6. *dis- + honest* _____

7. *dis- + connect* _____

8. *dis- + satisfied* _____

9. *dis- + belief* _____

10. *dis- + contented* _____

B. Practice: Complete the sentences below by adding the prefix *dis-* to each given word and writing each new word on the line.

1. Ellie (trusts) _____ Dr. Crawford's diagnosis.

2. Grandpa Jeremiah's stroke has caused a (ability) _____ that prevents him from doing chores on the farm.

3. In spite of his (comfort), _____ Grandpa is still able to tell his stories.

4. Macon values the stories and does not (courage) _____ Grandpa Jeremiah.

5. Ellie (agrees) _____ about the importance of these stories.

Challenge: In the story, Dr. Crawford makes a *diagnosis* of Jeremiah's illness. The word *diagnosis* is formed from the prefix *dia-* and the ancient Greek word *gnosis*. One meaning for the prefix *dia-* is *completeness* or *thoroughness. Gnosis* means *knowledge.* Dr. Crawford's complete knowledge of Jeremiah's condition enables him to tell exactly what is wrong with him; that is, to make a *diagnosis.* Another medical term the author could have used in the selection is *prognosis.* The Greek prefix *pro-* means *before* or *beforehand.* When the doctor says that Jeremiah probably will not live long, he is making a *prognosis;* that is, a prediction, telling what will happen before it actually does happen. Many English words are based on one or more Greek words. Below is a list of words derived from Greek. The Greek words and their meanings are in parentheses. In the space next to each word, write the letter of the correct definition from the list of definitions on the right.

_____ 1. biology (*bio* = life; *logy* = scientific study)

_____ 2. tyrant (*tyrannos* = king)

_____ 3. pharmacy (*pharmakon* = drug)

_____ 4. philanthropist (*philos* = love; *anthropos* = human being)

a. powerful ruler

b. person who helps others

c. the study of animals

d. drugstore

"Jeremiah's Song" by Walter Dean Myers

Build Grammar Skills: Pronouns

A **pronoun** is a word that takes the place of a noun. The noun that is replaced by the pronoun is called an *antecedent*. For example, in "Jeremiah likes summer. It is his favorite season." *His* is a pronoun replacing your *Jeremiah*, and *it* is a pronoun replacing *summer*. The most common pronouns are listed below.

Personal pronouns: pronouns that refer to the person speaking or writing (first person), to the person spoken or written to (second person), or to the person, place, or thing being spoken or written about.

> First person pronouns: *I, me, my mine, we, us, our, ours*
> Second person pronouns: *you, your, yours*
> Third person pronouns: *he, him, she, her, it, they, them, theirs*

Interrogative pronouns: pronouns that introduce questions. The five interrogative pronouns are *what, which, who, whom,* and *whose*.

Indefinite pronouns: pronouns that refer to people, places, and things, often without specifying which ones. Indefinite pronouns include such words as *all, both, few, no one, another, each, anyone, everyone, everything, anything, little, much, none, nothing, others, some, somebody,* and *several*. As you can see, these pronouns do not show a definite number (some, many, few) or definite person, place, or thing (someone, anything), which is why they are called indefinite.

A. Practice: Underline the pronouns in the following sentences.

1. I just knowed she wasn't gonna be liking him hanging around.

2. You couldn't do nothin' that was gonna please her.

3. I think his mama probably made him come at first, but you could see he liked it.

4. "They been asking about him in the church."

5. Who liked Grandpa's stories the best?

6. Everybody started tiptoeing around the house after that.

7. "Some got bent and some got twisted and a few fell . . . , but they didn't break."

8. What is going to happen to the farm after Grandpa Jeremiah's death?

9. Macon brought his guitar with him and played the new tune he had written.

10. It reminded listeners of other tunes Macon had played, but something was different.

B. Writing Application: Write three sentences of your own about the story. Use at least one personal pronoun, interrogative pronoun, and indefinite pronoun. Underline each pronoun.

1. _____
   _____

2. _____
   _____

3. _____
   _____

"Jeremiah's Song" by Walter Dean Myers

Reading Strategy: Using Context Clues

When you encounter an unfamiliar word while reading, you may not need a dictionary to determine its definition. You may be able to use **context clues** to make a fairly accurate guess about the word's meaning. Context is the text (words, sentences, or paragraphs) before and after the unknown word. The clue might be a word or phrase you *do* know, one that sheds light on the word you do *not* know. For example, in the following sentence from "Jeremiah's Song," where Ellie comments on Grandpa Jeremiah's health, the word *improving* might give you a hint that could help you if you did not know what *setback* means.

[examp text]

"Now that he's improving, we don't want him to have a setback."

The word *improving* tells you that Grandpa Jeremiah was feeling better. However, the negative comment "we don't want" lets you know that Ellie is concerned that the improvement might not continue. So you could guess that *setback* had something to do with stopping or reversing improvement.

Directions: Fill in the chart below to figure out the definitions of the italicized words in the following sentences. The first one has been done for you as an example.

1. Ellie thought that Dr. Crawford's medical knowledge was *obsolete* because she thought that he must be out of touch with new developments in medicine.

2. Deacon Turner probably enjoyed *hymns* that were sung in church more than the tunes that Macon played for the family.

3. Grandpa Jeremiah's illness had left him so *debilitated* that he was unable even to get out of bed.

4. Grandpa Jeremiah's *eerie* stories were enough to give the young narrator nightmares.

5. Ellie had no patience with the stories. She liked modern stories, not the *antiquated* tales from the past that Grandpa Jeremiah told.

Unfamiliar Word	Context Clue	Definition
1. obsolete	"out of touch with new developments"	out of date
2.		
3.		
4.		
5.		

"Jeremiah's Song" by Walter Dean Myers

Literary Analysis: First-Person Narrator

The **narrator** of a story is the teller of the story. Sometimes an author will use a character from the story as the narrator. That character calls herself or himself "I," and speaks directly to the reader, as if she or he were actually telling the story. Such a character is called **a first-person narrator**. It is important to remember that a first-person narrator does not know what other characters are thinking or planning, but only what those characters reveal through their words or actions. On the other hand, a first-person narrator can share with the reader private thoughts and feelings that only she or he would know. In "Jeremiah's Song," the first-person narrator is Grandpa Jeremiah's grandson. Referring to himself as "I," he tells you, the reader, what he, himself, thinks and feels. He also tells about events and actions he has experienced or heard about.

A. DIRECTIONS: Show which of the following sentences is spoken by a first-person narrator by writing the letters *FP* on the line. Write an *X* on the line if the sentence is not spoken by a first-person narrator.

_____ 1. I was the one who loved Grandpa Jeremiah the most and she didn't hardly even know him so I didn't see why she was crying.

_____ 2. The boy loved Grandpa Jeremiah the most, and so he couldn't understand why people who hardly knew his grandfather would be crying.

_____ 3. All the time Grandpa Jeremiah was talking, the boy could see Macon fingering his guitar.

_____ 4. All the time Grandpa Jeremiah was talking, I could see Macon fingering his guitar.

_____ 5. The boy was glad when the rain finally stopped.

_____ 6. When the rain stopped, I was pretty glad.

B. DIRECTIONS: In the space provided below, rewrite the following paragraph with the boy as the first-person narrator.

The boy sat by his grandfather's bed, listening to the old man's stories. He wondered if they were really true, but didn't ask. When he had asked in the past, his grandfather would just change the subject, so the boy didn't bother any more. The room was hot, and the boy felt perspiration trickle down his back. He could hear birds chirping outside and wished for a breeze. He thought about being old, and not being able to work or run around. He heard a knock on the door and Macon came in with a guitar. He was glad to see Macon, who smiled at him.

_____

_____

_____

_____

_____

"The King of Mazy May" by Jack London

Build Vocabulary

Using the Suffix -or

The suffix -or at the end of a word indicates "a person or thing that does something." For example, a person who *acts* is called an *actor*.

A. DIRECTIONS: In the space provided, write the new word formed by adding the suffix -or to each of the following words. Then write a sentence using each word.

1. edit + -or   = _____   4.   profess + -or   = _____

2. direct + -or   = _____   5.   sail + -or   = _____

3. govern + -or   = _____

6. _____

7. _____

8. _____

9. _____

10. _____

Using the Word Bank

toil	endured	prospectors	liable
poising	declined	summit	

B. DIRECTIONS: Circle the letter of the description that best fits each word in CAPITAL LETTERS.

1. PROSPECTORS: a. people who work in factories   b. people who look for gold
                    c. people who explore caves   d. people who climb mountains

2. TOIL: a. practice   b. rest   c. work   d. amusement

3. SUMMIT: a. top   b. crack   c. largest part   d. deep valley

4. DECLINED: a. took away   b. refused   c. rested   d. leaned to one side

5. LIABLE: a. useful   b. breakable   c. careful   d. likely

6. POISING: a. balancing   b. stopping   c. smiling   d. expressing

7. ENDURED: a. claimed to own   b. felt   c. suffered through   d. hardened

Recognizing Antonyms

C. DIRECTIONS: Circle the letter of the word or phrase that is most nearly *opposite* in meaning to the word in CAPITAL LETTERS.

1. DECLINED: a. accepted   b. climbed up   c. stood up straight   d. refused

2. SUMMIT: a. beginning   b. middle   c. bottom   d. worst

"The King of Mazy May" by Jack London

Build Spelling Skills: Spelling the *oy* Sound

Spelling Strategy Whenever the *oy* sound occurs in the middle of a one-syllable word, spell the sound with the letters *oi*. Whenever the *oy* sound occurs at the end of a word, spell the sound with the letters *oy*.

Examples: poise (*oy* sound in middle)   boy (*oy* sound at end)

A. Practice: Complete each of the following words correctly using *oi* or *oy*.

  1. ann_____   2. c_____n   3. j_____   4. n_____se   5. destr_____   6. p_____sing

B. Practice: Correct the misspelled italicized words in the following paragraph. Write a C in the blank if the word is spelled correctly.

   Although Walt was still a *boi* _____ he was able to *spoyl* _____ the plans of the men who tried to jump the claims of the prospectors near his camp. The men planned to *destroy* _____ the stakes that marked the claims and take the claims for themselves. He did not want those men to *enjoi* _____ the wealth that others had *toiled* _____ for. Walt knew that there was nobody nearby to *joyn* _____ him in stopping these men, so he would have to act on his own.

Challenge: When Walt wants the dogs to begin pulling the sled, he shouts to them, "Mush!" and "Mush on!" You may know that the word *mush* in this context means, "Go!" However, you may be surprised to learn that the word comes from the French word *marchons* meaning, "Let's go!" The English word *march* comes from the same French word. Many English words are de- rived from French. Match each French word on the left with the English word derived from it on the right. Then, use each English word in a sentence. **Hint:** If necessary, use a dictionary to find the precise meaning of each English word.

_____ 1. *chanter* (French for *sing*)   a. solely

_____ 2. *arbre* (French for *tree*)   b. chant

_____ 3. *beauté* (French for *beauty*)   c. fortify

_____ 4. *fort* (French for *strong*)   d. beautiful

_____ 5. *seul* (French for *only*)   e. arbor

6. _____

7. _____

8. _____

9. _____

10. _____

"The King of Mazy May" by Jack London

Build Grammar Skills: Pronouns and Antecedents

A **pronoun** is a word that takes the place of a noun or another pronoun. An **antecedent** is the noun or pronoun that has been replaced. Normally, an antecedent comes before a pronoun, but not always. Often, an antecedent is in a different sentence from the pronoun. However, a good writer will always make certain that a reader can tell to which antecedent a pronoun refers. In these examples, the pronoun is italic and the antecedent is underlined.

Examples: Walt headed for the men's camp. Once there, *he* picked out the best sled.
As *he* raced along, Walt wondered how to change the lead dog.

Personal pronouns (*he, you, they,* etc.) always have an antecedent (with *I, me, mine,* the antecedent would be the name of the writer or speaker). Interrogative pronouns *(what, which, who, whom, whose)* never have antecedents. For example, in the question "Who would do a thing like this?" we don't know to whom "who" refers. Indefinite pronouns (*some, one, anything,* etc.) sometimes have antecedents and sometimes don't. For example, in the sentence "Students generally enjoy sports, but some don't," *some* has the antecedent of *students.* However, in the sentence, "Everyone is going," there is no antecedent for *everyone.*

A: Practice: In the following sentences, the pronouns are in italics. On the lines, write each pronoun and its antecedent. If there is no antecedent for the pronoun, write *none.*

1. The Yukon was a rich land, with much to offer. However, *it* could also be dangerous.

_____

2. *What* brought men to this cold, remote place?

_____

3. *Some* came for the adventure, *others* came for the gold.

_____

4. Not all miners found riches, and *some* found nothing.

_____

5. Loren Hall was lucky. When *he* dug a shaft, there was gold in *it.*

_____

B: Writing Application: Rewrite each of the following sentences on the lines provided, replacing the repeated noun or nouns with the correct pronoun.

1. Walt studied the dogs, wondering which of the dogs would be the best leader.

_____

2. When the claim-jumpers reached the claim-jumper's sleds, the claim-jumpers chased Walt.

_____

3. The sled bounced and rocked as the dogs pulled the sled over the frozen ground.

_____

Unit 1: Growing and Changing

"The King of Mazy May" by Jack London

Reading Strategy: Recognizing Signal Words

As you read, watch for signal words, such as *but, so,* and *on account of.* They are clues that tell you how one part of a passage relates to another part. For example, look at the following sentence from the selection:

Loren Hall was an old man, and he had no dogs, so he had to travel very slowly.

In the sentence above, *so* is a signal word that tells you that what happens in the last part of the sentence is the effect of what happens in the first part. What happens in the first part of the sentence is the cause. In other words, the fact that Loren Hall had to travel very slowly is the effect of his being an old man and having no dogs. Some other signal words and phrases that show cause and effect are *for* and *because.*

DIRECTIONS: Find the signal word or phrase in each of the following sentences. Then fill in the chart below. The first row in the chart has been filled in as an example.

1. Walt wanted to stop the men from taking away Loren Hall's claim because he knew that stealing was wrong.

2. Walt Masters's father had recorded his claim at the start, so Walt had nothing to fear.

3. Evidently the men had agreed with their leader, for Walt Masters could hear nothing but the rattle of the tin dishes that were being washed.

4. The sled almost tipped over on account of the curving trail and the inexperience of the lead dog.

5. The men would be returning to their camp soon, so Walt did not have much time.

6. Walt knew a lot about sleds and dogs, for he had lived around them all his life.

Signal Word or Phrase	Cause	Effect
1. because	he knew that stealing was wrong	Walt wanted to stop the men from taking away Loren Hall's claim
2.		
3.		
4.		
5.		
6.		

"The King of Mazy May" by Jack London

Literary Analysis: Conflict Between Characters

In "The King of Mazy May," a group of men plans to steal another man's property. Walt Masters, who is only a young boy, is determined to stop them. This is the **conflict**, or struggle, that gives the story its tension and suspense. You, the reader, know that one side will win out in the end; the other will be defeated. As you read, you cheer for Walt because his thoughts and actions are good, kind, and honest. You root against the thieves because they think and act in an evil, cruel, and dishonest way. Often, in literature, as in this story, the conflict between characters is really a conflict between good and evil. Being aware of and understanding the conflict between characters in a story will increase your reading enjoyment.

DIRECTIONS: The following sentences from "The King of Mazy May" refer to either good or evil characters, thoughts, or actions. Under the appropriate headings, write the words in each sentence that let you know whether the sentence refers to the good or evil side of the conflict in the story. The first sentence has been done as an example.

	GOOD	EVIL
1. Last of all, he has a good heart, and is not afraid of the darkness and loneliness, of man or beast or thing.	he has a good heart	
2. But with the news of their discoveries, strange men began to come and go through the short days and long nights, and many unjust things they did to the men who had worked so long upon the creek.		
3. Yet, with the quickness of a cat, he had clutched the end of the sled with one hand, turned over, and was dragging behind on his breast, swearing at the boy and threatening all sorts of terrible things if he did not stop the dogs.		
4. In short, it was the old story, and quite a number of the earnest, industrious prospectors had suffered similar losses.		
5. They took greater care, and shot at him at the most favorable opportunities.		
6. He was only a boy, but in the face of the threatened injustice to old lame Loren Hall he felt that he must do something.		

"The Circuit" by Francisco Jiménez
"Hard as Nails" by Russell Baker

Build Vocabulary

Using Compound Nouns

A **compound noun** is a noun that is made up of at least two words, such as *milkshake*.

A. DIRECTIONS: Use the following compound words from "The Circuit" and "Hard as Nails" to complete the paragraph below.

outside   overturning   backbone   doorstep   necktie   salesman   doorbell

The inexperienced _____, who didn't have much

_____ for his job, stood on the _____

_____ the house. Nervously, he straightened his _____

and rang the _____. When no one answered; he heaved a sigh of relief

and hurried back to his car, _____ a flower-pot along the way.

Using the Word Bank

drone	instinctively	savoring	embedded
exhaust	sublime	immense	

B. DIRECTIONS: On the blanks, write the Word Bank word that matches each description.

1. _____ the sound that bees make

2. _____ very large

3. _____ the way you do something without having to think about it

4. _____ to use up

5. _____ enjoying the taste of, relishing

6. _____ firmly fixed in the surrounding material

7. _____ wonderful, causing awe

Recognizing Synonyms

C. DIRECTIONS: On the line, write the letter of the word that is closest in meaning to the word in CAPITAL LETTERS.

____ 1. IMMENSE: a. angry   b. huge   c. difficult   d. messy

____ 2. EXHAUST: a. soak   b. work   c. enlarge   d. use up

____ 3. SUBLIME: a. wonderful   b. funny   c. complicated   d. dull

____ 4. EMBEDDED: a. enlarged   b. cut in pieces   c. firmly planted   d. tied up

"The Circuit" by Francisco Jiménez
"Hard as Nails" by Russell Baker

Build Spelling Skills: Spelling Compound Nouns

Spelling Strategy To spell most compound nouns, combine the words from which they are formed into a single word.

Examples: draw + backs = drawbacks   gold + fish = goldfish

Exception: Some compound nouns use hyphens to link the words from which they are formed, and others are written as separate words. If you are uncertain of how to spell a specific compound noun, check a dictionary.

Examples: brother-in-law   home run
             right-hander   pen pal

A. Practice: On the lines provided, write the compound noun formed by combining each of the following pairs of words into one word. The first one has been done as an example.

1. ear + ring = earring _____

4. fire + place = _____

2. eye + lash = _____

5. green + house = _____

3. dish + washer = _____

6. smoke + stack = _____

B. Practice: Complete each of the following sentences by combining the words in parentheses and writing the resulting compound noun in the space provided.

1. Roberto in "The Circuit" wishes to be an ordinary (school + boy) _____.

2. But he is forced to begin work at (sun + rise) _____ each morning.

3. Instead of doing (home + work) _____, he spends his days picking grapes.

4. He cannot join other children while they have fun on the (play + ground) _____.

5. He does the same work as his father and (grand + father) _____ before him.

Challenge: In "The Circuit," Roberto calls his younger brother "Panchito." The father calls the family car "Carcanchita." In Spanish, the ending -ito or -ita is often added to a word to form an affectionate nickname. These endings, in Spanish, mean "little." A masculine word or name usually ends with the letter o, and a feminine word or name usually ends with the letter a. A family with a boy named Pablo is likely to call him Pablito, dropping the final o, and adding the ending -ito. If they have a girl named Teresa, they may call her Teresita, dropping the final a, and adding the ending -ita. In the space provided, write the Spanish nickname that can be made from each of the following names. Keep in mind that the names ending in o are masculine, and those ending in a are feminine.

1. Pedro _____

4. Juana _____

2. Carla _____

5. Carmela _____

3. Sancho _____

6. Manuelo _____

El Sereno Middle School
2839 North Eastern Avenue
Los Angeles, California 90032

"**The Circuit**" by Francisco Jiménez
"**Hard as Nails**" by Russell Baker

Build Grammar Skills: Pronoun-Antecedent Agreement

You already know that words such as *she, ours*, and *they* are pronouns, and that the words that pronouns replace are called antecedents. To make sense, however, **pronouns** and **antecedents** must **agree**. That is, the pronoun must always have the same **gender** (masculine, feminine, or neuter) and **number** (singular or plural) as its antecedent.

Example: Panchito's **mother** knew that **she** must cook the family's meals.

The noun *mother* identifies a single female individual, and the pronoun *she* identifies a single female individual. Therefore, *she* agrees with the antecedent *mother* in gender (feminine) and number (singular).

The most common agreement errors occur when compound nouns or indefinite pronouns are being replaced. For example, it makes a difference whether a compound antecedent contains *and* or *or*: *Bill and John* would take a plural pronoun, but *Bill or John* would take a singular pronoun. In addition, if the antecedent is an indefinite pronoun, the pronoun needs to agree in number with the pronoun. For example, in *One of the boys*, the antecedent is *one*, not *boys*, and the pronoun would be masculine singular: *One of the boys brought* his *book* (not *their book*).

A. Practice: In the following sentences, circle the pronoun in parenthesis that agrees with its antecedent.

1. Baker's mother told Mr. Deems that (she, it) thought that the age limit for work was silly.

2. The boys had to sell newspapers, but (he, they) also had time for fun.

3. The work was hard, but Baker knew that (it, they) was good for (her, him).

4. Many reasons were given for being proud of the work, and Baker believed all of (it, them).

5. Panchito and a top picker discover that (he, they) are both from Jalisco.

6. Each of the boys did (his, their) work when it was time to move.

7. Roberto or Papá will take (his, their) place in the cotton field.

8. "The family gathered around the table to enjoy the meal Mamá had prepared for (us, me)."

B. Writing Application: Rewrite the following sentences, supplying pronouns that matches antecedents.

1. Mamá was proud of _____ cooking pot.

_____

2. Roberto and Papá knew that _____ must continue to work.

_____

3. Each of the paper boys took _____ job seriously.

_____

"The Circuit" by Francisco Jiménez
"Hard as Nails" by Russell Baker

Reading Strategy: Reading With Expression

It is important that you read accurately. Otherwise, you may not understand what is happening or being said. Be careful not to skip over words, read words incorrectly, or ignore who is speaking. Breaking a sentence down into smaller parts may help. Punctuation or conjunctions can show you natural breaks in a sentence. Identify the subject or what the sentence is about. With compound or complex sentences, you may have to find more than one subject, one for each clause. Then, ask yourself what the rest of the sentence or clause tells you about the subject. Even with a sentence too short to be broken down, identifying the subject or topic and determining what the sentence says about it aids in reading accurately.

> My mother, in spite of believing that nothing came before homework at night, wasn't coldhearted enough to deny me a chance to see the city room of a great metropolitan newspaper.

Here, the subject is "my mother." The next long phrase shows that she believes that homework is important. If you skipped the words "in spite of," you might not realize that she was going to do something different than usual. Then, we learn that she was not going to deny her son a visit to the newspaper office. So, pulled together, we have a sentence that tells us that the writer's mother wants her son to do well in school, but lets him have fun, too.

> I held the front door open as Mamá carefully carried out her pot by both handles.

Here, there are two clauses joined by the conjunction *as*. In the first clause, *I* is the subject, and we learn that the writer is being helpful and holding the door. In the second clause, *Mamá* is the subject, and she is carrying a large cooking pot. Together, the two clauses tell us of both the writer and his mother.

Practice: Read the following sentences. Then, on the lines, write the subject of the sentence followed by a brief statement of what the sentence tells us about the subject. Break the sentence down by phrases, if necessary, to help you determine what is being said.

1. Papá listened to the motor, tilting his head from side to side like a parrot, trying to detect any noises that spelled car trouble.

   _____

   _____

2. Finally, after struggling for English words, I managed to tell the principal that I wanted to enroll in the sixth grade.

   _____

   _____

3. Mr. Deems, who spoke enthusiastically about the newspaper business and the important people who were behind it, encouraged selling, giving the newsboys extra papers each day and even coming up with a new-subscriber competition.

   _____

   _____

"The Circuit" by Francisco Jiménez
"Hard as Nails" by Russell Baker

Literary Analysis: Theme

A story usually has a **theme**, or central idea; it may be a thought or a belief about life that the story suggests. In many stories, such as "The Circuit" or "Hard as Nails," the author does not state the central idea directly but gives readers clues that they can use to figure it out. The clues may be found in the title of the story, in descriptions and explanations provided by the author, or in words spoken by the characters.

DIRECTIONS: For each of the following paragraphs, write the theme on the appropriate line. On the other lines, write three details from the paragraph that helped you to grasp the idea.

1. Whenever a school bus stopped near a field where Panchito was working, he had to hide. The law said that a boy of Panchito's age should be in school, but his family needed the money he earned working in the fields. From his hiding place he would watch enviously as the other children got on or off the bus, carrying their books and talking happily. Francisco had been to school. He had gone to several schools during the short periods of time when there was no farm work for him to do. He thought he could be a good student because he learned quickly and he enjoyed reading. But a boy did not get paid for going to school. So, after riding on a school bus for a few days, hoping to make some friends, Panchito would come home to find his family packing to leave once again.

Central Idea:

_____

Clues:

a. _____

b. _____

c. _____

2. Russell Baker was only twelve years old when he went into newspaper work. Baker did not mind having to work at the age of twelve; he was proud to be able to help his mother and sister by bringing some money home. Being a newsboy was not easy work. A newsboy had to get up very early in the morning, make deliveries in all kinds of weather, and constantly find ways to sell more papers. For four years, he sold newspapers, doubling the number of his subscribers. Over the years since that time, Russell Baker has remained in the newspaper business, becoming an award-winning columnist whose writing is read by millions. He is still proud of being in the newspaper business.

Central Idea:

_____

Clues:

a. _____

b. _____

c. _____

"How to Write a Letter" by Garrison Keillor
"How to Write a Poem About the Sky" by Leslie Marmon Silko
Build Vocabulary

Using the Suffix *-ory*

The suffix *–ory*, which means "having the quality or nature of," turns a noun into an adjective. Something that is *obligatory* has the quality or nature of an *obligation*. Here are some other examples:

satisfaction $\longrightarrow$ satisfact*ory*   migration $\longrightarrow$ migrat*ory*
explanation $\longrightarrow$ explanat*ory*   preparation $\longrightarrow$ preparat*ory*

A. DIRECTIONS: Complete each sentence with one of the above words ending in *-ory*.

1. Sandy traveled to South America to complete her study of _____ songbirds.

2. Elena plans to take some _____ courses before applying to medical school.

3. Mike was relieved to see that he had received a _____ score in the competition.

4. There are no directions for filling out this form because everything is self- _____ .

Using the Word Bank

confidence	anonymity	obligatory	episode	sibling	dense	membranes

B. DIRECTIONS: Use each of the Word Bank words in a sentence according to the instructions given.

1. Use *confidence* in a sentence about the members of a basketball team.

   _____

2. Use *anonymity* in a sentence about a movie star.

   _____

3. Use *obligatory* in a sentence about everyday chores.

   _____

4. Use *episode* in a sentence about a letter.

   _____

5. Use *sibling* in a sentence about your family or someone else's family.

   _____

6. Use *dense* in a sentence about a forest.

   _____

7. Use *membrane* (s) in a sentence about something you've studied in science.

   _____

"**How to Write a Letter**" by Garrison Keillor
"**How to Write a Poem About the Sky**" by Leslie Marmon Silko

Build Spelling Skills: Words That End in *ence*

Spelling Strategy The *ens* sound at the end of words is often—but not always—spelled *ence*, as it is in the Word Bank word *confidence*. Because the *ens* sound can be spelled in different ways, you may need to memorize the spelling of words that end in *ence*. Here are some other words in which the *ens* sound at the end is spelled *ence*.

intelligence	evidence	experience	occurrence	preference
residence	permanence	absence	correspondence	

A. Practice: Fill in each blank with a form of the underlined word ending in *ence*.

1. Ms. Waters was <u>confident</u> that we would raise enough money to buy new uniforms. Her _____ was reassuring.

2. <u>Evidently</u>, a crime had been committed. Therefore, the detective began to collect _____ .

3. I can understand why you would <u>prefer</u> to see Sam rather than Tony as class president. Just make sure that you express your _____ by voting.

4. Of course, my dog Sparky is <u>intelligent</u>. In fact, I think that he shows above-average _____ .

B. Practice: Complete the sentences by adding *ence* to each word part in parentheses. Write the new words on the lines.

1. Reading a poem can be a wonderful (experi) _____ .

2. Silko writes of a day when the sun's (abs) _____ makes the sky look like a frozen river.

3. Keillor tell us that any (occurr) _____ is a good topic for a letter.

4. The Postal Service delivers letters to your (resid) _____ daily.

Challenge: The word *anonymity* from the Word Bank means "the condition of being a stranger, not known by name." *Anonymity* is formed from a combination of the word root *-nym-*, meaning "name," the prefix *an-*, which means "without," and the suffix *–ity*, which means "state or condition." Here are two other words that contain the word root *-nym-*.

anonymous: given or written by a person whose name is unknown

pseudonym: a fictitious, or made-up, name used by an author

DIRECTIONS: Complete the following sentences using the word *anonymous* or the word *pseudonym*. Use each word once. Write your answers on the lines.

1. Mark Twain, the _____ of Samuel Clemens, is one of the most famous names in American literature.

2. Because no one knows who wrote this poem, the editors listed the author as "_____" in the table of contents.

Build Grammar Skills: Verbs

A **verb** is a word that expresses the action or condition of a person, place, or thing. No sentence is complete without a verb. In the following sentences, the verbs are underlined.

> So a shy person <u>sits</u> down and <u>writes</u> a letter.
> You <u>see</u> the sky now but the earth <u>is</u> lost in it.

The two main kinds of verbs are action verbs and linking verbs. **Action verbs** express physical action (walk, sit, talk, rise) or mental action (think, decide). **Linking verbs** express a state of being. They tell what the subject of a sentence is or is like by linking the subject to a word that further describes or identifies it. The most common linking verb is a form of *be* (*is, am, are*, etc.). Other linking verbs include *appear, become, seem, grow, look*. A good test to determine if a verb is a linking verb is to substitute a form of *be: I feel sick; I am sick.* If the substitute can be made, it is a linking verb. If it's an action verb, this substitution will give you a sentence that does not make sense: *I watch TV* and *I am TV* obviously do not mean the same thing, so *watch* is not a linking verb.

A. Practice: Underline the verbs in the following sentences. Then, above each one, write *A* if it is active, and *L* if it is linking.

1. She can read them twice and again tomorrow.

2. Few letters are obligatory.

3. Write the salutation, take a deep breath, and plunge in.

4. It is all a single breath.

5. The moment the wind shifts/sun splits it open.

B. Writing Application: Follow the directions below to write sentences about the specified topics.

1. Write a sentence about Garrison Keillor using the verb *write*.

_____

2. Write a sentence about sending or receiving letters using a linking verb.

_____

3. Write a sentence about Leslie Marmon Silko's poem using the verb *describe*.

_____

4. Write a sentence about the weather using an action verb.

_____

5. Write a sentence about a beautiful landscape using the verb *enjoy*.

_____

"How to Write a Letter" by Garrison Keillor
"How to Write a Poem About the Sky" by Leslie Marmon Silko

Reading Strategy: Reading Aloud With Expression

Reading aloud fluently and accurately may seem difficult, but if you combine the strategies you have already learned for reading fluently and reading accurately, it becomes much easier. Here, briefly, are the strategies you've already practiced.

- Read phrase by phrase rather than word by word.
- Use punctuation marks and conjunctions as guides for pausing.
- Identify the subject of a sentence or what the sentence is about, then determine what the rest of the sentence says about it.

To read fluently, you practiced marking off sentence sections to show where to pause. When reading aloud, it is important that these pauses are placed to emphasize meaning, and to make the reading sound more like normal speech. When reading poetry, it is tempting to pause at the end of each line, but if you read accurately, you may notice that words on different lines run together. For example, with the stanza that reads "You see the sky now/colder than the frozen river/so dense and white/little birds/walk across it." The slash marks indicate where the lines break for this poem, and for the first three lines, the offer good places to pause. However, the meaning of the last two lines makes it clear that "little birds walk across it" should be read as a phrase.

So you see, a combination of strategies can help you read aloud both fluently and accurately.

DIRECTIONS: Using a combination of strategies, prepare the following passages to be read aloud. After you have divided the passages up and determined the meaning, practice reading them aloud. Then pick one passage to read aloud with expression to a partner.

1. Let the letter cook along and let yourself be bold. Outrage, confusion, love—whatever is in your mind, let it find a way to the page. Writing is a means of discovery, always, and when you come to the end and write *Yours ever* or *Hugs and Kisses*, you'll know something you didn't when you wrote *Dear Pal*.

2. You see the sky now
   but the earth is lost in it
   and there are no horizons.
   It is all
   a single breath.

"How to Write a Letter" by Garrison Keillor
"How to Write a Poem About the Sky" by Leslie Marmon Silko

Literary Analysis: Informal Essay

An **informal essay** is a brief, casual discussion of a topic. The writer of this type of essay uses conversational language to create a relaxed and friendly feeling. Sometimes, as in "How to Write a Letter," humorous ideas and details—exaggeration, surprising analogies—help to create the informal feeling. In addition to creating a sense of casualness, Keillor uses contractions such as *we'll* and *it's* to create a sense of casualness.

A. DIRECTIONS: Read the following passage from "How to Write a Letter." Circle three words, phrases, or details within the passage that help to create a relaxed, informal feeling. On the lines below, write a sentence explaining what makes each of the items informal.

> A blank white eight-by-eleven sheet can look as big as Montana if the pen's not so hot—try a smaller page and write boldly. Or use a note card with a piece of fine art on the front; if your letter ain't good, at least they get the Matisse. Get a pen that makes a sensuous line, get a comfortable typewriter, a friendly word processor—whichever feels easy to the hand.

_____

_____

_____

B. DIRECTIONS: Look for more informal, humorous, and familiar words and phrases as you read, as well as other details that add to the essay's casual style. Use the organizer below to record your findings.

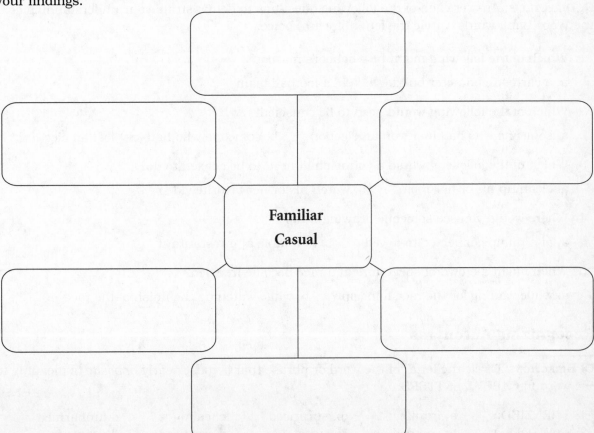

"Aaron's Gift" by Myron Levoy
"Water" by Helen Keller

Build Vocabulary

Using Related Words: Forms of *console*

The Word Bank word *consoled* means "comforted." As you can see, the following words are forms of the word *console*. All three words are related in meaning.

Consolation means "comfort."
Inconsolable means "unable to be comforted."

A. DIRECTIONS: Use one of the forms of *console* to complete each sentence.

1. The little boy cried for a long time after losing his favorite toy; he seemed to be
   _____

2. Losing the game was a disappointment, but knowing that we had enjoyed our best season ever was a _____

3. Tanya's friends _____ her when her beloved cat Rusty died.

Using the Word Bank

frenzied	mascot	coaxed	consoled	drawing

B. DIRECTIONS: Answer each of the following questions to demonstrate your understanding of the Word Bank words. Circle the letter of your choice.

1. Which of the following might be a school's mascot?

   a. a cartoon-character bulldog   b. a football team

2. Which of the following would need to be consoled?

   a. someone who had just won an election   b. someone who had just lost an election

3. Which of the following would a young child need to be coaxed to do?

   a. clean up his or her room   b. watch his or her favorite video

4. Where would you see someone drawing water?

   a. at a pump connected to a well   b. at a table at a restaurant

5. When might a crowd of spectators at a race become frenzied?

   a. while waiting for the race to begin   b. while watching the finish of the race

Recognizing Antonyms

C. DIRECTIONS: Circle the letter of the word or phrase that is most nearly *opposite* in meaning to the word in CAPITAL LETTERS.

1. FRENZIED: a. frantic   b. surprised   c. calm   d. unharmed
2. CONSOLED: a. soothed   b. upset   c. repaired   d. greeted

"**Aaron's Gift**" by Myron Levoy
"**Water**" by Helen Keller

Build Spelling Skills: Adding Endings to Words Ending in *y*

Spelling Strategy When adding an ending to a word that ends in *y*, follow these strategies:

- If a consonant precedes the final *y*, change the *y* to *i*. However, if the ending begins with *i*, the *y* does not change.

  try + *ed* = tried   try + *ing* = trying

  study + *ed* = studied   study + *ing* = studying

  happy + *est* = happiest   happy + *ness* = happiness

- If a vowel comes before the *y*, just add the ending.

  enjoy + *ed* = enjoyed   enjoy + *ing* = enjoying   enjoy + *ment* = enjoyment

  journey + *ed* = journeyed   journey + *ing* = journeying

A. Practice: Add the indicated ending to each word. Write the new word on the line.

1. buy + ing _____

2. fry + ing _____

3. apply + ed _____

4. weary + ness _____

5. scary + er _____

6. employ + er _____

7. spy + ed _____

8. survey + ing _____

9. sturdy + ness _____

10. annoy + ing _____

B. Practice: Complete the paragraph by adding the indicated ending to each given word. Write the new words on the lines provided.

   With the help of her teacher, Annie Sullivan, Helen Keller went on to live a life of remarkable

achievement. She continued (apply + ing) _____ herself to learning new

words and soon learned to speak, read, and write. She (study + ed) _____

hard and gained entrance to Radcliffe College, from which she graduated with honors in 1904.

In the years that followed, she (enjoy + ed) _____ a distinguished career

as a writer, lecturer, and civil rights advocate, (play + ing) _____ an

important role in winning public recognition for the needs and rights of visually disabled

people. The person who had, in her own words, been the wildest and (unruly + est)

_____ of children grew up to become one of the most famous and

influential people of our time.

"**Aaron's Gift**" by Myron Levoy
"**Water**" by Helen Keller

Build Grammar Skills: Verb Phrases

A **verb phrase** is a group of words that is made up of a main verb and one or more helping verbs. A **helping verb** is a verb that comes before the main verb and adds to its meaning. In a verb phrase, the main verb is the most important verb. There are many different helping verbs. The most common ones are shown in the chart below.

Common Helping Verbs	
Forms of *have*	has, have, having, had
Forms of *be*	am, is, are, was, were, being, been
Other helping verbs	do, does, did, may, might, must, can, could, will, would, shall, should

Look at these sentences. The verb phrase in each one is underlined. The main verb is in bold type. Note that, in one case, the word *not* interrupts a verb phrase.

The pigeon was **trying** to fly.

Aaron was not sure what his mother would **say** about his new-found pet.

Helen Keller *did* not ***know*** that, before day's end, she *would be **learning*** new words.

A. Practice: On the lines, write the verb phrase or phrases in each sentence. Then underline the main verb in each phrase.

1. Aaron had come to the park with his roller skates. _____

2. If you had seen him, you would have said that he is a fantastic skater.

   _____

3. Before coming to the U.S., Aaron's grandmother had lived in the Ukraine.

   _____

4. What would have happened to Helen without Miss Sullivan?

   _____

B. Writing Application: Complete the paragraph by writing a verb phrase in each blank. Use the verb phrases below or provide your own. When you are finished, underline the main verb in each verb phrase that you wrote.

   would bring   did bring   had made   had brought   will recall   could become

   About a month after Aaron _____ Pidge home, Carl, the gang leader, told him that he _____ a member if he _____ the bird to be the gang's mascot. Aaron _____ the pigeon to the club house, but he soon realized that he _____ a terrible mistake. The boys intended to throw Pidge into the fire while making Aaron swear a loyalty oath! As you _____, however, Aaron and Pidge managed to escape.

"Aaron's Gift" by Myron Levoy
"Water" by Helen Keller

Reading Strategy: Using Context to Clarify Meaning

Often, the only way you can determine precisely what a word or passage means is to consider its context. You may remember that **context** is the material that surrounds the word or passage you are trying to clarify. Often, the words or sentences immediately before and after an unfamiliar word, or a familiar word used in a novel manner, will provide all the context you need to clarify meaning. Sometimes a larger context needs to be considered, such as the subject of the story or the background of a character. For example, there is little in the sentences around the word *Cossacks* in this passage to let you know what it means.

> Aaron twisted and turned and kicked and punched back, shouting "Cossacks! Cossacks!" And somehow the word gave him the strength to tear away.

Looking up the word *Cossack* gives you more background: Cossacks are a people living on the steppes of Russia, noted as horsemen. However, that doesn't explain why Aaron would use this word—these bullies are not Russian horsemen. To clarify the meaning here, you need to consider the larger context of the story.

DIRECTIONS: Read the following excerpt from "Aaron's Gift," noting that it comes well before the scene described above. Then explain how it clarifies Aaron's use of the word "Cossacks." Write your answer on the lines below.

> Often, in the evening, Aaron's grandmother would talk about the old days long ago in the Ukraine, in the same way that she talked to the birds on the back fire escape. She had lived in a village near a place called Kishinev with hundreds of other poor peasant families like her own. . . .
>
> One day, a thundering of horses was heard coming toward the village from the direction of Kishinev. *The Cossacks! The Cossacks!* someone had shouted. The Czar's horsemen! Quickly, quickly, everyone in Aaron's grandmother's family had climbed down to the cellar through a little trapdoor hidden under a mat in the big central room of their shack. But his grandmother's pet goat, whom she'd loved as much as Aaron loved Pidge and more, had to be left above, because if it had made a sound in the cellar, they would never have lived to see the next morning. They all hid under the wood in the woodbin and waited, hardly breathing.
>
> *   *   *
>
> But they had been lucky. For other houses had been burned to the ground. And everywhere, not goats alone, nor sheep, but men and women and children lay quietly on the ground. The word for this sort of massacre, Aaron had learned, was *pogrom*. It had been a pogrom. And the men on the horses were Cossacks. Hated word. Cossacks.

_____

_____

_____

_____

_____

"Aaron's Gift" by Myron Levoy
"Water" by Helen Keller

Literary Analysis: Climax

The moment of high tension in a story is known as the **climax**, or turning point. It is the point at which the story could go one way or another. Writers who build up to climaxes shape their stories and accounts carefully. They present the events that lead up to this decisive moment in a part of a story known as the **rising action**. They also let readers know what happens after the climax; this part of the story is know as the **conclusion**.

DIRECTIONS: Use the diagrams below to record the events that lead up to the climaxes in "Aaron's Gift" and "Water." Also note what happens in each work's climax and conclusion in the spaces indicated.

"Aaron's Gift"

Climax

_____
Event

_____
Event

_____
Event

Rising Action

Conclusion

"Water"

Climax

_____
Event

_____
Event

_____
Event

Rising Action

Conclusion

In a sentence or two, identify the climax of each work.

"Aaron's Gift":

_____

_____

"Water":

_____

_____

"Zlateh the Goat" by Isaac Bashevis Singer

Build Vocabulary

Using the Prefix *ex-*

The prefix *ex-* means "out" or "away from." For example, the word *exhale* means "breathe out."

A. DIRECTIONS: In the space provided, write the word that fits the definition by combining the word part *ex-* with the main part of the word in parentheses. The first one has been done as an example.

_____ expel _____ 1. (-pel): to force out

_____ 2. (-tract) to take out

_____ 3. (-plode) to burst out or blow apart

_____ 4. (-tend) to reach out or away from

_____ 5. (-ile) to send away

_____ 6. (-clude) to leave out

Using the Word Bank

bound	conclusion	trace	rapidly	exuded

B. DIRECTIONS: Answer each of the following riddles by filling in the blank space with a word from the Word Bank.

1. What is the best way to escape from a hungry lion? _____

2. Why did the farmer tie up his cows? So that they were _____ to give milk.

3. Why did the children turn on the lamp after dark? Because the lamp _____ light.

4. How did the student finish the arithmetic problem? She reached a _____ .

5. Why couldn't the graffiti artist be found? He left without a _____ .

Recognizing Antonyms

C. DIRECTIONS: Circle the letter of the word or phrase most nearly *opposite* in meaning of the word in CAPITAL LETTERS.

1. CONCLUSION
   a. suspicion   c. reason
   b. introduction   d. question

2. BOUND
   a. free   c. curious
   b. eager   d. happy

3. RAPIDLY
   a. hopefully   c. slowly
   b. carefully   d. angrily

4. EXUDED
   a. broke   c. explored
   b. soaked up   d. welcomed

Unit 2: Reaching Out

"Zlateh the Goat" by Isaac Bashevis Singer

Build Spelling Skills: Spelling the Final *s* Sound With *ce*

Spelling Strategy Sometimes the *s* sound at the end of a word is spelled with *ce*, as in the following words: *force, ice, since.* Because there is no rule to tell you when to use *ce* to spell the *s* sound, look a word up in a dictionary if you are not sure of its spelling.

A. Practice: In each of the following sentences, choose the letter or letters from the ones in parentheses to spell the italicized word, and write the correctly spelled word in the space provided. The first one has been done as an example. Note: two of the words do not end with *ce*.

1. We liked the movie so much that we saw it *twi*(s, ce) _____twice_____ .

2. You can have your *choi*(s, ce) _____ of chocolate or vanilla ice cream.

3. We must learn to *expre*(ss, ce) _____ ourselves clearly.

4. I drink a glass of orange *jui*(s, ce) _____ every morning.

5. There was a *fen*(ce, s) _____ around the yard to keep the dog in.

6. Can you tell the difference between a duck and a *goo*(se, ce) _____ ?

7. The students decorated the room for their school *dan*(s, ce) _____ .

B. Practice: Complete each of the following sentences with one of the words below. Use each word only once.

price   choice   space   source   chance

1. Aaron did not want to take Zlateh to the butcher, but he knew that he had no _____ .

2. If Aaron and Zlateh had not found shelter from the snow, they would have had little _____ of survival.

3. There was just enough _____ in the haystack for Aaron and Zlateh.

4. After Zlateh saved Aaron's life, the family would not sell the goat for any _____ .

5. Zlateh was the _____ of the milk that Aaron drank.

Challenge: "Zlateh the Goat" mentions the Jewish holiday Hanukkah. The word *Hanukkah* means "dedication" in Hebrew, one of the oldest languages still in use. The Jewish new year is called *Rosh Hashanah* (Rohsh Hah-SHAH-nah), Hebrew for "beginning of the year."

Some English words come from Hebrew words. For example, the word "Sabbath," meaning "day of rest," comes from the Hebrew word *Shabat* (shah-BAHT). Have you ever heard the word *kosher* used to mean "acceptable"? *Kosher* (KOH-shuhr), means "proper" and applies to food that is acceptable for religious Jews to eat. Use the information above to fill in the blanks below.

1. The Jewish year begins on the holiday called _____ .

2. _____ food has been prepared according to special religious laws.

3. Many people do not work on the _____ , the day of rest.

"Zlateh the Goat" by Isaac Bashevis Singer

Build Grammar Skills: Principal Parts of Verbs

Every verb, or word that expresses an action or state of being, has four main forms, or **principal parts**. These parts show a verb's tense, letting you know when an action took place. Most verbs are **regular**, meaning that they all form their principal parts in the same way. Some verbs, however, are **irregular**, meaning that the forms of their principal parts do not conform to general rules. The principal parts of irregular verbs must be learned. See some examples in the chart below.

Principal Part	Regular Verbs	Irregular Verbs
Present tense	talk, jump, finish, expect	am/is/are, have/has, sing, become/becomes, bring, write
Past tense	Add *ed*: talk*ed*, jump*ed*, finish*ed*, expect*ed*	was/were, had, sang, became, brought, wrote
Present participle	Add *ing*: (am/is/are) talk*ing*, jump*ing*, finish*ing*, expect*ing*	(am/is/are) being, having, singing, becoming, bringing, writing
Past participle	Add *ed*:(has/have/had) talked, jumped, finished, expected	(has/have/had) been, had, sung, become, brought, written

A. Practice: For each of the following sentences, identify which principal part of the underlined verb is being used. The first one has been done as an example.

_____past_____ 1. The sun <u>shone</u> most of the time.

_____ 2. Reuven *is* <u>having</u> a bad year.

_____ 3. Aaron <u>knows</u> the way to Feivel's house.

_____ 4. He *has* <u>agreed</u> to take Zlateh there.

_____ 5. Aaron <u>placed</u> the rope around Zlateh's neck.

_____ 6. He *is* <u>feeling</u> sad.

_____ 7. Aaron and Zlateh *have* <u>gotten</u> lost in a storm.

_____ 8. The story <u>has</u> a happy ending.

B. Writing Application: On the lines provided, complete each of the following sentences, using the correct principal part of the verb in parentheses.

1. Reuven the furrier had _____decided_____ to sell the goat. (decide)

2. Feivel had _____ eight gulden for her. (offer)

3. While they were walking, Zlateh _____ Aaron's hand. (lick)

4. The snow had _____ Aaron's knees. (reach)

5. When the story ends, Aaron and Zlateh are _____ home. (return)

6. This is a story that _____ happily. (end)

"Zlateh the Goat" by Isaac Bashevis Singer

Reading Strategy: Summarizing

While you are reading, pause now and then. Go over in your mind the events that have taken place so far and think about why they happened. When you pause and think about a story in this way, you are **summarizing**, or reviewing the story up to that point.

A **summary** contains only the most important information about the events in the story. For example, read the passage below and the summary that follows it:

> The sun was shining when Aaron left the village. Suddenly the weather changed. A large black cloud with a bluish center appeared in the east and spread itself rapidly over the sky. A cold wind blew in with it. The crows flew low, croaking. At first it looked as if it would rain, but instead it began to hail as in summer. It was early in the day, but it became dark as dusk. After a while the hail turned to snow.

> **Summary:** When Aaron left the village, the sun was shining, but it suddenly grew cold, windy, and dark, and began to snow.

A. DIRECTIONS: One way of summarizing is to make a timeline on a sheet of paper and add to it each time you pause. Use the diagram below as a timeline for "Zlateh the Goat." In the spaces on the timeline, write the letters of the following events from the story in the order in which they occur. Start at the left end of the timeline and finish at the right.

a. Aaron digs a hole in the haystack so that he and Zlateh can take shelter from the blizzard.
b. Reuven the furrier decides to sell Zlateh to the butcher.
c. Aaron hears the ringing of sleigh bells.
d. A neighbor runs to tell Aaron's family that Aaron and Zlateh are on their way home.
e. It begins to snow heavily.

BEGINNING ┤──────────┼──────────┼──────────┼──────────├ ENDING
      1. _____   2. _____   3. _____   4. _____   5. _____

B. DIRECTIONS: On the lines provided, write a one-sentence summary of each of the following passages from "Zlateh the Goat."

1. In his twelve years Aaron had seen all kinds of weather, but he had never experienced a snow like this one. It was so dense it shut out the light of the day. In a short time their path was completely covered. The wind became as cold as ice. The road to town was narrow and winding. Aaron no longer knew where he was. He could not see through the snow. The cold soon penetrated his quilted jacket.

_____

_____

2. For three days Aaron and Zlateh stayed in the haystack. Aaron had always loved Zlateh, but in these three days he loved her more and more. She fed him with her milk and helped him keep warm. She comforted him with her patience. He told her many stories, and she always cocked her ears and listened. When he patted her, she licked his hand and his face. Then she said, "Maaaa," and he knew it meant, I love you too.

_____

_____

Name _____ Date _____

Literary Analysis: Conflict With Nature

A **conflict** is a struggle between two forces. The struggle may be between two people, a person and herself or himself, or between a person and something in nature. Often, part of the enjoyment of reading a story is waiting to find out who will win the conflict. In "Zlateh the Goat," the conflict is between Aaron and the snowstorm. Aaron, a character in the story, has to battle a blizzard, one of nature's most powerful and dangerous forces. The battle between Aaron and the blizzard creates tension and suspense, and Aaron's fight for survival tells readers a great deal about his bravery and resourcefulness.

DIRECTIONS: In the chart below, the left column contains passages from "Zlateh the Goat." For each passage, complete the second and third columns. In the second column, write the problem that Aaron faces. In the third column, write how Aaron solves the problem. The first row has been filled in as an example.

Passage	Danger	Solution
1. "He could not see through the snow."	Aaron is lost.	He finds the haystack.
2. "His hands were numb, and he could no longer feel his toes."		
3. "Aaron ate his bread and cheese, but after the difficult journey he was still hungry."		
4. "The snow had blocked up his window."		

"Door Number Four" by Charlotte Pomerantz
"Count That Day Lost" by George Eliot
"The World Is Not a Pleasant Place to Be" by Nikki Giovanni

Build Vocabulary

Using the Prefix *de-*

The prefix *de-* often means "down," as it does in the word *descending*. A person who is descending a flight of stairs, a ramp, or a ladder is going down.

A. DIRECTIONS: Complete each sentence by adding the prefix *de-* to each word part in parentheses. Write the words on the lines provided.

1. When you (de- + crease) _____ the volume on your radio, you turn the volume down.

2. If there is a (de- + cline) _____ in the popularity of a best-selling soft drink, the soft drink's popularity is going down.

3. If a boss decides to (de- + mote) _____ an employee, he or she decides to move the employee down in position or rank.

4. If you (de- + press) _____ a key on a keyboard, you push it down.

5. If a car (de- + celerates) _____ , it slows down.

Using Words from the Selection

The word *eased* is defined for you in the selection. Study these definitions of two other words you will find in the grouping.

    self-denying   the opposite of *selfish;* done without concern for one's own interests
    trace   find signs of, observe, discover

B. DIRECTIONS: Fill in the blanks with the word that best completes the sentence.

1. It had snowed, and I could no longer _____ the path taken by the deer.

2. In a burst of _____ kindness, Gregorio shoveled snow for two elderly neighbors.

3. When the sun came out, our minds were _____—there would be no more snow.

Analogies

C. DIRECTIONS: Each item consists of a related pair of words in CAPITAL LETTERS, followed by four lettered pairs of words. Circle the letter of the pair that best expresses a relationship similar to the one expressed in the pair in capital letters.

1. EASED : SOOTHED ::
   a. slept : awakened
   b. songwriter : song
   c. fixed : repaired
   d. snow : rain

2. SELF-DENYING : SELFISH ::
   a. full : empty
   b. bake : cake
   c. actor : act
   d. whale : animal

3. TRACE : FOOTPRINTS ::
   a. large : animal
   b. deer : hunt
   c. look : see
   d. shine : shoes

"**Door Number Four**" by Charlotte Pomerantz
"**Count That Day Lost**" by George Eliot
"**The World Is Not a Pleasant Place to Be**" by Nikki Giovanni

Build Spelling Skills: Spelling the *z* Sound With the Letter *s*

Spelling Strategy: Sometimes the *z* sound is spelled with the letter *s*. Look at the Word Bank word *eased,* for example. Notice that the *z* sound in this word is spelled *s.*

Each of the following words also contains a *z* sound that is spelled with an *s.* Read the words and then pronounce each one quietly to yourself: *whose, is, was, cause, those, pleasant, clouds, tears.*

A. Practice: Complete the words in these sentences by putting an *s* or a *z* in the blank. Two of the words do use a *z*: if you are unsure of the spelling, check a dictionary.

1. What i___ the weather going to be?

2. I heard that the temperature is going to drop, and tonight it will free___e.

3. The cloud___that are gathering show that it may snow.

4. A cold front coming in will cau___e the change.

5. Did you notice that the bree___e is getting stronger?

6. I found these gloves outside. Who___e are they?

B. Practice: Write each of the following words once to complete the sentences below.

        pause   clears   tease

1. Don't do that again—it isn't nice to _____ your little sister.

2. He worked for hours on the model, without a _____ even for lunch.

3. Though it is cloudy now, we all hope the sky _____ before the weekend.

Challenge: The word *pleasant,* which is used in this group, is a form of the word *please.* These words come from the Old French *plaisir,* which means to enjoy, take pleasure in, delight in doing. It may seem odd that we say *please* when asking for something, but this is actually a shortened form of "If you please," and so meant that you were asking the person to do something if they wished to do it or thought it was appropriate.

        please: (verb) be agreeable; to cause pleasure; wish or think appropriate;
        pleasure: (noun) a feeling of being pleased; enjoyment, delight
        pleasant: (adj.) giving enjoyment; agreeable

DIRECTIONS: Complete the following sentences using the appropriate words from this group.

1. It was such a _____ afternoon, we decided to go for a walk.

2. Did the grade you received _____ you?

3. I get a great deal of _____ from helping others.

"Door Number Four" by Charlotte Pomerantz
"Count That Day Lost" by George Eliot
"The World Is Not a Pleasant Place to Be" by Nikki Giovanni

Build Grammar Skills: Verb Tenses

You use verbs such as *deliver, play, be,* and *become* to express actions and states of being. To show when the actions and the states of being occur, you use forms of the verbs called **verb tenses**. For example, when you say, "I *played* a new computer game," "I *deliver* the newspapers every day," or "I *will* be at my friend's house," you are using verb tenses that tell when.

The three simple, or basic, tenses are the past, the present, and the future. The chart below shows three different verbs in each of these tenses.

TENSES			
Present	I listen	I speak	I become
Past	I listened	I spoke	I became
Future	I will listen	I will speak	I will become

The verb *listen* is known as a regular verb. Notice that the past tense of this verb is formed by adding -*ed.* Now notice that the past tense forms of *speak* and *become* are formed in a different way. These are irregular verbs. One of the most common irregular verbs is *be;* note these forms:

Present—*am, is, are;* Past—*was, were;* Future—*will be.*

Finally, look at the future tense of all three verbs. Notice that they all use the helping verb *will.*

A. Practice: Above each italicized verb in the following sentences, write *PR* if it is in the present tense, *PA* if it is in the past tense, and *F* if it is in the future tense.

1. George Eliot *was* the pen name of Mary Ann Evans.

2. This famous English writer *lived* during the 1800's.

3. Charlotte Pomerantz *is* a writer who *made* friends with young readers through her books.

4. If you *read* her poems, you *will understand* why her writing *won* many prizes.

5. Nikki Giovanni *writes* poems that *appeal* to readers of all ages.

B. Writing Application: Write a sentence about each topic provided below, using the verb and verb tense given.

1. Write a sentence about friendship, using the verb *be* in the present tense.

_____

2. Write a sentence about one of the poems, using the verb *make* in the past tense.

_____

3. Write a sentence about one of your friends using a verb of your choice in the future tense.

_____

"Door Number Four" by Charlotte Pomerantz
"Count That Day Lost" by George Eliot
"The World Is Not a Pleasant Place to Be" by Nikki Giovanni

Reading Strategy: Paraphrasing

When you **paraphrase** a difficult phrase, sentence, or passage from a poem, you "translate" it into your own words. Restating the poet's words in this way can help you clarify the poem's meaning. For example, here is one way you might paraphrase lines 1-2 of "Count That Day Lost."

> If you sit down at set of sun
> And count the acts that you have done. . . .

> **Paraphrase:** If you stop for a moment in the evening and think back over what you've done that day. . .

Notice that when you paraphrase lines like these, you can change the poet's words into simpler, more everyday words and ideas. You can also change the order of words and ideas if doing so helps you to clarify their meaning.

A. DIRECTIONS: Paraphrase each of the following excerpts of "Count That Day Lost."

1. But if, through all the livelong day,
   You've cheered no heart, by yea or nay—

_____

_____

2. If, through it all
   You've nothing done that you can trace
   That brought the sunshine to one face—

_____

_____

B. DIRECTIONS: Paraphrase "The World Is Not a Pleasant Place to Be" by Nikki Giovanni. Write your paraphrase, one section at a time, on the lines provided. Remember to convey the poet's message about friendship as you restate her ideas in your own words.

1. the world is not a pleasant place / to be without / someone to hold and be held by

_____

_____

2. a river would stop / its flow if only / a stream were there / to receive it

_____

_____

3. an ocean would never laugh / if clouds weren't there / to kiss her tears

_____

_____

"Door Number Four" by Charlotte Pomerantz
"Count That Day Lost" by George Eliot
"The World Is Not a Pleasant Place to Be" by Nikki Giovanni

Literary Analysis: Speaker

Who do you think is saying the following words from "Door Number Four" by Charlotte Pomerantz?

> Above my uncle's grocery store / is a pintu, / is a door. / On the pintu / is a number, / nomer empat, / number four.

The imaginary person who says the words of a poem is known as the poem's **speaker**. Based on the words above, you can gather that speaker of "Door Number Four" has an uncle and enjoys using and sharing words from another language. These facts, together with the simple and playful quality of the lines, might suggest to you that the speaker is a child.

Sometimes the speaker of a poem may be very much like the poet, and sometimes there are important differences. For example, an adult such as Charlotte Pomerantz may write a poem in which the speaker is a child. Or, a female poet might write a poem in which the speaker is a man, and vice versa. In other cases, the one who is speaking may not have a definite identity as a man, woman, or child. Instead, the speaker can be described as "a voice of wisdom" or "a voice of the heart."

DIRECTIONS: Answer the following questions based on the excerpts given.

1. How do the following lines from "Door Number Four" further suggest that the speaker is a child?

> In the door / there is a key. / Turn it, / enter quietly. / Hush hush, diam-diam, / quietly. There, in lamplight, / you will see / a friend / teman, / a friend, / who's me.

_____

_____

_____

2. Based on the following lines from "Count That Day Lost," who do you think the poem's speaker is? What words or ideas in the lines make you think so?

> If you sit down at set of sun / And count the acts that you have done, / And, counting, find / One self-denying deed, one word / That eased the heart of him who heard, / One glance most kind / That fell like sunshine where it went— / Then you may count that day well spent. /

_____

_____

_____

"Old Ben" by Jesse Stuart
"Feathered Friend" by Arthur C. Clarke

Build Vocabulary

Forms of *regulate*

Many words are forms of other words. For example, *regulate* means "to govern according to a rule." The following words are related in form and meaning to the verb *regulate*: the noun *regulation* means "a rule"; the noun *regulator* means "a person who regulates"; and the adjective *regulatory* means "having to do with regulations."

A. DIRECTIONS: Complete each of the following sentences by filling in the blank space with the correct form of *regulate*. Choose from the forms above.

1. There is a _____ that requires drivers to drive slowly near a school.

2. The factory employs a _____ to see that workers follow the rules.

3. Without umpires, there would be no one to _____ baseball games.

4. The government has a _____ agency that makes sure food is packaged according to strict health rules.

Using the Word Bank

scarce	regulation	fusing	ceased

B. DIRECTIONS: In the space provided next to each Word Bank word, write the letter of the word or phrase that is closest in meaning.

____ 1. FUSING: a. joining   b. hitting   c. breaking   d. cutting

____ 2. REGULATION: a. goal   b. question   c. problem   d. rule

____ 3. SCARCE: a. tricky   b. frightening   c. rare   d. useful

____ 4. CEASED: a. fastened   b. folded   c. stopped   d. arranged

Recognizing Antonyms

C. DIRECTIONS: On the line, write the letter of the word that is most nearly *opposite* in meaning to the word in CAPITAL LETTERS.

_____ 1. SCARCE: a. plentiful   b. useful   c. funny   d. dull

_____ 2. CEASED: a. cleaned   b. covered   c. began   d. asked

_____ 3. REGULATED: a. questionable   b. guided   c. clear   d. unruly

_____ 4. FUSING: a. bonding   b. separating   c. trusting   d. halting

"Old Ben" by Jesse Stuart
"Feathered Friend" by Arthur C. Clarke

Build Spelling Skills: Adding Suffixes to Words Ending in Silent *e*

Spelling Strategy When a word ends in silent *e*, drop the final *e* when you add a suffix that begins with a vowel. Keep the silent *e*, however, when you add a suffix beginning with a consonant. *ventilate* + *-ing* = *ventilating* *precise* + *-ly* = *precisely*

A. Practice: Add the suffix to each word. Write the new word on the line. Remember to use the rules above for adding suffixes that begin with vowels or consonants to words ending in silent *e*.

1. amaze + *-ing*   =   _____
2. rude + *-ly*   =   _____
3. brave + *-ly*   =   _____
4. hope + *-ful*   =   _____
5. write + *-ing* =   _____

6. skate + *-ing* =   _____
7. polite + *-ly* =   _____
8. drive + *-ing* =   _____
9. spite + *-ful* =   _____
10. shake + *-ing* =   _____

B. Practice: Complete the paragraph by adding the indicated suffix to each given word and writing each new word on the space provided.

While (take + -ing) _____ Old Ben home, the boy was not sure that his father would let him keep the snake. The boy thought that Old Ben would be (use + -ful) _____ on the farm, and eat the mice that were always (nibble + -ing) _____ the corn in the corncrib. However, his father had no (like + -ing) _____ for snakes. At first, his parents watched the snake (close + -ly) _____, because they did not know whether they could trust Old Ben. But, as time went by, the boy saw that his father was (come + -ing) _____ to like the snake. He even began (place + -ing) _____ bowls of water in the corncrib for Old Ben to drink.

Challenge: The author of "Old Ben" mentions two kinds of snake: the blacksnake and the copperhead. Both their names describe their appearance. The blacksnake is all black, and the copperhead has a copper-colored head. Below are some descriptions of other animals and a list of animal names. Write the letter of the animal name that matches each description.

a. yellow-bellied sapsucker   c. hammerhead shark   e. walking stick
b. praying mantis   d. calico cat   f. bottle-nosed dolphin

____ 1. a three-colored, brightly marked cat
____ 2. an insect that is protected by looking like a twig or stick
____ 3. a sea animal with a long, narrow snout
____ 4. a fish with a flat, wide head
____ 5. a bird with a belly the color of an egg yolk
____ 6. an insect that folds its front legs to look like a pair of praying hands

"Old Ben" by Jesse Stuart
"Feathered Friend" by Arthur C. Clarke

Build Grammar Skills: The Perfect Tenses

The perfect tenses of verbs give narrative writers three ways of relating an event to what came before it. The perfect tenses include a form of the verb to *have* plus the past participle of the main verb.

- The **present perfect tense** shows that an event **began in the past** and continues into the present. The present perfect includes a **present-tense** form of *have* plus the **past participle** of the main verb: I <u>have been</u> a lucky man.

- The **past perfect tense** shows that an event took place before another past event or time. It includes a **past-tense** form of *have* plus the **past participle** of the main verb: He <u>had cleaned</u> the corncrib of mice.

- The **future perfect tense** shows that an event will be completed before another future event or time. It includes a **future-tense** form of *have* plus the **past participle** of the main verb: You <u>will have learned</u> who committed the crime before you finish the book.

A. Practice: In the space provided, identify the tense of the italicized words as either present perfect, past perfect, or future perfect. The first one has been done as an example.

past perfect   1. The boy's father *had hated* snakes before he met Old Ben.

_____   2. I *have had* many pets, but never as good a pet as that snake.

_____   3. The Spacers *had adopted* the canary as their pet before she saved their lives.

_____   4. By the time the new stadium is built, the team *will have played* for thirty years in the old one.

_____   5. We *have enjoyed* many evenings in the park.

_____   6. By noon tomorrow, we *will have finished* our homework.

B. Writing Application: Rewrite each of the following sentences on the lines provided, filling in the specified perfect tense of the verb in parentheses. The first one has been done as an example.

1. We _____ the test before the bell rang. (past perfect, *finish*)
   We had finished the test before the bell rang.

2. The players _____ the locker room to start the game. (present perfect, *leave*)
   _____

3. By the end of the year, they _____ the whole book. (future perfect, *read*)
   _____

4. Before going to the store, we _____ to the bank. (past perfect, *go*)
   _____

5. The club _____ not to meet next week. (present perfect, *decide*)
   _____

"Old Ben" by Jesse Stuart
"Feathered Friend" by Arthur C. Clarke

Reading Strategy: Using Context Clues

Sometimes you can figure out the meaning of an unfamiliar word by using **context clues**. Context is the material—words, sentences, or paragraphs—that come before and after the new word. For example, in "Feathered Friend," Arthur C. Clarke writes that Sven Olsen *excelled* at space construction. If you have no idea what *excelled* means, you might look back at the statement that "Sven was one of our best construction men," and guess that excelled had something to do with being the best. In fact, *excel* means *do better than others,* so this would be an accurate guess. You may also sometimes find words that seem familiar but that are used in a way that is new to you. For example, in "Old Ben," the author mentions a *crib* several times. The fact that this crib is used on a farm, near the barn, and for corn, should alert you to the fact that this is a place to store grain, not a baby's bed.

When you come across a new word in your reading, or a word that is used in a new way, look for context clues and try to figure out what it means. Then, check your guess against the definition in the dictionary.

DIRECTIONS: In each of the following passages from the selections, there is an italicized word. Look for context clues in the passage that may give you a hint about the word's meaning. Then, write the context clue and the meaning of the word on the line provided. The first one has been done as an example.

1. There he lay coiled like heavy *strands* of black rope. He was a big bull blacksnake.

   Context clue: ____"of black rope"____ Meaning: __cords, pieces of rope__

2. The more I petted him, the more *affectionate* he became. He was so friendly I decided to trust him.

   Context clue: _____ Meaning: _____

3. . . . it was a skilled and difficult job, for a space suit is not the most convenient of *garbs* in which to work.

   Context clue: _____ Meaning: _____

4. . . . you will picture Sven at once as a six-foot-six Nordic giant. . . . Actually he was a *wiry* little fellow. . .

   Context clue: _____ Meaning: _____

5. Though of course there is no "day" and "night" when you are floating in *permanent* sunlight . . .

   Context clue: _____ Meaning: _____

6. My mind seemed to be very *sluggish* that morning, as if I was still unable to cast off the burden of sleep.

   Context clue: _____ Meaning: _____

Name _____ Date _____

"**Old Ben**" by Jesse Stuart

"**Feathered Friend**" by Arthur C. Clarke

Literary Analysis: Narratives

A **narrative** is a story made up of events linked together. The events may be nonfiction (true) like "Old Ben." They might be fiction (made up) like "Feathered Friend." One way in which many narrative events are linked is that one event causes, or leads to, another. When you read a narrative, you may find it useful to keep track of the events and how one leads to another by using a graphic organizer like the one below.

A. DIRECTIONS: The following events all occur in "Feathered Friend," but in a different order. In the graphic organizer below, write the number of each event in the order in which it occurs in the story. The first and last events have been filled in as examples.

1. Sven finds Claribel motionless and thinks the canary is dead.

2. Sven smuggles a canary on board a space station.

3. The narrator realizes that there is something wrong with the air in the space station.

4. Claribel revives after being given oxygen, but passes out again.

5. The narrator is startled to hear a bird song just behind his head while he is working.

6. Jim, the engineer, discovers that the air purifying system has not been working properly.

7. The crew make Claribel a company pet.

8. The narrator wakes up with a headache and feeling tired.

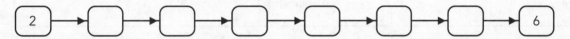

B. DIRECTIONS: On the lines below, write the events, thoughts, and statements of the narrator's father that show how his attitude toward Old Ben changes from the beginning of the narrative to the end. Write the events, thoughts, and statements in the order in which they occur in the narrative.

1. _____

2. _____

3. _____

4. _____

5. _____

6. _____

7. _____

from *The Pigman & Me* by Paul Zindel

Build Vocabulary

Using the Suffix *-tion*

The suffix *-tion*, meaning "the act, result, or condition of," generally changes a verb into a noun.

Examples: construct (to build); construction (the act or result of building)
imitate (to copy or ape); imitation (the act or result of copying or aping)

A. DIRECTIONS: In the first column of the following chart is a list of words. In the third column, each word has had the suffix *-tion* added to it. Fill in the blanks with the meanings of the words. (Hint: Each meaning in the last column will begin with "the act of . . . ," "the result of . . . ," or "the condition of . . . "). One example is provided.

Word	Meaning	Word with *-tion*	Meaning
1. educate	teach	education	the result of teaching
2. select		selection	
3. invite		invitation	
4. connect		connection	
5. subtract		subtraction	

Using the Word Bank

exact	tactics	undulating	goading
distorted	groveled		

B. DIRECTIONS: All the Word Bank words below have been scrambled. Unscramble the words, and write the letter of the correct Word Bank word next to the word's definition.

a. dgvrleoe   c. isdtroedt   e. gnaigod
b. xtace   d. duntigunal   f. scatsic

____ 1. pushing someone into action   ____ 4. methods used to achieve a goal

____ 2. take by force   ____ 5. crawled on the ground hoping
                                                         for mercy
____ 3. moving in waves
                                               ____ 6. twisted out of normal shape

C. DIRECTIONS: Circle the letter of the answer choice that means the same as the word in CAPITAL LETTERS.

1. CREATION: a. the act of creating b. to create c. creativity d. imagination

2. INSTRUCTION: a. to teach b. the act of learning c. the act of teaching d. learned

3. PROTECTION: a. to protect b. protecting c. desire to protect d. result of protecting

from *The Pigman & Me* by Paul Zindel

Build Spelling Skills: Spelling the Sound *shun* at the End of a Word

Spelling Strategy When the base form of a word ends with a *t* sound, usually use *-tion* to spell the sound *shun* as a suffix. Other words spell the final *shun* sound *-sion*.

Examples: promote + *shun* = promo**tion**

express + *shun* = expres**sion**.

Note that you need to change the spelling of most words before adding *-tion*. For example, the final e is dropped from *promote* to form *promotion*; the final s is dropped from *express* to form *expression*.

Exceptions: For many words, there is no clear rule for when to use *-tion* and when to use *-sion*. It is a good idea to check the spelling of such words in a dictionary if you're not sure of which spelling to use.

A. Practice: In the space provided, write the word formed by adding the *-tion* or *-sion* to the following words. Follow the instructions for how to change the spelling of each word before adding *-tion* or *-sion*. The first word has been done as an example.

1. prevent + shun = _____ prevention _____ (Drop the final *t*.)

2. confess + shun = _____ (Drop the final *s*.)

3. elevate + shun = _____ (Drop the final *te*.)

4. protect + shun = _____ (Drop the final *t*.)

5. interrupt + shun = _____ (Drop the final *t*.)

6. profess + shun = _____ (Drop the final *s*.)

7. provide + shun = _____ (Drop the final *de*.)

8. condemn + shun = _____ (Add a final *a*.)

B. Practice: Proofread the following paragraph. After each underlined word, write the letter "C" if the word is spelled correctly; if the word is spelled incorrectly, write the correct spelling on the line in parentheses. The first one has been done as an example.

Paul did not know how to handle the new complicasion (_____ complication _____) in his life. Because of some confution (_____) about playground rules, he had to choose between fighting another boy or getting the reputation (_____) of being a coward. He did not want to ask his friend for protection (_____), but he could not think of any way out of his situasion (_____). In desperasion (_____), he spoke to Nonno Frankie, but their discussion (_____) was not very helpful. Paul came to the sad conclution (_____) that he would probably have to fight John Quinn on Monday afternoon.

Name _____ Date _____

from *The Pigman & Me* by Paul Zindel

Build Grammar Skills: Adjectives

An **adjective** is a word that describes a noun by telling more about the person, place, or thing. Adjectives answer questions such as *What kind? Which one? How many?* and *How much?* In the following sentences, the adjectives are underlined.

They looked like the mob I had seen in a sixteenth-century etching. . . .

Sixteenth-century answers the question "**What kind** of etching?"

He once killed two million enemies in one hour.

Two million answers the question **"How many** enemies?" *One* answers the question **"How many** hours?"

This happened on the first Friday, during gym period.

First answers the question **"Which** Friday?" *Gym* answers the question **"Which** period?"

The most frequently used adjectives are the words *a, an,* and *the.* These three adjectives are called **articles.**

A. Practice: Underline the adjective in each of the following sentences. On the line following each sentence write the question the adjective answers: *What kind? Which one?* or *How many?* Then in parentheses, write any articles that appear in the sentence. The first sentence has been done as an example.

1. Paul was a new student at the school. __What kind?_____ (a, the)_____

2. Paul did not know that fifteen minutes was the limit for using a paddle. _____

3. It was Paul's first week of school. _____

4. A huge crowd was waiting to see the fight. _____

5. Paul tried to kick John on the left shin but missed. _____

6. Paul's brave sister saved him from an attack. _____

B. Writing Application: On each of the lines provided, write a sentence using the word in parentheses as an adjective, describing a person, place, or thing. The first one has been done as an example.

1. (energetic) __An energetic person will take on many projects._____

2. (dangerous) _____

3. (eighteen) _____

4. (chocolate) _____

5. (exciting) _____

6. (angry) _____

7. (difficult) _____

from *The Pigman & Me* by Paul Zindel

Reading Strategy: Recognizing Word Origins

As you read, you often meet words from other languages. That is because the English language always has been a borrower of words and expressions. Many of them become so familiar over time that their "borrowed" origins are forgotten. Others become familiar enough that they can be found in an English dictionary. Being able to **recognize word origins** will help you understand and enjoy what you read.

In *The Pigman & Me*, for example, Nonno Frankie urges Paul to say that John Quinn could wear an espresso cup like a sombrero. *Sombrero* is borrowed from Spanish; it refers to a hat with a high crown and a very wide brim. At the end of the story, Paul says that Nonno Frankie taught him karate. *Karate* is borrowed from Japanese; it refers to a form of self-defense known for its punching and kicking techniques.

A. Directions: Many words relating to clothing come from other languages. Complete each sentence using a "clothing" word from the box. Definitions and origins are in parentheses.

sequins	stilettos	kimono	bandanna	poncho

1. Eric wiped the sweat away with his red _____. (large handkerchief often worn around the head or neck [Hindi]).

2. The movie star's dress is covered with silver _____. (shiny, coin-shaped decorations [Arabic]).

3. It must be hard to walk on those _____, though. (shoes with high, thin, daggerlike heels [Italian]).

4. This silk _____ certainly is elegant. (wide-sleeved robe, worn with a sash [Japanese]).

5. I don't need an umbrella; this hat and this waterproof _____ will keep me dry. (blanket-like covering slipped over the head and worn as a sleeveless jacket [Araucanian Indian]

B. Directions: Many expressions come from other languages, too. Use a dictionary to find the meaning of each expression in the box. (The language of origin is in parentheses.) Then complete each sentence with the correct expression.

sotto voce (Italian)	faux pas (French)
cause célèbre (French)	mano a mano (Spanish)

1. A _____ on the school yard brought Paul into conflict with John Quinn.

2. After school they would not fight each other _____.

3. The _____ attracted a large crowd—and Paul's sister.

4. On the way home, Paul smiled at her and mumbled a _____ "Thank you."

from *The Pigman & Me* by Paul Zindel

Literary Analysis: Internal Conflict

In a story, a **conflict** is a struggle that take place between opposing characters or forces. An **internal conflict** takes place inside a person or character. For example, in *The Pigman & Me*, the narrator has a conflict within himself after John Quinn challenges him to a fight. On the one hand, he is a new student at school and does not want to look like he is a coward. On the other hand, he does not want to fight. His struggle is internal.

A. Directions: Answer the following questions on the lines provided.

1. What would happen if Paul simply chose to look courageous and not cowardly? _____
_____
_____

    Why would this outcome be undesirable for Paul? _____
_____

2. What would happen if Paul simply decided to avoid a fight? _____
_____
_____

    Why would this outcome be undesirable for Paul? _____
_____

B. Directions: The following quotations from *The Pigman & Me* demonstrate how Paul's internal conflict makes him feel. Choose one of these quotations, and use the lines provided to explain why Paul's conflict makes him feel the way he does.

1. By the time Monday morning came, I was a nervous wreck.

2. Nevertheless, my mind was numb with fear all day at school.

3. . . . I thought I was going to pass out.

_____
_____
_____
_____
_____
_____
_____

"**Thunder Butte**" by Virginia Driving Hawk Sneve

Build Vocabulary

Using Related Words: Forms of *vary*

The Word Bank word *variegated* is related to the familiar word *vary*, which means "to differ." Like all words related to *vary*, *variegated* includes the idea of "difference" in its meaning. Something that is variegated is marked with different colors, just like the agates that Norman finds on the butte. Here are some other words related to *vary*.

variety: a collection of different things
varied: of different kinds; many-sided
various: of different kinds; many or several
variable: tending to change or become different

A. Directions: Use the correct word to complete each sentence.

1. I don't know what kind of tape to get for Mark because his taste in music is so (variegated, variable) _____; one week all he listens to is classical music, and the next week he won't listen to anything but jazz.

2. I think I'll go to Music World to shop for something, because they have the greatest (variety, various) _____ of tapes.

3. After looking in (various, variable) _____ sections of the store, I decided to get something by the Beatles.

4. I thought that Mark would be sure to find something that he likes in their music, since their songs are so (variety, varied) _____.

Using the Word Bank

| meanderings | diminutive | variegated | heathen | adamant |

B. Directions: Match each word in the left column with its definition in the right column. Write the letter of the definition on the line next to the word it defines.

____ 1. variegated   a. not willing to give in

____ 2. adamant   b. not civilized

____ 3. meanderings   c. wanderings

____ 4. heathen   d. very small

____ 5. diminutive   e. marked with different colors

"Thunder Butte" by Virginia Driving Hawk Sneve

Build Spelling Skills: Adding Suffixes to Words Ending in y

Spelling Strategy Adding a suffix often means you must change the spelling of the original word. Use the following strategies:

- When adding a suffix that begins with a vowel to a word that ends in y preceded by a consonant, change the y to i before adding the suffix.

  vary + -ous = various   worry + -ed = worried
  (Exceptions: Do not change the y to i if the suffix begins with i—trying, babyish)

- When adding a suffix that begins with a vowel to a word that ends in y preceded by a vowel, keep the y before adding the suffix.

  portray + -al = portrayal   enjoy + -ed = enjoyed
  (Some Exceptions: pay + -ed = paid, say + -ed = said)

A. PRACTICE: Add the indicated ending to each word. Write the new word on the line.

1. fry + -ed   = _____

2. marry + -ing   = _____

3. study + -ous   = _____

4. fancy + -est   = _____

5. sturdy + -er   = _____

6. apply + -ed   = _____

7. merry + -est   = _____

8. journey + -ing   = _____

B. PRACTICE: Complete each sentence by writing the word in parentheses with the suffix indicated.

1. Norman (obey + -ed)_____the wishes of his grandfather.

2. The boy looked around the butte, (survey + -ing)_____his surroundings.

3. If Norman were careless on his trip up the butte, it would be a (betray + -al)
   _____of his mother's wishes.

4. While he was (hurry + -ing)_____to the west side, he collected agates,
   semiprecious stones.

5. Norman (pay + -ed)_____a tribute to his family's tribe when he recovered the
   coup stick.

"**Thunder Butte**" by Virginia Driving Hawk Sneve

Build Grammar Skills: Possessives as Adjectives

Adjectives are words that modify nouns or pronouns. They can answer the questions *what kind?* and *how many?* They can also answer the question *whose?* Look at these sentences.

The <u>sun's</u> rays heated the rocky landscape.

<u>Norman's</u> mother told him to be careful.

The boy found a Sioux <u>warrior's</u> *coup* stick on the butte.

In these sentences, the words *sun's*, *Norman's*, and *warrior's* are possessive nouns—nouns that show possession or ownership. These possessives function as adjectives because they answer the question *whose?* Now look at these sentences.

Norman examines the stick and *its* markings.   He showed the stick to *his* grandfather.

In these sentences, the words *its* and *his* are possessive pronouns—pronouns that show possession or ownership. Other possessive pronouns function as adjectives and include *my*, *your*, *her*, *our*, *their*. All can answer the question *whose?*

A. Practice: Circle the possessives that function as adjectives in the each of the following sentences. Remember that these words answer the question *whose?*

1. Norman dressed in his oldest clothes and pulled on worn boots to protect his feet.

2. "Guess I'll go," Norman said to his mother, who was pouring hot water into her dish pan.

3. Norman whistled, trying to echo the meadowlarks' happy song, as he left on his journey.

4. The boy's heart pounded as he realized that the stick had once belonged to the old ones.

5. Norman's grandfather explained the thunderbolt's meaning.

6. Grandfather said, "The Thunders favored a certain few of the young men who sought their vision on the butte."

B. Writing Application: Write a sentence about each topic provided below, using possessives as adjectives as suggested. When you are finished, reread your sentences and underline any additional possessives that you used as adjectives.

1. Write a sentence about a challenge that you have faced, using the possessive *my* as an adjective.

   _____

2. Write a sentence that tells something about a member of your family. Use the person's name in a possessive form.

   _____

3. Write a sentence about your school. Use the possessive *school's* as an adjective.

   _____

4. Write a question that you might ask someone whom you recently met. Use the possessive *your* as an adjective.

   _____

"Thunder Butte" by Virginia Driving Hawk Sneve

Reading Strategy: Understanding Shades of Meaning

What's the difference between *looking* and *searching*, between *knew* and *understood*, between *instruction* and *command*? In each pair, the words are similar in meaning but are not exactly the same. Each word has a slightly different sense. For example, *searching* seems more intense than *looking*, *understood* suggests deeper or more careful thought than *knew*, and *command* seems more forceful than *instruction*. These differences often are called "shades of meaning."

Writers choose their words carefully. (For example, Virginia Driving Hawk Sneve used *looking*, *understood*, and *command* in the first few paragraphs of "Thunder Butte.") When you read, therefore, try to **understand shades of meaning** in the words you meet. If you do, you will have a clearer picture of what the writer is sharing.

DIRECTIONS: Think about the underlined word in each of these passages from "Thunder Butte." Write a word that has a similar meaning. (Check a dictionary, if you wish.) Then, write a sentence or two explaining how the shade of meaning in that word helps you understand the story better.

1. Sarah <u>grunted</u> scornfully, "No one believes in dreams or any of those old superstitious ways anymore."

   _____   _____

   _____

   _____

2. Then Norman smiled as he remembered his grandfather's command to climb the south trail that <u>wound</u> to the top.

   _____   _____

   _____

   _____

3. His grandfather's tent was a white shoe box in its clearing, and beside it stood a <u>diminutive</u> form waving a white flag.

   _____   _____

   _____

   _____

4. "This," he said, holding the *coup* stick upright, "is a <u>relic</u> of our people's past glory when it was a good thing to be an Indian."

   _____   _____

   _____

   _____

"Thunder Butte" by Virginia Driving Hawk Sneve

Literary Analysis: Atmosphere

Atmosphere is the feeling or mood of a work of literature. Through a careful choice of details, phrases, and images, a writer can create an atmosphere that is light-hearted or serious, cheerful or threatening, silly or mysterious.

A. DIRECTIONS: Read the following passage, and circle the images, phrases, or details that help to create a certain atmosphere. One the lines below, write a sentence describing the atmosphere that the details convey.

1. He was afraid that the cane may have plunged into a rattlesnake den. Carefully he pulled at the stout branch, wiggling it this way and that with one hand while he dug with the other. It came loose, sending a shower of rocks down the hill, and Norman saw that something else was sticking up in the hole he had uncovered.

_____

2. "Sarah," he said as he put the tools away, "think of the stick as an object that could be in a museum, a part of history. It's not like we were going to fall down on our knees and pray to it." His voice was light and teasing as he tried to make peace.

But Sarah stood stiffly at the stove preparing supper and would not answer. Norman felt sick. His appetite was gone. When his mother set a plate of food before him he excused himself saying, "I guess I'm too tired to eat," and went to his room.

_____

B. DIRECTIONS: Use the organizer below to record other details in the story that help to create atmosphere. Use the space in the center to name the mood or feeling you sense. Jot down the details that contribute to this atmosphere.

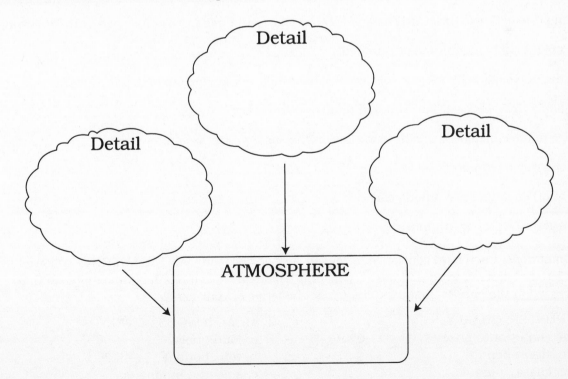

© Prentice-Hall, Inc.

Build Vocabulary

Using the Prefix *mono-*

The prefix *mono-* means "one," as you can see in the meaning of the Word Bank word *monotonous*. Something that is monotonous is tiresome because it has one sound or quality that does not vary. Here are some other words that contain the prefix *mono-*.

monograph: a scholarly book or article focusing on one specific subject
monologue: a long speech made by one speaker or one character in a play
monopoly: the control of an entire business by one company
monorail: a railway with a single track
monosyllables: words of one syllable

A. DIRECTIONS: Complete each sentence using one of the words listed above.

1. Paul is rehearsing his _____ for the school play.

2. Now there are two gas stations in town, and no one has a _____.

3. Professor Dawes is writing a _____ about ancient Egyptian mummies.

4. My little brother was mad and barely speaking to me, and whenever I tried to ask him questions, he answered in _____.

5. In only five minutes, the _____ will take you to the airport terminal.

Using the Word Bank

scuttled	quarry	fostering	veterans	monotonous	dispute	clamor

B. DIRECTIONS: Write the Word Bank word that you would use to describe each of the following.

1. an animal being hunted or pursued: _____

2. the noise made by six-year-old twins who loudly refuse to go to bed: _____

3. like a tiresome task that you had to do over and over: _____

4. committee members who have worked on the same project year after year: _____

5. the way a chipmunk moved: _____

6. another way to say "taking care of": _____

7. another word for "argument": _____

C. DIRECTIONS: Each item consists of a related pair of words in CAPITAL LETTERS, followed by four lettered pairs of words. Choose a pair that best expresses a relationship similar to that expressed in the pair in capital letters. Circle the letter of your choice.

1. HUNTER : QUARRY
   a. contestant : prize
   b. tiger : lion
   c. chase : pursue
   d. farmer : weather

2. MONOTONOUS : LIVELY
   a. loud : noisy
   b. top : bottom
   c. smooth : bumpy
   d. pleased : joyful

Name _____ Date _____

Build Spelling Skills: *There, Their,* and *They're*

Spelling Strategy The English language has many examples of words that sound alike but have different spellings and different meanings. Such words are called homophones. *There, their,* and *they're* are a good example of homophones that often are confused. Note the correct spellings and meanings:

The wolves gather over *there*, at Council Rock. (adverb)

How *their* eyes glow in the moonlight! (possessive pronoun)

I think that *they're* discussing the fate of Mowgli, the man's cub. (pronoun-verb contraction)

Make sure that the spelling of the word you use matches the meaning that you want to express.

A. Directions: Complete each sentence using *there, their,* or *they're.*

1. The wolves barely hide _____ dislike of Shere Khan.

2. _____ he goes now, with Tabaqui by his side.

3. Father Wolf thinks that _____ up to no good.

4. What will become of _____ plan to take back the man's cub?

5. Akela speaks to the wolves, and _____ all ignoring Shere Khan.

6. Mowgli is sitting _____, playing in the center of the wolves' circle.

7. He smiles at the wolves, not knowing that _____ deciding his fate.

B. Directions: If the underlined word in a sentence is used and spelled correctly, write *Correct* on the line. If it is incorrect, write the correct spelling.

_____ 1. Wolf cubs must have <u>there</u> Pack membership supported by two adults.

_____ 2. <u>There</u> are the adult wolves, watching Mowgli with great interest.

_____ 3. <u>Their</u> waiting to see who will speak for the man's cub.

_____ 4. Will <u>they're</u> be anyone who will support him?

_____ 5. Suddenly, all the wolves turn <u>they're</u> heads toward Baloo.

_____ 6. <u>They're</u> all respectful of the wise old bear.

_____ 7. They sense that <u>their</u> is great wisdom in Baloo's advice.

Name _____ Date _____

Build Grammar Skills: Adverbs

Adverbs modify verbs, adjectives, and other adverbs. They answer the questions *how? when? where?* and *to what extent?*

Adverb	Word it modifies	Question it answers
We waited <u>patiently</u>.	waited (verb)	How did we wait?
He <u>often</u> travels by train.	travels (verb)	When does he travel by train?
She goes <u>there</u> on foot.	goes (verb)	Where does she go on foot?
Were you <u>very</u> tired from your trip?	tired (adjective)	To what extent were you tired?

A. Practice: Underline the adverb in each of the following sentences and draw an arrow to the word that it modifies. Then, on the line below the sentence, write the question that the adverb answers. One example is given

1. Father Wolf awoke <u>early</u>.

    When did Father Wolf awaken?

2. He scratched himself, stretched his paws, and yawned loudly.

    _____

3. He looked at the moonlit sky and declared that he must now hunt.

    _____

4. The voice of the jackal Tabaqui greeted him softly.

    _____

5. Father Wolf allowed him to enter but told him that he would find no food there.

    _____

6. Tabaqui declared that his needs were extremely modest.

    _____

7. A dry bone would make a perfectly adequate meal for a poor, lowly jackal.

    _____

B. Writing Application: Write a short paragraph about a tiger catching and eating its dinner. Use at least five of the following adverbs.

silently	here and there	suddenly	rapidly	hungrily
later	afterward	contentedly	happily	very

_____

_____

_____

_____

Name _____   Date _____

"Mowgli's Brothers" by Rudyard Kipling
Reading Strategy: Predicting

As you read an exciting story like "Mowgli's Brothers," you will probably find yourself predicting what characters will do or what events will occur next. The **predictions** you make are logical guesses based on information you encounter in the story.

As an active reader, you will also find yourself revising your predictions at times. For example, suppose that at one point in your reading, you predicted that Mother and Father Wolf would hurt the human child. What effect would these words, spoken by Mother Wolf, have on your prediction?

> "The man's cub is mine, Lungri—mine to me! He shall not be killed. He shall live to run with the Pack and to hunt with the Pack. . . . "

Based on this new information, you would revise, or change, your prediction. You would conclude that just because Mother and Father Wolf are capable of killing the "man's cub," it doesn't necessarily mean that they will choose to do so.

DIRECTIONS: Use the chart below to make and check predictions as you read "Mowgli's Brothers." Use the first and second columns to jot down your predictions and the details that helped you make them. In the third column, note the evidence from the story that helped you to confirm or revise your prediction. One entry has been modeled for you, based on the example given above.

Prediction	Reasons	Was I Right or Wrong?
Mother and Father Wolf will hurt the child.	Father Wolf says: "I could kill him with a touch of my foot" and "The man's cub is ours—to kill if we choose."	Wrong—Mother Wolf decides to protect the child because she wants to defy Shere Khan.

Unit 3: Proving Yourself

© Prentice-Hall, Inc.

Selection Support **69**

"Mowgli's Brothers" by Rudyard Kipling

Literary Analysis: Animal Characters

Most of the characters in "Mowgli's Brothers" are animals. **Animal characters** behave according to their animal characteristics, but they also have human traits. Reread the opening passage from the story. What animal characteristics do you see in the characters being introduced? What are their human characteristics?

You probably noticed that Mother and Father Wolf do several things that are consistent with the behavior of wolves: they sleep, yawn, stretch, and keep an eye on their cubs. However, Father Wolf also displays one trait that is definitely human: he speaks, expressing his thoughts in words. As the story unfolds, Mother and Father Wolf will reveal more animal and human traits, as will other animal characters.

A. DIRECTIONS: Read the following passage. Then write a sentence or two to answer the questions below.

> It was the jackal—Tabaqui the Dishlicker—and the wolves of India despise Tabaqui because he runs about making mischief, and telling tales, and eating rags and pieces of leather from the village rubbish-heaps....
>
> "Enter, then, and look," said Father Wolf, stiffly; "but there is no food here."
>
> "For a wolf, no," said Tabaqui; "but for so mean a person as myself a dry bone is a good feast. Who are we, the Gidur-log [the jackal-people], to pick and choose?" He scuttled to the back of the cave, where he found the bone of a buck with some meat on it, and sat cracking the end merrily.
>
> "All thanks for this good meal," he said, licking his lips. "How beautiful are the noble children! How large are their eyes! And so young too! Indeed, indeed, I might have remembered that the children of Kings are men from the beginning."
>
> Now, Tabaqui knew as well as anyone else that there is nothing so unlucky as to compliment children to their faces; and it pleases him to see Mother and Father Wolf look uncomfortable.

1. What characteristics does Tabaqui show that reflect the way real jackals behave?

   _____

   _____

   _____

2. What characteristics does he show that normally belong only to humans?

   _____

   _____

3. Identify two human characteristics that Mother and Father Wolf display in this passage.

   _____

   _____

"Names/Nombres" by Julia Alvarez
"The Southpaw" by Judith Viorst
"Alone in the Nets" by Arnold Adoff

Build Vocabulary

Using the Prefix *trans-*

The prefix *trans-* means "over," "through," or "across." Knowing the meaning of this prefix can help you remember that the Word Bank word *transport* means "to carry over or across a distance." It can also help you figure out the meanings of the following words:

transplant   transparent   transcontinental   transmitter

A. DIRECTIONS: Complete each sentence by writing one of the words listed above. Look in a dictionary if you are not sure of the meaning of any of the words.

1. Our _____ railroad trip started in Atlanta, Georgia, and ended in Seattle, Washington.

2. The _____ plastic wrap lets you see exactly what is in the bowl.

3. A radio _____ is a device that sends radio signals though the air.

4. Early spring and late fall are the best times to _____ these shrubs.

Using the Word Bank

| transport | inevitably | chaotic | inscribed | opposition | evaporate |

B. DIRECTIONS: Match each word in the left column with its definition in the right column. Write the letter of the definition on the line next to the word it defines.

____ 1. chaotic   a. disappear

____ 2. inevitably   b. confused; messy

____ 3. evaporate   c. carry from one place to another

____ 4. transport   d. unavoidably

____ 5. opposition   e. written on

____ 6. inscribed   f. other side in a conflict

Recognizing Antonyms

C. DIRECTIONS: Circle the letter of the answer choice that is most nearly opposite in meaning to the word in CAPITAL LETTERS.

1. INEVITABLY: a. finally   b. avoidably   c. never   d. invisibly

2. CHAOTIC: a. attractive   b. noiseless   c. tiny   d. orderly

Unit 3: Proving Yourself

"Names/Nombres" by Julia Alvarez
"The Southpaw" by Judith Viorst
"Alone in the Nets" by Arnold Adoff

Build Spelling Skills: *Your* and *You're*

Spelling Strategy Homophones are words that sound alike but have different spellings and different meanings. Make sure that the spelling of the word you use matches the meaning that you want to express.

Here, from "The Southpaw," are examples of the commonly confused homophones *your* and *you're*.

Here is *your* stupid Disneyland sweatshirt, if that's how *you're* going to be.

Your is a possessive pronoun, but *you're* is a contraction of *you* and *are*.

A. DIRECTIONS: Circle the word in parentheses that correctly completes each sentence.

1. When you play sports, (your, you're) attitude is very important.

2. If (your, you're) a baseball fan, for example, you know the value of teamwork.

3. Teamwork is a theme that (your, you're) going to find in "The Southpaw."

4. Richard, don't you want (your, you're) team to win more games?

5. (Your, You're) also in need of help because some players are out sick.

6. Janet, I admire (your, you're) determination.

7. If you and Richard combine (your, you're) talents, (your, you're) sure to have a great team.

B. DIRECTIONS: Complete each sentence (based on "Alone in the Nets") using *your* or *you're*.

1. The goalie thought, "If you like this cold, rainy weather, _____ crazy."

2. "Watch how you run, forward, or _____ going to slip."

3. "You wouldn't want to get _____ cleats all muddy."

4. "Coach, _____ mistaken if you think I can save this game!"

5. Goalie, why is _____ mind so troubled?

6. _____ a good player, so don't doubt _____ abilities.

7. There— _____ save was great, so _____ happy once again.

Names/Nombres" by Julia Alvarez
"The Southpaw" by Judith Viorst
"Alone in the Nets" by Arnold Adoff

Build Grammar Skills: Adverbs Modifying Adjectives and Adverbs

In addition to modifying verbs, **adverbs** can modify adjectives and other adverbs.

Adverb *eagerly* modifies the verb *read*:
Julia Alvarez <u>eagerly</u> read books, stories, and poems when she was in high school.

Adverb *sometimes* modifies the verb *appear*:
Judith Viorst's children <u>sometimes</u> appear as characters in her books.

Adverb *very* modifies the adverb *touchingly* and answers the question *how?*:
Julia Alvarez writes <u>very</u> touchingly about her family.

Adverb *rather* modifies the adjective *unusual* and answers the question *to what extent?*:
Arnold Adoff describes a soccer game in a <u>rather</u> unusual way.

Here are some adverbs commonly used to modify adjectives and other adverbs:

almost	too	so	very	rather	usually	quite

A. Practice: Look at the underlined adverb or adverbs in each sentence. Draw an arrow to the word that each one modifies, and write whether it is an adjective or another adverb. One example is given.

1. Julia Alvarez's family names changed <u>almost</u> immediately. _____ adverb _____

2. Julia was <u>too</u> shy to correct people who mispronounced her name. _____

3. By the time she got to high school, she was <u>very</u> confident. _____

4. "Southpaw" presents a <u>rather</u> different kind of situation. _____

5. Two <u>usually</u> close friends exchange a series of angry letters. _____

6. The goalie in "Alone in the Nets" speaks <u>quite</u> nervously. _____

7. At the end, she was not <u>too</u> nervous to save the ball. _____

B. Writing Application: Revise the paragraph below so that it contains adverbs that modify adjectives and other adverbs. Choose from the following adverbs.

extremely	very	so	quite

Julia Alvarez loved literature and wanted to become a writer. When she was in high school, she read _____ frequently that her parents called any well-known author her "friend," as in "your friend Shakespeare." Their teasing was not meant to embarrass her, however. On the contrary, it was _____ gentle and loving. When Julia graduated from high school, her parents gave her a(n) _____ thoughtful gift. It was a typewriter for writing her stories and poems. Some day, they told her, her name would be _____ famous throughout the United States.

Names/Nombres" by Julia Alvarez
"The Southpaw" by Judith Viorst
"Alone in the Nets" by Arnold Adoff

Reading Strategy: Set a Purpose for Reading

Setting a purpose for reading means giving yourself a focus for your thoughts and reactions as you read. Often, special features and qualities of the work you are reading will help you set a particular purpose. For example, a story that is full of suspenseful clues and details will encourage you to keep making predictions about what will happen next or how a mystery will be solved. Works such as these three poems, which present interesting situations from distinctive viewpoints, encourage you to look at events through other people's eyes.

DIRECTIONS: Jot down notes on the lines below to keep track of viewpoints and reactions in "Names/Nombres," "Southpaw," and "Alone in the Nets." One set of notes, based on the beginning of "Southpaw," has been modeled for you.

What Happens

Richard does not allow Janet to play on the Mapes Street baseball team. _____
_____
_____
_____

How Character Reacts

Janet gets mad. She tells Richard that she doesn't want to be friends anymore. Richard defends his decision.
_____
_____
_____
_____

Character's Point of View (Reason for His or Her Reaction)

Janet thinks the decision is unfair. Richard says that girls have never been allowed on the team and that
things should continue that way. _____
_____
_____
_____

Do I Sympathize With Character's Point of View?

I agree (disagree) with Janet. _____
_____
_____
_____
_____

"Names/Nombres" by Julia Alvarez
"The Southpaw" by Judith Viorst
"Alone in the Nets" by Arnold Adoff

Literary Analysis: Narrator's Perspective

The narrator—or person who tells a story—presents his or her own **perspective** on the events that he or she is describing. For example, in "Names/Nombres," Julia Alvarez writes from her own perspective about experiences that she had as a recent immigrant to the United States. The two "former friends" who are the narrators of "Southpaw" present two different perspectives on a disagreement about who should and should not play on a certain baseball team. The Narrator in "Alone in the Nets" offers a unique perspective on a soccer game.

A. DIRECTIONS: Read the following passage from "Names/Nombres." One the lines below, use your own words to identify the situation or event that the narrator is describing. Then identify two different feelings or reactions that she reveals as part of her perspective.

These relatives had such complicated names and there were so many of them, and their relationships to myself were so convoluted. There was my Tía Josefina, who was not really an aunt but a much older cousin. And her daughter, Aida Margarita, who was adopted, una *hija de crianza*. My uncle of affection, Tío José, brought my *madrina* Tía Amelia and her *comadre* Tía Pilar. My friends rarely had more than a "Mom and Dad" to introduce.

_____

_____

_____

B. DIRECTIONS: Read the following passage from "The Southpaw." Then answer the questions below.

Dear Janet,
    Ronnie caught the chicken pox and Leo broke his toe and Elwood has these stupid violin lessons. I'll give you first base, and that's my final offer.
    Richard

Dear Richard,
    Susan Reilly plays first base, Marilyn Jackson catches, Ethel Kahn plays center field, I pitch. It's a package deal.
    Janet
    P.S. Sorry about your 12-game losing streak.

1. What specific issue or situation do Richard and Janet disagree about?

_____

_____

2. What is Richard's position on this issue?

_____

_____

3. What is Janet's position?

_____

_____

"Adventures of Isabel" by Ogden Nash
"I'll Stay" by Gwendolyn Brooks
"Wilbur Wright and Orville Wright"
by Rosemary and Stephen Vincent Benét
"Dream Dust" by Langston Hughes

Build Vocabulary

Using the Suffix *-ous*

The suffix *-ous* means "having the qualities of" or "full of." For example, *virtuous* means "full of virtue," and *famous* means "having the quality of fame."

A. DIRECTIONS: In the space next to each of the following definitions in the left column, write the letter of the word from the right column that best fits the definition.

____ 1. angry, full of fury   a. miraculous

____ 2. risky, full of danger   b. disastrous

____ 3. terrible, like a catastrophe c. furious

____ 4. wonderful, delightful   d. dangerous

____ 5. amazing, like a miracle   e. glorious

Using the Word Bank

ravenous	cavernous	rancor	grant

B. DIRECTIONS: Complete the crossword puzzle below. Hint: The Across list contains the answers for the clues in the Down list; the Down list contains the answers for the clues in the Across list.

Across

3. admit
4. hungry
6. big and empty
8. hate

Down

1. cavernous
2. rancor
5. ravenous
7. admit

Sentence Completions

C. DIRECTIONS: Fill in each blank with the word that best completes the sentence.

grant   ravenous   cavernous

1. After their long hike, the campers were _____.

2. The kids had to _____ that the clever magician had fooled them.

3. The fans' voices echoed in the _____ arena.

Name _____ Date _____

"**Adventures of Isabel**" by Ogden Nash
"**I'll Stay**" by Gwendolyn Brooks
"**Wilbur Wright and Orville Wright**"
by Rosemary and Stephen Vincent Benét
"**Dream Dust**" by Langston Hughes

Build Spelling Skills: Spelling Words That Use the Suffix *-ous*

Even though you do not hear the *o* sound in the suffix *-ous*, be sure to use an *o* when you spell any words ending in that suffix.

ravenous   delicious   poisonous

A. Practice: Write the word ending in *-ous* that fits each of the following definitions in the space provided. The first one has been done as an example.

1. evil, having the qualities of a villain ____villainous_____

2. happy, full of joy_____

3. large and empty, having the qualities of a cavern_____

4. very loud, having the quality of thunder _____

5. funny, full of humor _____

B. Practice: Complete each of the following sentences by filling in the blank with a word formed by adding the suffix *-ous* to the word in parentheses. Hint: If you are not sure of the spelling, check a dictionary. The first sentence has been done as an example.

1. Ogden Nash wrote many (humor) ____humorous_____ poems, such as "Adventures of Isabel."

2. Isabel seems like a very (adventure) _____ girl.

3. She finds herself in some (ridicule) _____ situations.

4. Wilbur and Orville Wright realized that flying can be (danger) _____.

5. The people who flew the first airplanes were (courage) _____.

Challenge: In "Adventures of Isabel," Isabel eats zwieback, a kind of biscuit that is first baked and then toasted. The fact that it is cooked twice gives it its name, which is German for "twice baked." In fact the word *biscuit* comes from the French—*bis* (twice) *cuit* (cooked). Many other foods get their names from the ways in which they are prepared or how they look. Below is a list of some tasty foreign dishes. Can you match each with its description? If you're unsure of the meaning of a word, look in a dictionary.

____ 1. French: croissant   a. rolled, stuffed tortilla, covered with chili sauce

____ 2. Chinese: lo mein   b. long, thin pasta, whose name means "worms"

____ 3. Italian: vermicelli   c. chopped cabbage that has been pickled in sour vinegar

____ 4. Spanish: enchilada   d. crescent-shaped roll

____ 5. German: sauerkraut   e. noodles mixed with various other foods

Selection Support **77**

"Adventures of Isabel" by Ogden Nash
"I'll Stay" by Gwendolyn Brooks
"Wilbur Wright and Orville Wright"
by Rosemary and Stephen Vincent Benét
"Dream Dust" by Langston Hughes

Build Grammar Skills: Adjective or Adverb?

Adjectives describe nouns and pronouns; they answer questions such as *Which? What kind?* and *How many?* **Adverbs** describe verbs, adjectives, or other adverbs; they answer questions such as *How? When? Where?* and *To what extent?*

Adjectives:

The <u>first</u> real airplane really flew . . . (**Which** airplane?)
Isabel met a <u>hideous</u> giant. (**What kind of** giant?)
There never were <u>two</u> brothers more devoted . . . (**How many** brothers?)

Adverbs:

Isabel <u>calmly</u> cured the doctor. (**How** did she cure the doctor?)
They <u>sometimes</u> skinned their noses. (**When** did they skin their noses?)
They glided <u>here</u>, they glided <u>there</u>. (**Where** did they glide?)
Wilbur and Orville were <u>completely</u> loyal to each other. (**To what extent** were they loyal?)

Keep in mind that some words can be adjectives *or* adverbs, depending on how they are used in a sentence. In "This is an *early* class," *early* is an adjective that describes the noun *class* and answers the question **What kind** of class? But in "The class starts *early*," *early* is an adverb that describes the verb *starts* and answers the question **When** does the class start?

A. Practice: In each of the following sentences, you will find an italicized adjective or adverb. If it is an adjective, write *adj* in the space provided. If it is an adverb, write *adv*.

_____ 1.   We worked *tirelessly* to finish our project on time.

_____ 2.   Ramon is a very *capable* student.

_____ 3.   We were *really* glad when vacation time came.

_____ 4.   My sister is an *excellent* tennis player.

_____ 5.   My bicycle is still *fairly* new.

B. Writing Application: On the lines provided, write sentences using each of the following adjectives or adverbs. In each sentence, underline the word the adjective or adverb modifies. The first two have been done as examples.

1. beautiful (adjective) _She grew beautiful <u>flowers</u> in her garden_____

2. carefully (adverb) _The boy carefully <u>set</u> the model ship on its stand._____

3. slightly (adverb)_____

4. several (adjective) _____

5. anywhere (adverb) _____

6. gentle (adjective) _____

"Adventures of Isabel" by Ogden Nash
"I'll Stay" by Gwendolyn Brooks
"Wilbur Wright and Orville Wright"
by Rosemary and Stephen Vincent Benét
"Dream Dust" by Langston Hughes

Reading Strategy: Interpreting Meaning

Because poetry is a compact form of expression, poets do not always spell out all the ideas and feelings they hope to convey. Understanding poetry is a lot easier if you try to interpret the meaning behind the images that the poet does provide. Use these questions to guide you:

- What do you see, hear, feel, and think as you read each line?

- Do you get a picture that reminds us of something from your own life or from literature?

- How does the poet use language to create these images?

Poets often depend on readers to interpret poems by providing answers to questions like these as they read.

DIRECTIONS: Use the graphic organizer to help you think about connections between words, the world of the poem, and your world. Choose a poem from the grouping. In the innermost circle, write words or phrases from the poem that give you a sensory image. In the next circle outward, describe the picture or sense that the image gives you. Finally, in the outer circle, write what that image reminds you of in your own life.

The World of the Poem

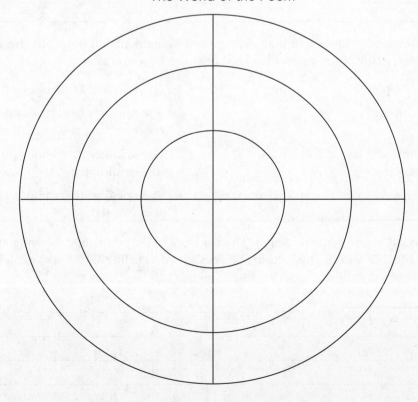

"Adventures of Isabel" by Ogden Nash
"I'll Stay" by Gwendolyn Brooks
"Wilbur Wright and Orville Wright"
by Rosemary and Stephen Vincent Benét
"Dream Dust" by Langston Hughes

Literary Analysis: Stanzas

A prose paragraph focuses on a single main idea, and is separated by indenting or spacing from other paragraphs. **Stanzas** in poetry are similar to paragraphs in prose. They are groups of lines that usually focus on one main idea and are separated by spaces from other groups of lines. The stanzas in many poems are regular; they have the same number of lines and the same rhythm and rhyme pattern. In this grouping of poems, both "Adventures of Isabel" and "Wilbur Wright and Orville Wright" are written in regular stanzas. Stanzas can be irregular, which is true of "I'll Stay." The stanzas in this poem do not follow a regular pattern. Each one, however, focuses on a central idea. A one-stanza poem, like "Dream Dust," has just one central idea.

A. DIRECTIONS: In what ways are the stanzas of "Adventures of Isabel" alike, other than having the same number of lines and the same rhythm and rhyme patterns? Write your answer in the space provided. Hint: The first pair of lines in each stanza tells you about the person or creature Isabel meets. Look at the third and fourth, fifth and sixth, seventh and eighth, and ninth and tenth lines of each stanza. Think about what kind information you get from each pair.

_____

_____

_____

_____

B. DIRECTIONS: Below are the first four lines from the stanzas in "I'll Stay." In the space next to each line, write the letter of the main idea that best fits that stanza.

____ 1. I like the plates on the ledge

____ 2. I am confident.

____ 3. My name will be Up in Lights!

____ 4. Mother says "You rise in the morning—"

a. The speaker talks about her future.

b. The speaker describes an image representing self-confidence.

c. The speaker gives one source of her self-confidence.

d. The speaker talks about the way she sees herself.

C. DIRECTIONS: What is the central idea of "Dream Dust"? Do you think that one stanza is enough for that idea, or would you add to the poem if you could? Write and explain your answers in the space provided.

_____

_____

_____

_____

"Lob's Girl" by Joan Aiken
"The Tiger Who Would Be King" by James Thurber
"The Lion and the Bulls" by Aesop

Build Vocabulary

Using Forms of *decide*

To *decide* means "to make up one's mind," or "to reach a conclusion about a question." Other words that are related to *decide* are *decision*, meaning "the act of making up one's mind" or "a conclusion that a person reaches," and *decisive*, meaning "positive" or "firm."

A. DIRECTIONS: Fill in the blank in each of the following sentences with one of the words below.

decisive   decide   indecision   decisively   decision

1. It was a difficult _____, but we finally chose apple pie for dessert.

2. The home team scored a _____ victory over the visiting team.

3. Once you _____ which book you want to read, get it from the library.

4. The officer stated _____ that there was no cause for alarm.

5. We have no time for your _____. Either come along, or stay at home.

Using the Word Bank

decisively	atone	resolutions	melancholy	intimated
aggrieved	prowled	repulse	slanderous	

B. DIRECTIONS: In each flower petal, write the Word Bank word whose definition matches the number of the petal.

1. hinted, made known

2. offended, wronged

3. untrue and damaging

4. with determination

5. intentions, things decided

6. crawled quietly and secretly

7. repel at attack, drive back

8. make up for a wrong

9. sad, gloomy

Unit 4: Seeing It Through

"**Lob's Girl**" by Joan Aiken
"**The Tiger Who Would Be King**" by James Thurber
"**The Lion and the Bulls**" by Aesop

Build Spelling Skills: *ie* or *ei*?

Spelling Strategy To spell words in which the letters *i* and *e* appear together, remember this rule:

Spell *i* before *e*: rel<u>ie</u>ve, gr<u>ie</u>f, p<u>ie</u>ce

Except after *c*: re<u>ce</u>ive, con<u>ce</u>ited, de<u>ce</u>it

Or when the sound is *ay* as in: n<u>ei</u>ghbor, w<u>ei</u>gh

Notable exceptions: w<u>ei</u>rd, s<u>ei</u>ze, s<u>ei</u>zure, l<u>ei</u>sure, h<u>ei</u>ght, <u>ei</u>ther, n<u>ei</u>ther, forf<u>ei</u>t

A. Practice: Use the rules above to work out the spelling of the following incomplete words. Write the complete words on the lines provided.

1. A person who steals is a th____ ____f.   _____

2. A room usually has a floor, four walls, and a c____ ____ling.   _____

3. It is hard to bel____ ____ve that people have actually walked on the

   moon.   _____

4. The h____ ____ght of the skyscraper was awesome.   _____

5. Tigers and bears can be very f____ ____rce animals at times.   _____

6. He has a very w____ ____d sense of humor.   _____

7. Have you ever taken a sl____ ____gh ride on a winter

   evening?   _____

8. The lion dec____ ____ed the bulls.   _____

B. Practice: Fill in the blanks in each of the following sentences with the correctly spelled version of the word in parentheses.

1. Mr. Dodsworth travels hundreds of miles to (retrieve, retreive) _____ his dog.

2. Finally, he (percieves, perceives) _____ that Lob wants to stay with Sandy.

3. Sandy's family is (seized, siezed)_____ with (greif, grief) _____.

4. The tiger (beleives, believes) _____ that he ought to be the king of the beasts.

5. The lion does not want to (yield, yeild) _____ his place as king.

6. In Aesop's fable, a lion (weighs, wieghs) _____ his chances and

   creates some (beleivable, believable) _____ lies.

7. At the end, the lion (acheives, achieves) _____ his goal.

"Lob's Girl" by Joan Aiken
"The Tiger Who Would Be King" by James Thurber
"The Lion and the Bulls" by Aesop

Build Grammar Skills: Prepositional Phrases

A **prepositional phrase** is a group of words that begins with a preposition and ends with a noun or pronoun. The noun or pronoun at the end of the phrase is called the **object of the preposition**. For example, in "The Tiger Who Would Be King," Thurber writes that "the tiger prowled through the jungle. . . ." *Through the jungle* is a prepositional phrase, in which *through* is the preposition, and *jungle* is the object of the preposition.

A. Practice: Draw a circle around the prepositional phrase in each sentence. Then underline the preposition once and the object of the preposition twice. The first one has been done as an example.

1. Everyone cleaned up after the party.

2. The cat escaped and ran up a tree.

3. Yesterday, I got a postcard from my sister.

4. No one may talk during the test.

5. The train reached the end of the line.

6. The tired campers crawled into their tents.

7. Among Aesop's fables, "The Fox and the Grapes" is my favorite.

8. She squeezed between her parents and watched the parade.

9. The acrobat balanced herself on one hand.

10. I saved my dessert for my brother.

B. Writing Application: Complete each sentence with a prepositional phrase.

1. The sun was hidden _____

2. She threw the litter _____

3. When he had finished reading, he replaced the book _____

4. Ferdinand Magellan led the first sailing expedition _____

5. We brought the flowers especially _____

6. The painters leaned the ladder _____

7. We hung our coats _____

8. That afternoon, she played _____

9. The dog ran _____

10. We do not attend school _____

"Lob's Girl" by Joan Aiken
"The Tiger Who Would Be King" by James Thurber
"The Lion and the Bulls" by Aesop

Reading Strategy: Comparing and Contrasting Characters

Like real people, fictional characters are alike in some ways and different in others. When you study the ways in which they resemble each other in behavior, thought, and feelings, you **compare** characters. When you concentrate on differences between characters, you **contrast** them. A Venn diagram can help you sort out the details for your comparison/contrast. The diagram consists of two overlapping circles, one for each character you are examining. Write the qualities both characters share in the area where the circles overlap. In the part of each circle that does not overlap, write those qualities that are true only of the character represented by that circle.

DIRECTIONS: Fill in the Venn diagram to compare and contrast Mr. Dodsworth and Sandy from "Lob's Girl." Use the results to answer the questions below.

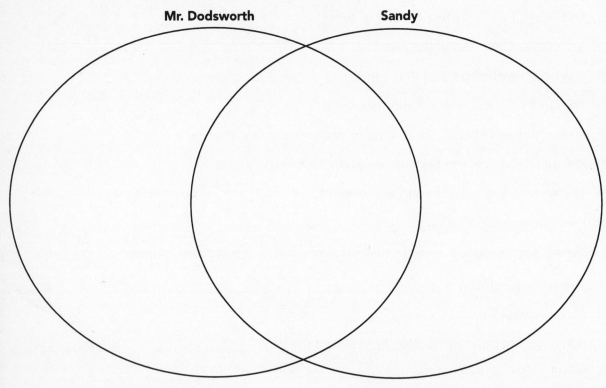

Mr. Dodsworth　　　　　**Sandy**

1. How are the feelings of Mr. Dodsworth and Sandy towards Lob different? How are they similar?

   _____

   _____

   _____

2. What qualities in Sandy might make her a more suitable owner for Lob than Mr. Dodsworth is?

   _____

   _____

"Lob's Girl" by Joan Aiken
"The Tiger Who Would Be King" by James Thurber
"The Lion and the Bulls" by Aesop

Literary Analysis: Foreshadowing

When an author makes hints that suggest what may take place later in a story, he or she is using a technique called **foreshadowing**. You might find such hints in dialogue, description, narrative, or even in a title. The purpose of foreshadowing may be to create or heighten suspense, or to provide a warning to readers that the story may take a sudden turn in mood or action. If you have not yet read these stories, look for hints of things to come and think about what they foretell. If you have read them already, look through them again to find places where the authors used foreshadowing.

A. DIRECTIONS: On the lines provided, answer the following questions.

1. What does the title, "Lob's Girl," foreshadow in the story?

   _____

   _____

2. What does this paragraph from "Lob's Girl" lead readers to think might take place in the story?

   > Some people choose their dogs, and some dogs choose their people. The Pengelly family had no say in the choosing of Lob; he came to them in the second way, and very decisively.

   _____

   _____

B. DIRECTIONS: In each of the following passages from "Lob's Girl," underline the detail that foreshadows events in the story. In the lines provided, write what the underlined details foreshadow.

1. As usual, each member of the family was happily getting on with his or her own affairs. Little did they guess how soon this state of things would be changed by the large new member who was going to erupt into their midst.

   _____

   _____

2. Suddenly, history repeating itself, there was a crash from the kitchen. Jean Pengelly leaped up, crying, "My blackberry jelly!"

   _____

   _____

"Greyling" by Jane Yolen

Build Vocabulary

Using Related Words: Forms of *grief*

The Word Bank word *grief* is a noun that means "deep sadness or distress." In this story, the fisherman keeps his grief, or deep sadness, to himself, instead of burdening his wife with it. Other words related to the word *grief* convey the same meaning of deep sadness. For example, the word *grieve* is a verb that means "to feel deep sadness or to mourn."

People may *grieve* when they lose someone they love.

Grievous is an adjective that means "serious enough to cause sadness or distress."

The boy's *grievous* actions caused his friends to feel great distress.

A. DIRECTIONS: Use one of the following words to complete each of the sentences below: *grief, grievous,* and *grieve.*

1. Spreading unkind rumors about a person is a _____ act.

2. Kyla was filled with _____ when her dog Dakota died.

3. The fisherman and his wife _____ because they do not have a child.

Using the Word Bank

grief	slough	wallowed	sheared

B. DIRECTIONS: Using context clues, fill in the blank in each sentence with the correct word from the Word Bank.

1. When we studied reptiles in science class, we saw a snake _____ off its old skin.

2. At the zoo, a mother hippopotamus and her baby _____ in the mud.

3. With several strong strokes of the razor, the rancher_____ off the sheep's woolly coat.

4. The fisherman brought the seal pup home, hoping it would end his wife's _____.

Recognizing Synonyms

C. DIRECTIONS: Circle the letter of the answer choice that is closest in meaning to the word in CAPITAL LETTERS.

1. SLOUGH   a. shed   b. energetic   c. put on   d. swamp

2. SHEARED   a. saw through   b. tilted   c. cut   d. thought about

3. WALLOWED   a. digested   b. permitted   c. rolled around   d. wandered around

4. GRIEF   a. extreme happiness   b. deep feeling   c. intense anger   d. deep sadness

"Greyling" by Jane Yolen

Build Spelling Skills: The Sound *uff* Spelled *ough*

Spelling Strategy The Word Bank word *slough*, meaning "to cast off," or "get rid of," is one of a few English words that spell the *uff* sound with *ough*. Here are some others:

rough   not gentle
tough   very strong or sturdy
enough   plenty

The *uff* sound may also be spelled -*uff*, as in *stuff* and *fluff*. Use a dictionary if you are not sure which way to spell the *uff* sound.

A. Practice: On the lines provided, write four sentences using each of the following words in each: *slough*, *rough*, *tough*, and *enough*.

1. _____
2. _____
3. _____
4. _____

B. Practice: Proofread the following paragraph. Look for words in which the *uff* sound is spelled incorrectly. Cross out each incorrectly spelled word and write the correct spelling above it.

Just as the fisherman's wife thought no one would risk entering the ruff sea to save her

huband, Greyling decided he'd had enuff. Though it was a steep drop to the water below, the

boy plunged from the cliffs into the churning sea and fought his way to his father's floundering

boat. The waves made the going tuff. The water pushed against him, pulling off his clothes and

shoes. Finally, the boy seemed to sluff off his skin, and he swam swiftly toward his father.

Challenge: In the story "Greyling," the word for the color of the boy's hair and eyes is spelled *grey*. Most dictionaries, however, list *gray* as the preferred spelling for this word, and *grey* as a second spelling that is also considered correct. Several words in English have more than one acceptable spelling. Dictionaries usually list the preferred spelling of the word first. In your own writing, it is usually best to use the first spelling of these words. Here are some other examples of words with two acceptable spellings. In each pair, the preferred spelling is listed first:

theater, theatre   glamour, glamor   dialogue, dialog

Use each word in the above list in a sentence. Use the preferred spelling of each word.

1. _____
2. _____
3. _____

© Prentice-Hall, Inc.   Selection Support **87**

Unit 4: Seeing It Through

Build Grammar Skills: Interjections

An **interjection** is a word or group of words that expresses emotion. An emotion is a feeling such as surprise, pain, joy, or disappointment. An exclamation point (!) usually follows an interjection that expresses a strong emotion. A comma (,) usually follows an interjection that expresses a mild emotion.

Examples: _Wow!_ That's wonderful!   _Oh,_ that's okay.

A. Practice: Rewrite each sentence. Correct the punctuation when necessary. Underline the interjection in the sentence you wrote.

1. Ugh. there are no fish today.

   _____

2. Well! what do you think?

   _____

3. My goodness. the boy is such a great swimmer!

   _____

4. Oh no. The boy is missing?

   _____

5. Aha. Greyling is a selchie!

   _____

B. Writing Application: Write sentences that you think a character from "Greyling" might say. Use each interjection and the correct punctuation in your sentence.

1. oh my

   _____

2. aaack

   _____

3. okay

   _____

4. whew

   _____

5. now

   _____

"Greyling" by Jane Yolen

Reading Strategy: Predicting

Predict means "make a logical guess." As you read, you can use story details to predict what might happen next. You might revise, or change, your predictions as your reading leads you to new details—new events, descriptions of characters, statements that characters make, and so on. Making predictions as you read makes you want to read on to see if your predictions will come true. In the following passage from "Greyling," for example, you are given some details that help you predict what Greyling will do next.

> As Greyling disappeared beneath the waves, little fingers of foam tore at his clothes. They snatched his shirt and his pants and his shoes and sent them bubbling away to the shore. And as Greyling went deeper beneath the waves, even his skin seemed to slough off till he swam, free at last, in the sleek grey coat of a great grey seal.
>
> The selchie had returned to the sea.

You have learned a new detail: that Greyling has become a seal again, at home in the stormy sea. When you add this to the details you've already gathered from the story — that Greyling is a devoted son and that he's willing to risk his life to help his family — you might make the prediction that Greyling will swim to the boat and rescue his father. Or is it possible that the call of the sea will prove stronger than Greyling's loyalty to his father? Perhaps Greyling will disappear under the waves and leave the fisherman to his fate. The possibility that your prediction could be wrong provides suspense. You want to read on to find out what will happen next. Making predictions and revising them actively involves you in a story as you read.

A. DIRECTIONS: Use the chart below to keep track of details and make predictions as you read. The first row has been filled in as an example.

Detail	New Detail	My Prediction
The fisherman's wife is lonely.	The fisherman brings home a seal pup.	They will keep the seal pup.

"Greyling" by Jane Yolen

Literary Analysis: Conflict and Resolution

Characters in stories often struggle with each other, with nature, or with their own feelings or problems. A struggle like one of these is called a **conflict.** In "Greyling," for example, the fisherman has an **internal conflict** as he struggles to look cheerful when he actually feels very sad. He later has an **external conflict** as he struggles against a powerful storm.

Conflicts can make a story exciting to read. You want to read on to find each **resolution**—that is, the way that each conflict turns out.

A. DIRECTIONS: Read each of the following sentences and decide whether it is an example of internal conflict or external conflict. On the line, write whether the conflict is internal (I) or external (E).

_____ 1. Greyling did not know whether to stay with his mother or dive into the beckoning sea.

_____ 2. It was hard for him to swim: Enormous waves pushed against him as he tried to move forward.

_____ 3. The fisherman's wife cries over Greyling's disappearance but finally accepts what has happened.

B. Directions: For each of the following quotations from "Greyling," explain the conflict that is going on. Then explain the resolution—how that conflict turns out. The first example has been done for you.

1. "She would weep and wail and rock the cradle that stood by the hearth."

    The fisherman's wife wanted a baby, but she does not have one. Her desire for a child
    is resolved when she decides to raise Greyling as her own.

2. " . . . he knew how his wife had wanted a child. And in his secret heart, he wanted one, too. Yet he felt, somehow, it was wrong."

    _____

    _____

3. "But though he often stood by the shore, . . . looking and longing and grieving his heart for what he did not really know, he never went into the sea."

    _____

    _____

4. "'Let the boy go,' said one old man. . . . But the fisherman's wife clasped Greyling in her arms. She did not want him to go into the sea. She was afraid he would never return."

    _____

    _____

"Abuelito Who" by Sandra Cisneros
"The Open Road" by Walt Whitman
"Life Doesn't Frighten Me" by Maya Angelou
"who knows if the moon's" by E. E. Cummings

Build Vocabulary

Compound Transition Words

Compound words are two or more words joined together. When they are used to connect one thought, idea, or event to the next, they are called **compound transition words**. Examples include *however*, *meanwhile*, and *moreover*. Generally, compound transition words are set off by commas from the rest of the sentence. Look at these examples:

> **The compound transition word *however* means "yet" or "in spite of that."**
> My grandparents left late for the airport. <u>However</u>, they still made their flight.
> **The compound transition word *meanwhile* means "at the same time."**
> Lisa watched the moon through her telescope. <u>Meanwhile</u>, Leon looked at a photograph of the moon in a science magazine.
> **The compound transition word *moreover* means "in addition to what has been said; also."**
> The road was narrow and winding; <u>moreover</u>, it was covered with stones.

A. Directions: Use *however*, *meanwhile*, or *moreover* to complete each sentence.

1. The day was hot and humid; _____, there wasn't a cloud in the sky.

2. The wind was cold. _____, Sheila was warm in her parka.

3. I prepared the meal. _____, my brother set the table.

4. The dessert looked delicious; _____, I was too full to eat it.

5. I have tons of homework tonight. _____ I have band practice, too.

Using the Word Bank

henceforth	whimper	querulous

B. Directions: Use one word from the Word Bank to replace the underlined word or words in each sentence below. Rewrite the words on the lines provided.

1. My dog used to <u>make a low whining sound</u> when he wanted to go out. _____

2. Today I missed the bus. <u>From now on</u>, I'll wear my watch. _____

3. The team was in a <u>complaining</u> mood after losing the game. _____

Recognizing Antonyms

C. Directions: Circle the letter of the answer choice that is most nearly opposite in meaning to the word in capital letters.

1. HENCEFORTH   a. because   b. in addition   c. never again   d. from this time on
2. WHIMPER   a. whine   b. giggle   c. beat up   d. listen to
3. QUERULOUS   a. complaining   b. not careful   c. talented   d. approving

"Abuelito Who" by Sandra Cisneros
"The Open Road" by Walt Whitman
"Life Doesn't Frighten Me" by Maya Angelou
"who knows if the moon's" by E. E. Cummings

Build Spelling Skills: Compound Transition Words

Spelling Strategy When combining words to form a compound transition word, the spelling of each word in the compound usually remains the same. This is true whether the compound transition word is formed from two or more words.

For example: hence + forth = henceforth   never + the + less = nevertheless

A. Practice: In each sentence, below, join the words in parentheses to spell a compound transition word. Write the compound transition word on the line next to each sentence.

1. One day our dog ran away. (There, after), we kept her on a leash. _____

2. The theater was crowded. (None, the, less), we all got seats. _____

3. You vacuum the living room. (Mean, while), I'll make the beds. _____

4. We finished our jobs; (there, fore), we had time to play. _____

5. Speak loudly when you give a speech; (how, ever), don't shout. _____

6. I was late for school again. (Hence, forth), I will get up earlier. _____

B. Practice: Complete the following short passages with compound transition words. Choose six of the compound transition words that you wrote on the lines above. Some compound transition words have similar meanings, so try not to use a transition word more than once. If you are not sure of the meaning of a compound transition word, use your dictionary.

1. Sandra Cisneros grew up in a poor neighborhood in Chicago, Illinois. _____, the difficult times in her early life did not deter her from developing her talents as a writer. In "Abuelito Who," she lovingly describes her grandfather's habits. _____, she expresses her love for him and the great sense of loss she feels after his death.

2. E. E. Cummings ("e. e. cummings") was a painter and a playwright. _____, it is through his poetry that he is best known. He experimented with form, phrasing, and punctuation (or lack of it), sometimes splashing lines across, down, and diagonally on a page.

3. Walt Whitman had strong feelings about freedom, democracy, and America. He _____ wrote of his beliefs in his poetry. His poem "The Open Road" expresses his feelings about taking new paths.

4. Maya Angelou found fame in 1970 with *I Know Why the Caged Bird Sings.* _____, she wrote many books. Angelou continues to write today. _____, she also teaches, speaks in public, and occasionally acts in television and movies.

Name _____ Date _____

"**Abuelito Who**" by Sandra Cisneros
"**The Open Road**" by Walt Whitman
"**Life Doesn't Frighten Me**" by Maya Angelou
"**who knows if the moon's**" by E. E. Cummings

Build Grammar Skills: Subordinating Conjunctions

A **subordinating conjunction** is a word that joins two complete ideas and shows that one idea is more important than another. In the examples, the subordinating conjunctions are circled.

Before I go to bed, I read some poetry.   I enjoy reading poetry whenever I can.

less important idea   more important idea   more important idea   less important idea

When the less important idea comes first, it is followed by a comma. When the more important idea comes first, it is not followed by a comma.

These are some of the subordinating conjunctions that often appear in sentences.

after	as if	before	than	whenever
although	as soon as	if	unless	where
as	because	since	when	wherever

A. Directions: Circle the subordinating conjunction in each sentence. Draw a line under the more important idea.

1. E. E. Cummings wonders if the moon is a balloon.

2. He talks about "a keen city" where it always is Springland.

3. Although I enjoy E. E. Cummings's poems, I like Maya Angelou's even more.

4. I understand her when she talks about frightening things.

5. I often feel as if she and I have a lot in common.

6. Since the speaker in "Life Doesn't Frighten Me" is brave, I live life bravely, too.

B. Writing Application: Join each pair of sentences with a subordinating conjunction that makes sense. Write the new sentence on the line, placing the comma correctly. The first example has been done for you.

1. Cummings's poems are imaginative. Whitman's poems have more energy. _____
      Although Cummings's poems are imaginative, Whitman's poems have more energy. _____

2. He travels the open road. Whitman's speaker is "strong and content." _____
   _____

3. Sandra Cisneros's Abuelito may have been like that. He was a young man. _____
   _____

4. Abuelito now is gone. His granddaughter must be satisfied with her memories. _____
   _____

Unit 4: Seeing It Through

"Abuelito Who" by Sandra Cisneros
"The Open Road" by Walt Whitman
"Life Doesn't Frighten Me" by Maya Angelou
"who knows if the moon's" by E. E. Cummings

Reading Strategy: Drawing Inferences

To understand what you read, you need to **draw inferences**, or educated guesses, based on the information you are given and your own knowledge and experience. In poetry, especially, meanings are not always obvious. You have to use the images and other details the poem provides to infer the underlying meaning of the poem. For example, in the poem "Abuelito Who," you read that Abuelito "is dough and feathers." What does that really mean?

The poet wants you to think about the kind of person Abuelito is. First, you need to think of the qualities of dough and feathers: Dough is a somewhat soft and pliable; feathers are light, airy, warm, and often colorful, and they feel gentle against the skin. You can infer from the qualities of dough that Abuelito is a yielding and giving person. You can infer from the qualities of feathers that Abuelito is a warm, uplifting, and kind person.

When you read poetry, you often will draw inferences based on the images the poet creates. Remember to use the stated words and your own knowledge and experience to decide what the poet wants you to figure out about a person, event, or idea.

DIRECTIONS: In the left-hand column of the chart below, you will find details from the poems you read. Complete the chart by filling in the right-hand column with your inferences. Go back and reread the poems to find the details listed so that you can make inferences.

Detail	Inference
1. Abuelito doesn't live here anymore.	
2. Abuelito is blankets and spoons and big brown shoes.	
3. we'd go up higher with all the pretty people than houses and steeples and clouds:	
4. Strong and content, I travel the open road.	
5. Don't show me frogs and snakes And listen for my scream,	

Name _____ Date _____

"**Abuelito Who**" by Sandra Cisneros
"**The Open Road**" by Walt Whitman
"**Life Doesn't Frighten Me**" by Maya Angelou
"**who knows if the moon's**" by E. E. Cummings

Literary Analysis: Free Verse

Free verse is a form of poetry in which there is no formal pattern of lines that rhyme or regular rhythmic pattern. A free-verse poem may take any shape and be any length to express the poet's ideas. What makes the poem effective is the sound, sense, and rhythm created by the following:

- choice and position of words

- use of repeated words or use of rhyming words close together

- varied length of lines

- special use of, or lack of, punctuation

The poems in this group are free verse. Each has its own shape and length, as well as the other qualities listed above. Each expresses very different ideas and emotions. For example, in "Abuelito Who," Cisneros repeats the word *who* numerous times. This repetition gives the poem a sense of sound and creates a rhythm of its own.

DIRECTIONS: Read the excerpt from each poem. On the lines provided, write the rhyming and/or repeated words used by the poets.

from "**Abuelito Who**"

is tired shut the door
doesn't live here anymore
is hiding underneath the bed
who talks to me inside my head
is blankets and spoons and big brown shoes
who snores up and down up and down up and
    down again

1. Rhyming Words:

   _____

2. Repeated Words:

   _____

from "**The Open Road**"

Henceforth I ask not good-fortune, I myself
am good-fortune,
Henceforth I whimper no more, postpone
no more, need nothing.

5. Repeated Words:

   _____

   _____

from "**who knows if the moon's**"

who knows if the moon's
a balloon, coming out of a keen city . . .
. . .
go sailing
away and away sailing into a keen
city which nobody's ever visited.

3. Rhyming Words:

   _____

4. Repeated Words:

   _____

from "**Life Doesn't Frighten Me**"

Dragons breathing flame
On my counterpane
That doesn't frighten me at all.
. . .
Life doesn't frighten me at all.

6. Rhyming Words:

   _____

7. Repeated Words:

   _____

Unit 4: Seeing It Through

"A Backwoods Boy" by Russell Freedman
"Jackie Robinson: Justice at Last"
by Geoffrey C. Ward and Ken Burns

Build Vocabulary

Using the Prefix *re-*

The Word Bank word *retaliated* contains the prefix *re-*, which means "back." The word means "got revenge" or "paid back." Like many other prefixes, *re-* can have additional meanings, such as "again." Here are some other words using the prefix *re-*. Notice the way in which each one is used in the example sentence.

return: go back or give back
We *return* to school in the fall.   Will you please *return* the book to the library?

renew: make new again, make like new
The sun and rain will *renew* the wilted plant and make it thrive again.

reflect: turn back or throw back
A mirror can *reflect* your image, making it seem that you are looking back at yourself.

A. DIRECTIONS: Combine the underlined words with the prefix *re-*. Write the new words on the lines provided.

1. After making it disappear, the magician <u>produced</u> _____ the egg.

2. The historian <u>traced</u> _____ the steps of Lewis and Clark.

3. We were eager to <u>unite</u> _____ with our friends after the summer.

4. Matt <u>placed</u> _____ the clothes in the closet after cleaning it out.

Using the Word Bank

aptitude	intrigued	treacherous	integrate	retaliated

B. DIRECTIONS: Match each word in the left-hand column with its definition in the right-hand column. Write the letter of the definition on the line next to the word it defines.

_____ 1. treacherous   a. fascinated

_____ 2. aptitude   b. remove barriers and allow access to all

_____ 3. retaliated   c. natural ability

_____ 4. intrigued   d. dangerous

_____ 5. integrate   e. harmed someone in return for an injury

Analogies

C. DIRECTIONS: Circle the letter of the pair of words that expresses the same relationship as the pair in CAPITAL LETTERS.

1. SUNSET : BEAUTIFUL
   a. heart : integrate
   b. mystery : intrigued
   c. flood : treacherous
   d. forgave : retaliated

2. MUSIC : TALENT
   a. math : aptitude
   b. curious : intrigued
   c. combine : integrate
   d. angry : retaliated

"A Backwoods Boy" by Russell Freedman
"Jackie Robinson: Justice at Last"
by Geoffrey C. Ward and Ken Burns

Build Spelling Skills: The Suffix -tude

Spelling Strategy Words that end in the suffix -tude are always spelled with one t, never a double t. Examples include the Word Bank word aptitude as well as attitude, gratitude, and solitude.

A. Practice: Write the word from the following list that best completes each sentence.

   gratitude   solitude   altitude   fortitude   multitude   aptitude   attitude

1. The highest peak in the mountain had an _____ of 4,000 feet.

2. We expressed our _____ to our teacher by giving her a dozen roses.

3. Max has a poor _____ in class and rarely completes his homework.

4. The soldier showed his _____ when he carried his wounded comrade to safety.

5. Martha has a great _____ for music and was playing the piano by age six.

6. We pushed our way through the great _____ of people in the shopping mall.

7. All alone in the library, Henry enjoyed the _____ as he read his book.

B. Practice: Complete the following paragraph. Choose six words from the list above to fill in the blanks.

   Abraham Lincoln and Jackie Robinson shared some of the same character traits. Both men had a positive _____ that helped them struggle against great obstacles. They also showed great _____ and courage in fighting slavery and racism in their times. Both were rewarded with the _____ of a nation for their achievements, although both were criticized during their lifetime. Men of action, Lincoln and Robinson were also thoughtful and enjoyed _____ to escape the demands of the _____ of people who often surrounded them. Of course, they had their differences, too. Lincoln's _____ lay in politics and speech making, while Robinson's gift was his athletic ability.

Challenge: In the first syllable of the Word Bank word treacherous the short e sound that you hear in the word red is spelled ea. That sound is spelled the same way in such words as leather and ready. Often, however, the ea combination is pronounced as a long e, as in bead. In the chart below, list the following words in the correct column, according to whether the short e sound is spelled with an e or with ea, or whether the ea combination is pronounced as a long e.

health	stream	seven	cream	fear	level	head	dear	steady
neat	intend	instead	treat	tread	deaf	never	kept	wedding

Short e sound spelled e	Short e sound spelled ea	Long e sound spelled ea

Unit 4: Seeing It Through

"A Backwoods Boy" by Russell Freedman

"Jackie Robinson: Justice at Last"

by Geoffrey C. Ward and Ken Burns

Build Grammar Skills: Conjunctions Joining Sentences

Conjunctions are words that link single words or groups of words. Conjunctions can also indicate the relationships between the ideas they join together in sentences. For example, the conjunction *and* indicates that a word or group of words is linked to another by *addition*. In the sentence below, the conjunction *and* indicates "in addition to."

He supported his family by living off his own land, *and* he watched for a chance to better himself.

In other words, Lincoln supported his family; *and in addition to that*, he planned to better himself.

The conjunction *but* indicates a *contrast* between two ideas. The conjunction *so* indicates a *cause-and-effect* relationship.

He stayed with his family through this first prairie winter, *but* he was getting restless.

There wasn't much business at Offutt's store, *so* he could spend long hours reading as he sat behind the counter.

In the first sentence, the two ideas are in contrast with each other. Lincoln stays with his family, *in spite of the fact* that he felt restless. In the second sentence, the two ideas are related by cause-and-effect. Lincoln had time to read *because* there was little business at the store.

A. Practice: Underline the conjunction in each of the following sentences. On the line, identify the relationship between the two parts of the sentence. Write A for addition, C for contrast, or CE for cause and effect.

_____ 1. Baseball was loved by America, but the major leagues were for white men only.

_____ 2. The invasion began, and the governor called for volunteers.

_____ 3. New Salem was still a small place, but it was growing.

_____ 4. He knew nothing about surveying, so he bought couple of books on the subject.

_____ 5. Thomas built a coffin, and nine-year-old Abraham whittled the pegs.

B. Writing Application: Write a two-part sentence about the topics below, using the conjunctions indicated to join the two parts together.

1. Write a sentence about something that happened to you when you were younger, using the conjunction <u>and</u>.

_____

2. Write a sentence about two of your favorite sports, using the conjunction <u>but</u>.

_____

3. Write a sentence about the life of a person you admire, using the conjunction <u>so</u>.

_____

"A Backwoods Boy" by Russell Freedman
"Jackie Robinson: Justice at Last"
by Geoffrey C. Ward and Ken Burns

Reading Strategy: Determining Main Ideas

Details make a piece of writing interesting to read. Good readers, however, know that writers supply these details not only to capture your interest, but to lead up to or support their ideas. For example, in "A Backwoods Boy," the main idea is that Abraham Lincoln went from being a poor backwoods farm boy to President of the United States. The following details help you identify that main idea:

- Lincoln was born in a log cabin with one window, one door, and a dirt floor.
- His parents couldn't read or write.
- Lincoln went to school only a few months a year.

DIRECTIONS: Use the following organizer to help you better understand the main ideas in "A Backwoods Boy" and "Jackie Robinson: Justice at Last." Read each passage below. In the first column of the organizer, fill in at least two details that help you identify the main idea of each passage. Then write the main idea of the passage in the second column. The first two passages are about Abraham Lincoln, and the third is about Jackie Robinson.

1. He would carry a book out to the field with him, so he could read at the end of each plow furrow, while the horse was getting its breath. When noon came, he would sit under a tree and read while he ate. "I never saw Abe after he was twelve that he didn't have a book in his hand or in his pocket," Dennis Hanks remembered. "It didn't seem natural to see a feller read like that."

2. To support himself, he worked at all sorts of odd jobs. He split fence rails, hired himself out as a farmhand, helped at the local gristmill. With the help of friends, he was appointed postmaster of New Salem, a part-time job that paid about fifty dollars a year. Then he was offered a chance to become deputy to the local surveyor. He knew nothing about surveying, so he bought a compass, a chain, and a couple of textbooks on the subject. Within six weeks, he had taught himself enough to start work—laying out roads and townsites, and marking off property boundaries.

3. When Rickey met Jackie Robinson, he thought he'd found the right man. Robinson was 28 years old, and a superb athlete. In his first season in the Negro leagues, he hit .387. But just as importantly, he had great intelligence and sensitivity. Robinson was college-educated, and knew what joining the majors would mean for blacks. The grandson of a slave, he was proud of his race and wanted others to feel the same.

	Detail	Main Idea
Passage 1		
Passage 2		
Passage 3		

Unit 4: Seeing It Through

"**A Backwoods Boy**" by Russell Freedman

"**Jackie Robinson: Justice at Last**"
by Geoffrey C. Ward and Ken Burns

Literary Analysis: Historical Accounts

In a **historical account**, an author tells you facts, or true information, about an event or a person. But just a list of facts would not be very interesting to read. By adding details, an author can interpret or explain facts. In other words, an author includes details to express what he or she thinks those facts really mean.

Read the following passage from "A Backwoods Boy."

> Yes, the law intrigued him. It would give him a chance to rise in the world, to earn a respected place in the community, to live by his wits instead of by hard physical labor.

In the passage, the author states a fact: **Abraham Lincoln was interested in the law**. He adds the following details to **explain** why Lincoln developed this interest:

1. Being a lawyer would give him a chance to rise in the world.

2. He would be respected by the community.

3. He would be able to earn a living without doing hard physical labor.

DIRECTIONS: Read the following two passages. The first is about Abraham Lincoln's journey to New Orleans with a friend. The second is the last paragraph of "Jackie Robinson: Justice at Last." On the lines below each passage write the fact stated in the passage and three details that explain or interpret that fact.

1. To support himself, he worked at all sorts of odd jobs. He split fence rails, hired himself out as a farmhand, helped at the local gristmill. With the help of friends, he was appointed postmaster of New Salem, a part-time job that paid about fifty dollars a year.

Fact:

_____

Details:

1. _____

2. _____

3. _____

2. Many fans and players were prejudiced—they didn't want the races to play together. Rickey knew the first black player would be cursed and booed. Pitchers would throw at him; runners would spike him. Even his own teammates might try to pick a fight.

Fact:

_____

Details:

1. _____

2. _____

3. _____

"The Fun They Had" by Isaac Asimov

Build Vocabulary

Using the Prefix *non-*

The Word Bank word *nonchalantly* contains the prefix *non-*, which means "not" or "without." In the story, Tommy answers Margie's question *nonchalantly*, meaning "casually" or "without much interest." Because *non-* means "not" or "without," it gives the opposite meaning to a word to which it is attached. For instance, *non + sense = nonsense*, meaning, "without sense." *Non + stop = nonstop*, which means "not stopping" or "without stopping." *Non + fiction = nonfiction*, or "fact." *Non + existent = nonexistent*, or "not existing."

A. DIRECTIONS: Complete each sentence by adding *non-* to the word in parentheses.

1. The concerned students held a (violent) _____ protest.

2. Dieters often choose (fat) _____ ice cream.

3. Because of the (stop) _____ arguments, the meeting was (productive) _____.

4. Most charities are (profit) _____ organizations.

Using the Word Bank

calculated	loftily	dispute	nonchalantly

B. DIRECTIONS: The underlined words in this paragraph don't make sense because they are not where they ought to be. Use clues in each sentence to decide which underlined word best fits the meaning of each sentence. Then rewrite the paragraph on the lines or on a separate sheet of paper. Write the underlined words where they will make sense.

Brian <u>dispute</u> boasted that he could finish the arithmetic quiz by the time the bell rang. He <u>loftily</u> picked up his pencil and began on the first problem. No one could <u>calculated</u> that he was good at math. He had <u>nonchalantly</u> all of the answers ten minutes ahead of schedule.

_____

_____

_____

_____

Recognizing Synonyms

C. DIRECTIONS: Circle the letter of the answer choice that is closest in meaning to the word in CAPITAL LETTERS.

1. CALCULATED: a. guessed b. figured c. understood d. subtracted

2. NONCHALANTLY: a. without interest   c. without regret or sorrow
                  b. without anger or rage   d. without concern or excitement

3. LOFTILY: a. speedily b. proudly c. dreamily d. foolishly

4. DISPUTE: a. agree b. reason c. argue d. accept

"The Fun They Had" by Isaac Asimov

Build Spelling Skills: Using *ch* to Spell the *sh* Sound

Spelling Strategy *Ch* can be used to spell words that have the *sh* sound. This is the soft sound that is found in the Word Bank word *non<u>ch</u>alant*. Learn the spelling of these words as you come across them in your reading.

Examples: nonchalantly, chateau, chaperone, pistachio, chauffeur

Contrast hard *ch* sound: chair, chain, rich, much

A. Practice: The following words contain the soft *sh* sound spelled *ch* or *sh* or a hard *ch* sound spelled *ch*. Write each word in its proper column in the chart below. One example of each is given.

mustache shoe pistachio such dash choose chef crash nonchalant child shell
chauffeur approach shed champion wishes machine chandelier chateau charge

Soft *sh* Spelled *ch*	Soft *sh* Spelled *sh*	Hard *ch* Spelled *ch*
chandelier	crash	child

B. Practice: In the words below, the letters that spell the sound *sh* have been left out.

non___alantly *(ch)*   ma___ *(sh)*ed   ___auffeur *(ch)*   cra___ing *(sh)*   ma___ine *(ch)*

The letters in parentheses next to each word tell how the *sh* sound should be spelled in that word. Complete the paragraph below with the word from above that makes sense.

Margie and Tommy live in the age of the _____. A nonhuman robot can pre-

pare scrambled eggs or _____ potatoes. The family car can be operated by an

electronic _____, who can drive without _____. The people of

the future are not surprised by these developments and regard it all _____.

Challenge: In the Word Bank word *calculated* the *u* has a long *y$\overline{oo}$* sound. You can find this sound spelled differently in other English words. On the lines below, write at least two words in which the long *y$\overline{oo}$* sound is spelled with the letters indicated. Look in a dictionary for help if necessary.

1. **u**_____

2. **you** _____

3. **yu**_____

4. **eu**_____

"The Fun They Had" by Isaac Asimov

Build Grammar Skills: Simple Subjects and Predicates

The **simple subject** of a sentence is the main word in the complete subject. The simple subject is a noun or a pronoun that shows the person, place, or thing the sentence is about. In the following examples the simple subject is underlined. Sometimes the simple subject is the complete subject, as *Margie* and *It* are in the examples below.

                complete subject

Examples: Today's arithmetic lesson is on the addition of proper fractions.

                 Margie was disappointed. It was a very old book.

The **simple predicate** of a sentence is the main word or words in the complete predicate. The simple predicate is a verb that tells what the subject does or is.

In the following sentences, the complete predicate is in italics. The simple predicate is underlined twice.

Example: Tommy *screamed with laughter*. Today Tommy *found a real book*.

A. Practice: In the sentences below, underline the simple subject once and the simple predicate twice. The first exercise has been done for you.

1. The lucky students of long ago had human teachers.

2. The human teachers instructed groups of students.

3. They had a special building called a "school."

4. All the kids went there for classes.

5. They used a computer for a teacher.

6. This computer gave lessons and tests.

7. A real teacher was much more interesting.

8. Education was boring and lonesome.

B. Writing Application: Write three sentences telling which you would rather have—a real teacher or a robot—and why. Draw a line under the simple subject and two lines under the simple predicate in each sentence.

1. _____

    _____

2. _____

    _____

3. _____

    _____

Unit 5: Mysterious Worlds

"**The Fun They Had**" by Isaac Asimov

Reading Strategy: Evaluating the Author's Message

In many stories, as in "The Fun They Had," the author has a message to communicate to readers. Rather than directly stating that message, the author gets his or her point across by including certain details, such as things the characters do or say. Good readers use those details to figure out the author's points and then decide for themselves whether or not they agree. That is, they **evaluate** the author's message. For example, in "The Fun They Had," the author makes his main point, that computers do not make good teachers, by having the characters do and say things that let the reader know they are not enjoying or getting much out of their education.

DIRECTIONS: As you read "The Fun They Had," use the following chart to help you understand the author's message and express your own ideas about it. Fill in the chart with details the author includes and the points he makes by including those details. Write in whether you "agree" or "disagree" with each point, and then add your reasons. The first row in the chart has been filled in as an example.

Detail	Message	Agree/Disagree	Reason
Margie has to write out her homework in a punch code.	Doing homework on a computer is too hard and boring.	Disagree	We use computers, but we don't have to use punch codes.

"The Fun They Had" by Isaac Asimov

Literary Analysis: Science Fiction

Science fiction is a special type of literature that usually focuses on the science and technology of the future. Because most science fiction stories take place in the future, authors have to combine what they know about technology at the time they are writing with how they imagine technology will advance at a later time. When Isaac Asimov wrote "The Fun They Had," he was sure that computers, which were in an early stage of use at that time, would be used for education. He had to imagine, however, exactly how they would be used. He predicted some details correctly and others incorrectly.

DIRECTIONS: Look through "The Fun They Had." Look for details about computers that the author predicted correctly. Look for others that the author imagined, but predicted incorrectly. List the details you find on the chart below. The first two examples have been filled in for you.

Predicted Correctly	Predicted Incorrectly
Math problems on screen	No such thing as real books

"A Dream Within a Dream" by Edgar Allan Poe
"The Spring and the Fall" by Edna St. Vincent Millay
"Ankylosaurus" by Jack Prelutsky

Build Vocabulary

Using the Prefix *in*–

The prefix *in*- means *not*. When you add the prefix *in*- to most words, it changes the meaning of the word to its opposite. For example, if you add the prefix *in*- to the base word *capable*, which means *able*, the word becomes *incapable*, which means *not able*. Usually, you can figure out the meaning of a word that begins with the prefix *in*- if you know the meaning of the base word. Just add "not" to the base word.

Not all words starting with *in*- follow this rule, however. The word *indebted*, for example, means the condition of being *in debt*, of owing something, rather than *not* owing something. If you are not sure what a word starting with *in*- means, look it up in a dictionary.

A. DIRECTIONS: In the chart below, base words and their meanings are given in columns 1 and 2. In column 3, rewrite each base word, adding the prefix *in*-, and in column 4, write the new meaning. The first one has been done as an example.

Base Word	Meaning	Add *in*-	New Meaning
1. consolable	able to be comforted	inconsolable	not able to be comforted
2. edible	able to be eaten		
3. constant	staying the same		
4. compatible	able to get along		
5. credulous	believing		
6. humane	kind		

Using the Word Bank

deem	bough	raucous	inedible	cudgel

B. DIRECTIONS: In the blank, write the word that best replaces the word or phrase in parentheses.

1. The crowd at the game grew (rough and harsh-sounding) _____.

2. The tough meat was (not capable of being eaten) _____.

3. He looked frightening, waving his (thick club) _____.

4. The (branch) _____ was bent by the heavy snow.

5. I do not (judge) _____ this situation dangerous.

"A Dream Within a Dream" by Edgar Allan Poe
"The Spring and the Fall" by Edna St. Vincent Millay
"Ankylosaurus" by Jack Prelutsky

Build Spelling Skills: The Sound *ow* Spelled *ough*

Spelling Strategy The words *bough* and *drought* use *ough* to spell the sound *ow*. However, the *ow* sound is usually spelled *ow*, as in *vow*, or *ou* as in *noun*.

Examples: b<u>ough</u>, dr<u>ough</u>t, pl<u>ough</u>/pl<u>ow</u>, gr<u>ou</u>nd, h<u>ou</u>se, f<u>ou</u>nd, ab<u>ou</u>t, <u>ou</u>t, h<u>ow</u>, n<u>ow</u>, v<u>ow</u>, all<u>ow</u>

Exceptions: Not all words spelled with *ough* make the *ow* sound. The words *cough*, *though*, and *through* are three examples.

A. Practice: Add the letters *ough*, *ou*, or *ow* to the incomplete word in each sentence.

1. I made a v_____ to always to tell the truth.

2. It finally rained, ending the month of dr_____t.

3. He lives in the h_____se on the corner.

4. The farmer went out to pl_____ the field.

5. I will all_____ her one more chance.

6. The b_____ was covered with pink blossoms.

B. Practice: In the following paragraph, cross out each misspelled word and write it correctly above the line.

In "A Dream Within A Dream," the poet has fownd owt something important abought

life: time changes everything. Like sand, everything he cares about slips through his fingers,

no matter hough tightly he grasps it. Nou, as he comes to this realization, he feels boughed

doun with sadness.

Challenge: In most words, the *ow* sound is spelled *ou* or *ow*. However, some words that have the *ow* sound are spelled with *au*. These are German words that have made their way into the English language and are used both in German-speaking and English-speaking countries.

hausfrau, a housewife
sauerkraut, shredded, salted cabbage
landau, an enclosed, four-wheeled carriage

DIRECTIONS: Use the information above to complete the sentences, filling in the blanks with one of the above words borrowed from German.

1. I like _____ on my hot dog.

2. Queen Elizabeth rode in a _____.

3. A _____ works hard managing a home.

Name _____ Date _____

"A Dream Within a Dream" by Edgar Allan Poe
"The Spring and the Fall" by Edna St. Vincent Millay
"Ankylosaurus" by Jack Prelutsky

Build Grammar Skills: Complete Sentences

A **complete sentence** expresses a complete thought and has at least one subject and one predicate, or verb. If a sentence is missing a subject or verb, you can tell that the sentence is incomplete.

Complete sentence: The poet writes about the seasons.

The subject is *poet*. The verb is *writes*. The sentence expresses a complete thought.

Incomplete sentence: Uses beautiful words.

There is no subject. The verb is *uses*. The thought is incomplete.

Incomplete sentence: But she, only she

The subject is *she*. There is no verb. The thought is incomplete.

Incomplete sentence: Although the words rhyme.

The subject is *words*, the verb is *rhyme*, but there is no complete thought. More words are needed: *Although the words rhyme, I don't like their sound.*

While it is usually considered incorrect to use incomplete sentences, they are often used in dialogue, and in poetry to produce a special effect. For example, in "A Dream Within a Dream," Edgar Allan Poe uses the incomplete sentence "Grains of the golden sand—How few!"

A. Practice: In the blanks, write C if the sentence is complete or I if it is incomplete.

_____ 1. I weep.   _____ 4. He hurt her in little ways.

_____ 2. A deep feeling of loneliness.   _____ 5. Stomped around the forest making noise.

_____ 3. This enormous dinosaur.   _____ 6. Sand crashes in the wave.

B. Writing Application: Write complete sentences using the subjects and verbs given.

1. flower / gives _____

2 bough / broke _____

3. ankylosaurus / waddled _____

4. she/ grasped _____

5. friend / laughed _____

"A Dream Within a Dream" by Edgar Allan Poe
"The Spring and the Fall" by Edna St. Vincent Millay
"Ankylosaurus" by Jack Prelutsky

Reading Strategy: Drawing Inferences

Rather than plainly and directly stating exactly what they mean, poets often use language that is indirect and words that can have several meanings. The reader is expected to **draw inferences**, about the meaning, based on details in the poem. When you do so, you arrive at a deeper understanding of a poem and find greater pleasure in reading it.

DIRECTIONS: As you read the poems, use the chart below to note details and draw inferences based on those details. Three details are given, and the first inference has been made for you.

"A Dream Within a Dream"

Detail	Inference
The speaker gives someone a parting kiss.	The poet is sad to say good-bye to someone he once cared for deeply.

"The Spring and the Fall"

Detail	Inference
"He laughed at all I dared to praise."	

"Ankylosaurus"

Detail	Inference
"Ankylosaurus was built like a tank."	

Unit 5: Mysterious Worlds

"A Dream Within a Dream" by Edgar Allan Poe
"The Spring and the Fall" by Edna St. Vincent Millay
"Ankylosaurus" by Jack Prelutsky

Literary Analysis: Rhyme

Words that **rhyme** end with the same sound. For example, the word *bough* rhymes with *allow* because both end with the sound *ow*, even though the sound is spelled differently in each word.

- Rhyming words may be spelled alike: *cake, make, sake, mistake.*
- They may be spelled differently: *go, know, toe, although.*
- Some words have similar spellings, but do not rhyme: *earth, hearth; wear, near.*

A. DIRECTIONS: For each line, circle the letter of the line that rhymes with it.

1. The ankylosaurus grew in weight

   a. More quickly than it grew in height   b. The more it ate and ate and ate

2. He made a vow

   a. That I'll allow   b. When he felt low

3. It stomped through forests long ago

   a. It had so many things to do   b. The sky above, the earth below

4. In the fall of the year

   a. It was hard to bear   b. She shed a tear

5. He broke a bough

   a. She remembers it now   b. And she'd had enough

B. DIRECTIONS: In the paragraph below, circle all the words that rhyme with the word *show*.

   The violinist's career had been slow to grow, but he had made a vow that he would allow

himself five years to achieve success. Now the time had come for him to wow his audience.

Every row in the concert hall was filled. With a slight bow of his head, he raised his bow,

and the sounds began to flow. By the end of the evening, he would know if he'd made it.

from *Exploring the* Titanic by Robert Ballard

Build Vocabulary

Using Compound Adjectives

When two or more words work together as one to modify a noun or pronoun, the word is called a **compound adjective**. The word *airtight*, for example, combines two words, *air* and *tight*. This word describes something so tight no air can get in.

Compound adjectives are useful in writing, because they can replace a whole phrase or group of words. For example, it's shorter and clearer to say "The compartment was airtight," than "The compartment was so tight that no air could get into it." Here is another example.

It was breezy, so I packed up my jacket *that was light in weight* and red.
It was breezy, so I packed up my *lightweight* red jacket.

A. DIRECTIONS: Replace the italicized words with a compound adjective from the list below.

watertight   carefree   windblown

1. The passengers had a *free of care* conversation. _____

2. The ship's compartments were *made tight so that no water could get in.* _____

3. I need a comb because my hair is *blown by the wind.* _____

Using the Word Bank

majestically	collision	novelty	watertight

B. DIRECTIONS: Use a word from the Word Bank above to answer the following riddles, filling in the blank space.

1. How is a high, snow-capped mountain like a king wearing velvet robes? They are both _____ dressed.

2. Two skaters with bad vision might have a _____.

3. To someone who studies all the time, having no homework is a _____

4. A fish is very happy inside a _____ container.

Recognizing Antonyms

C. DIRECTIONS: Circle the letter of the word that is most *opposite* in meaning to the word in CAPITAL LETTERS.

1. WATERTIGHT: a. dry b. damp c. leaky d. desert

2. MAJESTICALLY: a. modestly b. grandly c. magically b. sadly

3. COLLISION: a. crash b. separation c. plot d. collection

Name _____ Date _____

Build Spelling Skills: The Sound *zhun* Spelled *-sion*

Spelling Strategy The Word Bank word *collision*, meaning "a crash," spells the *zhun* sound with *-sion*. Other words that have this sound and spelling include *illusion*, *vision*, and *confusion*.

• **Exception:** If the *-sion* is preceded by an *s*, it is pronounced *-shun*: admi<u>ssion</u>, discu<u>ssion</u>.

A. Practice: Add *-sion* to the word parts in parentheses; then use each word in a sentence.

1. (deci) _____

2. (confu) _____

3. (explo) _____

4. (inva) _____

5. (illu) _____

B. Practice: In the paragraph below, fill in the blanks with a word that uses the spelling *-sion* from the following list:

vision   conclusion   collision   illusion

Most people on the Titanic were under the _____ that the Titanic was

"unsinkable". A passenger remembers that the night was brilliant and starry. Apparently

there was a clear line of _____ from the crow's nest, but the lookout only

saw the iceberg seconds before the _____ occurred. The

_____ of the voyage was a disaster rather than a celebration.

Challenge: In *Exploring the* Titanic, the ship's radio is called a "wireless set." In Great Britain today, a radio is still called a "wireless." Though Americans and the British share a common language, you may find when reading English literature that some words are used differently in Great Britain. Here are some examples of British words and their American equivalents.

lorry (truck)   **torch** (flashlight)   **boot and bonnet** (car trunk and hood)

lift (elevator)   **chips** (French fries)   **crisps** (potato chips)

DIRECTIONS: Write a sentence using each of the above words in its British meaning.

1. _____

2. _____

3. _____

4. _____

5. _____

6. _____

from *Exploring the* **Titanic** by Robert Ballard

Build Grammar Skills: Kinds of Sentences

A **sentence** is a group of words that expresses a complete thought. There are four kinds of sentences: declarative, imperative, interrogative, and exclamatory. Each kind of sentence begins with a capital letter.

- A **declarative** sentence makes a statement:
  Bride watched the crewmen steer the ship towards New York.

- An **imperative** sentence commands:
  Go back to your cabins.

- An **interrogative** sentence asks a question and ends with a question mark:
  Why were the iceberg warnings ignored?

- An **exclamatory** sentence expresses abruptness or excitement and ends with an exclamation mark:
  How quickly water poured into the forward holds!

A. Practice: Circle the letter of the sentence that correctly answers the question about its type.

1. Which sentence below is interrogative?

   a. When did the temperature start to drop?   b. When he got the message he passed it on.

2. Which sentence below is imperative?

   a. Reverse the engines.   b. Reverse the engines?

3. Which sentence below is declarative?

   a. The crew braced for the collision.   b. Turn the ship's wheel hard.

4. Which sentence below is exclamatory?

   a. There weren't enough lifeboats for everyone.   b. What a tragedy this was!

B. Writing Application: On the lines provided, rewrite the following sentences, changing each to the type of sentence indicated in parentheses. Be sure to capitalize each sentence correctly. The first sentence is done for you.

1. Jack Thayer put on his coat. (imperative)

   Put on your coat, Jack Thayer.
   _____

2. Harold Bride was only twenty-two years old. (interrogative)

   _____

3. Was Captain Smith on duty on the bridge? (declarative)

   _____

4. Were the stars shining brightly? (exclamatory)

   _____

5. Will you send the call for assistance? (imperative)

   _____

Name _____ Date _____

from *Exploring the* **Titanic** by Robert Ballard

Reading Strategy: Distinguishing Between Fact and Opinion

Nonfiction writing, such as *from Exploring the* Titanic, is based on **facts**, information that is true and can be proven. For example, the following sentence expresses a fact:

The *Titanic* sank.

In addition to facts, nonfiction writers express **opinions**, or statements about what someone thinks or believes. Opinions cannot be proven, but can be supported, or backed up, by reasons and arguments. For example, the sentence below expresses an opinion:

The captain of the *Titanic* acted foolishly.

This statement can't be proven, but it can supported, or backed up, by saying, "He should have paid more attention to the warnings." You might disagree with this opinion by arguing, "But he believed the ship was unsinkable."

A piece of nonfiction writing that includes opinions is more interesting than one that includes facts only. Opinions give the reader more to think about. It's important to know the difference between facts and opinions so that you can think about whether you agree with the writer's opinions rather than simply accept them as proven facts. *Exploring the* Titanic contains both facts and opinions.

A. DIRECTIONS: Identify the following passages from the selection as fact or opinion by writing *F* or *O* on the lines provided.

_____ 1. It was a sunny but cold Sunday morning. . . .

_____ 2. It was the kind of night that made one feel glad to be alive.

_____ 3. At 7:30 P.M., the radio room received three more warnings. . . .

_____ 4. . . . such a close call at the beginning of a maiden voyage was a very bad omen.

_____ 5. As it was Sunday, church services had been held in the morning. . . .

B. DIRECTIONS: Robert Ballard fills *Exploring the* Titanic with many kinds of interesting facts. Read through the selection, and find at least two facts to fill in at each category in the chart below.

1. Facts about the collision:
2. Facts about the officers and crew:
3. Facts about the passengers:

Name _____ Date _____

from *Exploring the* **Titanic** by Robert Ballard

Literary Analysis: Atmosphere, Suspense

Atmosphere is the emotional feeling that a passage of literature or a literary work creates in the reader. A piece of writing may cause a reader to feel happy, for example, or sad, or relieved. When a piece of writing creates a sense of nervous expectation in the reader, the writing is said to have an atmosphere of **suspense.** For example, you know that the *Titanic* sank. You feel suspense when you read that it was in danger of colliding with another ship first, however, because you want to know if the collision actually occurred.

DIRECTIONS: As you read the passage from *Exploring the* Titanic, use the chart below to help you note elements that add an atmosphere of suspense to the writing. The left-hand column, **What I Know,** lists details you learn as you read. In the right-hand column, list what each detail makes you **want to know.** The first example has been done for you.

What I Know	What I Want to Know
The pull created by the *Titanic* broke the docking ropes of another ship.	Did the two ships collide?
Bride gives an iceberg warning to the captain.	
The lookouts were ordered to watch for ice.	
The watertight compartments were closed.	
The stokers were hit by a jet of icy water.	

"**Breaker's Bridge**" by Laurence Yep

Build Vocabulary

Using Related Words: Forms of *execute*

The Word Bank word *executioner* is a noun that means "one who carries out a death penalty." It is a form of the word *execute*, which means "put to death." The word *execute* has other meanings as well. It can be used to mean "carry out," or simply "do."

The death penalty in a state allows it to *execute* convicted criminals. (*execute* = put to death)

We worked hard to *execute* our plan. (*execute* = carry out, do)

Several other English words are based on the word *execute*. Here are some of them:

The convicted man's *execution* will take place at midnight. (*execution* = putting to death)

The *executive* worked hard to make his company successful. (*executive* = person who manages)

Fred was the *executor* of our project. (*executor* = person who performs a job or assignment)

A. DIRECTIONS:

Use one of the words above to complete each of the sentences below.

1. The highest _____ in state government is the governor.

2. The school principal will _____ the order for a school uniform.

3. The _____ felt pity for the condemned man, but carried out the sentence.

4. The prisoner was allowed to choose the means of his _____.

Using the Word Bank

obstacle	writhing	piers	executioner	immortals

B. DIRECTIONS: Use one word from the Word Bank to replace the word or words in parentheses in the following sentences.

1. The town closed the bridge when several of its (supports) _____ cracked.

2. The dead hero is now one of the (beings who live forever) _____.

3. The biggest (barrier) _____ to our baseball team reaching the championship was a rival team.

4. The kite was (twisting and turning) _____ in the strong winds.

5. The identity of the (person who carries out the death sentence) _____ is often kept a secret.

Sentence Completions

C. DIRECTIONS: Circle the letter of the word that best completes each sentence.

1. If a car breaks down on a busy road, it could become a dangerous ____ .
   a. writhing   b. piers   c. immortals   d. obstacle

2. I was ____ with pain as the doctor examined my injured shoulder.
   a. writhing   b. piers   c. immortals   d. obstacle

"Breaker's Bridge" by Laurence Yep

Build Spelling Skills: *i* Before *e* Rule and Exceptions

Spelling Strategy A famous rhyme says, "Put *i* before *e* except after *c*, or when sounded like *a* as in *neighbor* and *weigh*."

Examples: ***i* before *e*** — piers, piece, believe, field
except after *c* — receive, conceited, deceive
or when sounded like *a* — rein, sleigh, neighbor, weigh

Here are some exceptions to the rhyme:

either	financier	foreign	forfeit	height	heir	leisure
sheik	sovereign	their	weird	neither	protein	seize

A. Practice: Complete the words by adding *i* and *e* in the correct order.

1. It is better to give than to rec____ve.

2. My little brother has a w____rd way of tying his shoelaces.

3. I grabbed the r____ns of the horse and held tight.

4. The arrow p____rced the bull's eye on the target.

5. The American people bel_____ve in the principles of democracy.

B. Practice: Proofread the following paragraph carefully, looking for misspelled words containing the *ie* combination. Cross out each misspelled word, and write it correctly above the line.

Engineers have concieve and build impressive suspension bridges. Some, such as the Golden Gate Bridge in San Francisco and the Verrazano Narrows Bridge in New York City, span waterways at a great height. The cheif users of these bridges are commuters on thier way to and from work. Some beleived the wide lanes would help them receive some releif from rush-hour congestion. However, to their greif, traffic still creeps along, morning and evening.

Challenge: In the Word Bank word *writhing*, and in other words beginning with *wr*, the *w* is silent. On the lines below, write five sentences using the following *wr* words.

wrong   write   wrath   wreath   wrap

1. _____

2. _____

3. _____

4. _____

5. _____

Name _____ Date _____

Build Grammar Skills: Direct and Indirect Objects

You know that a verb is the action word in a sentence. A **direct object** is a noun or pronoun that *receives* the action of the verb. In other words, the verb tells what happens. The thing or person the action *happens to* is the direct object. It answers the question *what?* or *whom?*

The old man *held* the <u>crutch</u>.

What was held? A crutch. The crutch *receives* the action of the verb *held*.

Indirect objects are nouns or pronouns that name the person or thing *to whom* or *for whom* an action is done. Indirect objects may come before or after the direct object. Now look at these sentences:

The old man gave <u>the emperor</u> advice.   The old man gave advice <u>to the emperor</u>.

In the sentence, *gave* is the verb. *Advice* is the direct object. *To whom* did the old man give the advice? The answer is *the emperor*. *Emperor* is the indirect object of both sentences.

A. Practice: In each of the following sentences, underline the direct object once. Underline the indirect object twice. On the lines following each sentence, write the question each object answers. Choose from the questions *What? To whom?* and *For whom?* The first example has been done for you.

1. The old man gave <u>Breaker</u> the <u>pellets</u>.

Question answered by direct object <u>what?</u> Question answered by indirect object <u>to whom?</u>

2. Breaker built the emperor a bridge.

Question answered by direct object_____ Question answered by indirect object_____

3. Breaker offered the old man the crutch.

Question answered by direct object_____ Question answered by indirect object_____

4. The emperor wrote him a letter.

Question answered by direct object_____ Question answered by indirect object_____

B. Writing Application: Combine each of the following sentence pairs into one sentence with both a direct object and an indirect object. The first sentence has been done for you.

1. My sister threw the ball. She threw it to the puppy.
   My sister threw the puppy the ball. _____

2. My father built a desk. He built it for me.

   _____

3. I gave a wonderful present. I gave it to my best friend.

   _____

4. The babysitter told a bedtime story. She told it to the children.

   _____

Name _____ Date _____

"**Breaker's Bridge**" by Laurence Yep

Reading Strategy: Determining Cause and Effect

It's time for school and you're running late. You'd be on time if you'd remembered to turn on your alarm clock. The alarm clock's failure to go off is a cause. The effect was that you were late for school. A **cause** is a reason that something happens. An **effect** is the thing that happens.

Recognizing cause-and-effect relationships when you read helps you to connect one event to another in a story. For example, in "Breaker's Bridge," the dam on the river breaks. The effect is that the water rushes down and destroys the two piers Breaker has built for his bridge.

DIRECTIONS: Read each passage below. On the lines following each passage, write the cause and the effect. The first one has been modeled for you.

1. "But Breaker was as clever as he was clumsy. When he grew up, he managed to outlive his nickname. He could design a bridge to cross any obstacle. No canyon was too wide. No river was too deep. Somehow the clever man always found a way to bridge them all.
   Eventually the emperor heard about this clever builder and sent for him."

Cause: Breaker proves himself a clever bridge builder. _____

Effect: The emperor sends for Breaker. _____

2. "The river was too wide to span with a simple bridge. Breaker would have to construct two piers in the middle of the river. The piers would support the bridge like miniature stone islands."

Cause: _____

Effect: _____

3. "The old man looked at the branches that grew from the sides of his new crutch. `A little splintery.'
   Breaker angrily took his cut finger from his mouth. `Don't insult someone who's doing you a favor.'"

Cause: _____

Effect: _____

Selection Support   **119**

"**Breaker's Bridge**" by Laurence Yep

Literary Analysis: Character Traits

Character traits are the qualities that make up an individual's personality. Fictional characters demonstrate their character traits through how they act and speak. Read the following passage from "Breaker's Bridge" about Breaker.

> Although it was hard to see, Breaker found a tall-straight sapling and tried to trim the branches from its sides; but being Breaker, he dropped his knife several times and lost it twice among the old leaves on the forest floor. He also cut each of his fingers. By the time he was ready to cut down the sapling, he couldn't see it. Of course, he cut his fingers even more.

In the passage, Breaker drops his knife and loses it and cuts his fingers twice. Based on this behavior, you could say that clumsiness is one of Breaker's character traits.

A. Directions: On the lines below each excerpt, write the actions of the character as described. Then write a word or words describing the character trait that these actions illustrate.

1. But before Breaker could straighten, the old man's left hand shot out and caught hold of Breaker's wrist. The old man's grip was as strong as iron. "Even the least word from me will remind that river of the law."
   Breaker tried to pull away, but as strong as he was, he could not break the old man's hold. "Let me go."
   But the crooked old man lowered his right hand so that Breaker could see that he had rubbed some of the dirt and sweat from his skin. "We are all bound together," the old man murmured, "and by the same laws."

The Old Man's Actions

1. _____

2. _____

3. _____

Character Trait: _____

2. "There is a river in the hills," the emperor said to him. "Everyone tells me it is too swift and deep to span. So I have to go a long way around it to get to my hunting palace. But you're famous for doing the impossible."
   The kneeling man bowed his head to the floor. "So far I have been lucky. But there is always a first time when you can't do something."
   The emperor frowned. "I didn't think you were lazy like my other bridge builders. You can have all the workers and all the materials you need. Build the bridge and you'll have your weight in gold. Fail and I'll have your head."

The Emperor's Actions and Words

1. _____

2. _____

3. _____

Character Trait: _____

"The Loch Ness Monster" by George Laycock
"Why the Tortoise's Shell Is Not Smooth" by Chinua Achebe

Build Vocabulary

Using Forms of *orate*

The words *orate* and *oration* are related to the Word Bank word *orator*. Look at the meaning of each word. Which one is a verb? Which one is an adjective? Which two are nouns?

orate: to deliver a speech
orator: speaker
oratorical: having to do with formal speaking
oration: formal speech

A. DIRECTIONS: Use one of the forms of *orate* to complete each sentence. Write your answers on the lines provided.

1. Pericles, a leader in ancient Greece, was a famous _____.

2. He was known to _____ on many subjects; sometimes he spoke in tribute of people he knew, and sometimes he tried to persuade others to agree with his views on government.

3. His most famous _____ honored a fellow Greek at the time of his funeral.

4. Everyone who heard Pericles speak was impressed by his _____ gifts.

Using the Word Bank

elusive	abundant	famine	orator	eloquent

B. DIRECTIONS: Match each word in the left column with its definition in the right column.

____ 1. abundant   a. always escaping

____ 2. eloquent   b. shortage of food

____ 3. elusive   c. speaker

____ 4. orator   d. able to speak effectively

____ 5. famine   e. plentiful

Sentence Completions

C. DIRECTIONS: Circle the letter of the word that best completes each sentence.

1. I think that Felicia should join debating team because she is such a(n) ___ speaker.
        a. abundant   b. elusive   c. orator   d. eloquent

2. The villagers held a feast to celebrate the unusually ___ harvest that they enjoyed.
        a. eloquent   b. abundant   c. famine   d. elusive

3. The rains ended the drought that had caused years of ___.
        a. oratory   b. famine   d. eloquence   d. abundance

Unit 5: Mysterious Worlds

"The Loch Ness Monster" by George Laycock
"Why the Tortoise's Shell Is Not Smooth" by Chinua Achebe

Build Spelling Skills: Words Ending in *ent* and *ant*

Spelling Strategy The letters *ent* and *ant* usually have the same sound at the end of words—*eloquent* and *abundant*, for example. There is no easy way to know when to use *ent* or *ant*; therefore, it is important to try to learn the correct spelling of these words when you come across them. If you're not sure whether a word is spelled with *ent* or *ant*, look in a dictionary.

A. Practice: Use the clues in the sentences below to help you correctly complete the spelling of the following words. Write the complete word on the lines provided. You can use a dictionary to check your work..

intellig __ __ __   independ __ __ __   descend __ __ __

assist __ __ __   oppon __ __ __   excell __ __ __

1. This word means "free from the control of others" and is spelled with three e's in a row.
   _____

2. This word means "outstandingly good" and also is spelled with three e's in a row.
   _____

3. This word is similar in meaning to the word *aunt*, because both have to do with family relationships; its ending is spelled with an *a*, as in *aunt*. _____

4. This word means "smart" and is spelled with two *i*'s and two *e*'s. _____

5. This word means "one who opposes" and, like *opposes*, is spelled with an e in its ending.
   _____

6. This word means "helper"; like *abundant*, it has an *a* at its beginning and in its ending.
   _____

B. Practice: Revise the following sentences to correct the errors in the spelling of words that have the *nt* sound. Write any misspelled words correctly on the lines. If there are no misspelled words in a sentence, write *no error*. Use a dictionary to check your spelling, if you wish.

1. The tortoise in "Why the Tortoise's Shell Is Not Smooth" is an eloquant speaker.
   _____

2. One day, he thinks of a brilliant plan. _____

3. He persuades the birds to invite him to their feast by insisting that he is a changed man.
   _____

4. He also tricks the birds into helping him make an efficiant pair of wings.
   _____

5. The clever and confidant tortoise manages to eat most of the food. _____

6. It becomes apparant to the birds that the tortoise has not changed after all.
   _____

"The Loch Ness Monster" by George Laycock
"Why the Tortoise's Shell Is Not Smooth" by Chinua Achebe

Build Grammar Skills: Subject Complements

A **linking verb** is a word such as *be*, *feel*, *appear*, or *seem* that tells what the subject of a sentence is or is like. A **subject complement** is a word that comes after a linking verb and identifies or describes the subject. In the following sentences, the subject complement is underlined.

Loch Ness is a <u>lake</u> in Scotland. (*identifies* the subject, Loch Ness)

Loch Ness is very <u>deep</u>. (*describes* Loch Ness)

Two common kinds of subject complements are predicate nouns and predicate adjectives. A **predicate noun** follows a linking verb and identifies or renames the subject. A **predicate adjective** follows a linking verb and describes the subject.

A. Practice: Look at the underlined subject complement in each sentence. Draw an arrow to the word or phrase that it renames or describes. Then write whether the subject complement is a *predicate noun* or a *predicate adjective*. The first one is modeled for you.

1. George Laycock is a professional <u>writer</u>. _____ predicate noun _____

2. He also is an avid <u>photographer</u>. _____

3. He became <u>curious</u> about the Loch Ness monster. _____

4. The creature is <u>famous</u> throughout Scotland and throughout the world. _____

5. Nessie is the <u>nickname</u> that most people use when referring to it. _____

6. Nessie appears <u>huge</u> in several famous photos. _____

7. According to one theory, Nessie is a giant <u>reptile</u> that surfaces to breathe. _____

8. The tales of the Loch Ness Monster are <u>fascinating</u>. _____

9. In fact, Nessie has become the most valuable <u>animal</u> in all of Scotland. _____

10. No one has proved its existence, and so Nessie remains a <u>mystery</u>. _____

B. Writing Application: Complete the following sentences with phrases of your choice. After you have completed each sentence, underline the subject complement that you used. Then, after the sentence, write *PN* if it is a predicate noun or *PA* if it is a predicate adjective.

____ 1. To me, the Loch Ness monster is _____.

____ 2. The scientists who study Nessie are _____.

____ 3. To those who have seen the Loch Ness monster, Nessie looks

_____.

____ 4. The waters of Loch Ness must feel _____.

____ 5. It seems _____ to many that the Loch Ness monster really exists.

"The Loch Ness Monster" by George Laycock
"Why the Tortoise's Shell Is Not Smooth" by Chinua Achebe

Reading Strategy: Evaluating Logic

Both in stories and in real life, persuasion can be hard to resist. Therefore, when a character (real or imaginary) tries to get others to *think* something or *do* something, it's time to stop and evaluate: Is the character using good logic? Often, the answer is NO. For example, the character may fail to support the ideas that he or she suggests are true. Even if there is support, it may not be reliable. The character may use propaganda—misleading statements—instead of honest facts. See if the logic is true, not tricky!

A. DIRECTIONS: On the lines below, explain why each of these statements from "The Loch Ness Monster" does—or does not—have good logic.

1. Other sightings even included an observation by a driver who saw Nessie in the beam of his headlights on a dark night as the monster crossed the highway near the loch.

_____

_____

2. But the lecturer who was to tell us about the Loch Ness monster that night in Oxford, Ohio, had brought scientific methods to the search for Nessie, and people were eager to hear his message.

_____

_____

DIRECTIONS: In "Why the Tortoise's Shell Is Not Smooth," the birds ask Tortoise why they should agree to take him to the sky. Tortoise gives this persuasive reply:

I am a changed man. I have learned that a man who makes trouble for others is also making it for himself.

The birds do not stop to evaluate Tortoise's logic.

On the lines below, write two questions that you think they should have asked before agreeing to his plan.

_____

_____

_____

_____

"The Loch Ness Monster" by George Laycock
"Why the Tortoise's Shell Is Not Smooth" by Chinua Achebe

Literary Analysis: Oral Tradition

The Nigerian tale "Why the Tortoise's Shell Is Not Smooth" is part of the **oral tradition.** Stories, songs, and poems that belong to this tradition are passed from generation to generation by word of mouth. They may be hundreds or even thousands of years old. Today, writers such as Chinua Achebe collect and write down these traditional works so that today's readers and future generations will continue to know and enjoy them.

DIRECTIONS: Answer the following questions about how the oral tradition is reflected in "Why the Tortoise's Shell Is Not Smooth" and "The Loch Ness Monster." Write your responses on the lines provided.

1. Explain in your own words what is happening in the opening passage from "Why the Tortoise's Shell Is Not Smooth," which is reprinted below. In what way does the action illustrate what happens in the oral tradition?

> Low voices, broken now and again by singing, reached Okonkwo from his wives' huts as each woman and her children told folk stories. Ekwefi and her daughter, Ezinma, sat on a mat on the floor. It was Ekwefi's turn to tell a story.
> "Once upon a time," she began, "all the birds were invited to a feast in the sky…

_____
_____
_____
_____
_____
_____

2. Chinua Achebe has written, "Our ancestors created their myths and legends and told their stories for a purpose. . . . Any good story, any good novel, should have a message." In a sentence or two, summarize what you think is the message of "Why the Tortoise's Shell Is Not Smooth."

_____
_____
_____

3. Which of the following do you think is part of the oral tradition—George Laycock's article about the Loch Ness monster or the stories of sailors and other people in Scotland that described sightings of the creature? Explain your answer.

_____
_____
_____

"Dragon, Dragon" by John Gardner

Build Vocabulary

Using Forms of *tyrant*

The Word Bank word *tyrant* means "a cruel, unjust ruler." Look at the meanings of the following words related to *tyrant*. What idea or ideas do all of them have in common?

tyranny: a cruel, unjust reign or rule   **tyrannize:** to rule unjustly and cruelly
tyrannical: having the qualities of one who rules unjustly and cruelly
tyrannically: in the manner of one who rules unjustly and cruelly

A. DIRECTIONS: Use one of the forms of *tyrant* to complete each sentence.

1. The king in "Dragon, Dragon" declared that he was not a _____.

2. He did not believe in behaving _____; therefore, he did not feel he could force his knights to slay the dragon.

3. The king did believe that if the dragon were to gain complete control of the kingdom, he would surely _____ everyone who lived in it.

4. Fortunately, the young man who won half of the kingdom was wise and fair; he was not at all _____.

Using the Word Bank

plagued	ravaged	tyrant	reflecting	craned

B. DIRECTIONS: Choose the word from the Word Bank that answers each question below. Write your answers on the lines.

1. Which word names the way someone might have moved his or her neck? _____

2. Which word could describe an unfair and unpopular ruler? _____

3. Which word might you use if you were talking about someone who is thinking seriously about his or her future? _____

4. Which word might you use if you were looking for another way to say that a kingdom was "tormented by a dragon"? _____

5. Which word could name the way that a powerful hurricane affected an area? _____

Analogies

C. DIRECTIONS: Circle the letter of the pair of words that expresses a relationship most similar to that expressed by the pair in CAPITAL LETTERS.

1. CRANED : NECK
   a. snapped : fingers   b. washed : soap   c. removed : gone   d. whistled : ears

2. RAVAGED : DESTROYED
   a. built : rebuilt   b. led : followed   c. poured : dripped   d. helped : assisted

Name _____ Date _____

"Dragon, Dragon" by John Gardner

Build Spelling Skills: Spelling the Long *i* Sound With a *y*

Spelling Strategy The long *i* sound is sometimes spelled with a *y*, as it is in the word *tyrant*. Pronounce each of the following words to yourself. Notice that in each one the long *i* sound is spelled with a *y*.

dynamic   why   bicycle   typhoon   rhyme   deny   style   type

A. Practice: Use the clues to fill out the puzzle below. *Hint:* You can find all of the words in the above list.

Across

4. energetic, forceful
5. for what reason?
6. fashion

Down

1. The words *bad, sad, glad,* and *dad* do this
2. a vehicle with two wheels and pedals
3. another word for *hurricane*
7. kind

B. Practice: Revise the following sentences to correct the errors in the spelling of words that have the long *i* sound. Cross out each misspelled word and write it correctly above the line. Write C next to the sentence if it contains no errors.

_____ 1. The king in "Dragon, Dragon" does not wish to be thought of as a tierant.

_____ 2. Forcing his knights to slay the dragon is not his stile, so he looks for someone else.

_____ 3. The cobbler's three dinamic sons step forward to apply for the job.

_____ 4. Only one of them, however, was the tipe of person the king wanted.

_____ 5. You can't deny that this story took place in bygone days.

El Sereno Middle School
2839 North Eastern Avenue
Los Angeles, California 90032

"Dragon, Dragon" by John Gardner

Build Grammar Skills: Clauses

A **clause** is a group of words that contains a subject and verb. An **independent clause** can stand on its own as a complete sentence. A **subordinate clause** cannot stand on its own; it needs an independent clause to complete its meaning. Subordinate clauses begin with **subordinating conjunctions**. Here are some common subordinating conjunctions: *who, after, as, because, if, unless, whenever, when,* and *where.*

In the following example, the subject of each clause is underlined once and the verb twice; the subordinating conjunction is in italics.

> ┌─────subordinate clause─────┐┌─────independent clause─────┐
> *When* everything was ready, the son went for a last talk with his father.

A. Practice: Circle the independent clause in each sentence. Then underline the subordinate clause.

1. The dragon caused trouble wherever it went.

2. The king's wizard was unable to help because he had misplaced his book of spells.

3. After the king called everyone in the kingdom together, he asked for help.

4. As we know, a cobbler in the village had three sons.

5. Although he thought of himself as an unimportant person, the cobbler came to the king's meeting.

6. The king began his speach when all the people were assembled.

7. The frustrated ruler had put up with the dragon as long as he could.

8. The terrible monster would remain a problem unless a hero appeared.

9. Because a volunteer was needed, the king offered a huge reward.

10. If anyone could get rid of the dragon, he would win half of the kingdom and the princess's hand in marriage.

B. Writing Application: Build your own sentences by adding a subordinate or independent clause to each clause given below. After you have completed each sentence, circle the independent clause and underline the subordinate clause.

1. The king stared at the queen _____ .

2. _____ , the cobbler's eldest son volunteered to go out and slay the dragon.

3. The cobbler's middle son decided that it was his turn to try

   _____ .

4. Although he was nervous and timid, _____ .

5. The youngest son was glad for his father's advice

   _____ .

"**Dragon, Dragon**" by John Gardner

Reading Strategy: Comparing and Contrasting

When you read a story that has many characters or other details, you probably will find it helpful to do some comparing and contrasting. When you **compare,** you look for similarities among certain things—that is, ways in which the things are alike. When you **contrast,** you look for differences. By doing so, you often can figure out some story ideas.

In "Dragon, Dragon," for example, you can compare and contrast the actions that make the dragon a threat. When you do, you can figure out that the dragon does several different things. Still, some actions are the same because they affect people and others are the same because they affect property. You also can figure out that some of the actions are minor problems whereas others cause big problems for everyone.

DIRECTIONS: Use this chart to help you compare and contrast the cobbler's sons. In each column, jot down details about each of the three sons. Note anything that two of the three brothers have in common. Then study your notes. Beneath the chart, write two story ideas that you figured out because of those notes.

	Eldest Son	**Middle Son**	**Youngest Son**
Attitude toward fighting	Eager to fight dragon	Eager to fight dragon	Reluctant to fight dragon
Strength and ability to kill dragon			
Response to father's advice			
Outcome of fighting with dragon			

STORY IDEAS

_____

_____

_____

_____

"Dragon, Dragon" by John Gardner

Literary Analysis: Plot

When you read a story like "Dragon, Dragon," you follow a series of events in which a problem is introduced and characters try to solve it. This sequence of events is known as the story's **plot**. As the characters attempt to solve their problem, the events lead to a climax, or turning point; this is the moment of highest tension in the story. The events are then wrapped up in a part of the story known as the resolution or conclusion.

DIRECTIONS: Use the organizer below to identify the problem, significant events, the turning point and the conclusion as you read "Dragon, Dragon." Note that two of the events have been filled in for you as examples.

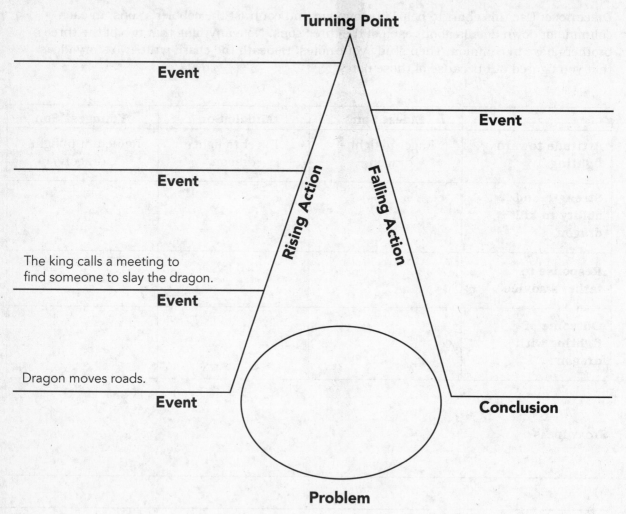

Name _____ Date _____

"Becky and the Wheels-and-Brake Boys" by James Berry

Build Vocabulary

Using Regional Synonyms

Speakers of the same language may use different words to name or describe something. Depending upon the area in which you live, you might call the same tasty breakfast food a *pancake*, a *flapjack*, or a *griddle cake*; you might call the same big sandwich a *hero*, a *hoagie*, a *grinder*, or a *sub*. These words are called **regional synonyms** because the word you use depends on the region, or area, in which you live. The Word Bank word *veranda* and the word *porch* are examples of regional synonyms.

A. Directions: Replace each underlined word with one of the following regional synonyms.

seesaw   frying pan   sofa   handbag

1. The two children enjoyed going up and down on the underlined teeter-totter. _____

2. Their parents sat on the underlined couch and watched them from the window. _____

3. Mrs. Brown searched in her underlined purse for her shopping list. _____

4. She needed a new underlined skillet because the old iron one was rusty. _____

Using the Word Bank

veranda	menace	reckless

B. Directions: Complete each sentence below by writing the correct Word Bank word.

1. Becky's mother considered the boys on bicycles to be a _____ to the neighborhood.

2. Becky's grandmother rested on the _____ while Becky played.

3. They watched a particularly _____ boy do dangerous tricks on his bike.

Recognizing Synonyms

C. Directions: Circle the letter of the word that is the **synonym** of the underlined word.

1. The bully was a underlined menace to the smaller children in the class.
   a. threat   b. help   c. teacher   d. pest

2. The family often gathered on the underlined veranda after dinner and greeted their neighbors.
   a. attic   b. front lawn   c. porch   d. pavement

3. The parents in the neighborhood did not like the underlined reckless way some of the children rode their bicycles and scooters.
   a. careful   b. sloppy   c. ridiculous   d. careless

"Becky and the Wheels-and-Brake Boys" by James Berry

Build Spelling Skills: *ace* and the *is* Sound

Spelling Strategy The letters *ace* are sometimes used to spell the *is* sound when it comes at the end of a word. The Word Bank word *menace*, for example, spells the *is* sound with the letters *ace*. The words *surface* and *necklace* are other examples. Some words, however, spell the *is* sound at the end of a word with the letters *iss*, as in *miss*; some use the letters *is*, as in *Paris*.

Remembering that the *is* sound is sometimes spelled with *ace* may help you to avoid some spelling mistakes. If you are not sure how to spell the *is* sound at the end of a word, look up the word in a dictionary until you find the correct spelling.

A. Practice: Fill in the following words on the chart below. Sort the words into columns according to the way they spell the *is* sound.

menace   palace   kiss   tennis   dismiss   terrace   grimace   synopsis   Swiss

ace	iss	is

B. Practice: Proofread the following paragraph about Becky. Correct any misspelled words.

Becky did not want an expensive neckliss or a new dress to wear. She did not care to live in a mansion or a palis. She only wanted a bicycle of her own. Becky did not plan to be a menice to the neighborhood. She would never ride on the sidewalk, but only on the paved surfiss of the road. She knew she would always be careful.

Challenge: Unscramble each of the following words in Column A. Write the word on the line next to the correct definition in Column B. Clue: Every word on the list can be found in the story "Becky and the Wheels-and-Brake Boys."

Column A	Column B
namece	careless of danger _____
ndavera	opposite of "outdoors" _____
sebuol	another word for "firefighter" _____
leksrcses	a girl's shirt _____
doinros	threat or danger _____
nmaefri	porch of a house _____

"Becky and the Wheels-and-Brake Boys" by James Berry

Build Grammar Skills: Independent Clauses

An **independent clause** must have both a subject and a verb, and make sense by itself as a complete sentence. In the following sentences from "Becky and the Wheels-and-Brake Boys," the independent clause is underlined.

I only want a bike because I want it and want it and want it.
When she can borrow a bike, Shirnette comes too.

The groups of words that are not underlined in the sentences above are called **subordinate clauses**. Even though a subordinate clause has a subject and a verb, it doesn't make sense when you read it by itself. It needs to be joined with an independent clause. Notice that the independent clause does not always come first and is not necessarily the longest clause in a sentence. Notice, too, that when a subordinate clause begins a sentence, it is followed by a comma.

A. Practice: Underline the independent clause in each of the following sentences. Then write its subject and the verb on the lines provided.

1. Becky wanted a bicycle badly although her mother and grandmother were against it.
   Subject_____   Verb_____

2. The Wheels-and-Brake Boys had so much fun when they rode together.
   Subject_____   Verb_____

3. After she watched the boys ride, Becky asked her mother for a bicycle.
   Subject_____   Verb_____

4. Although she felt sorry for Becky, her mother said no at first.
   Subject_____   Verb_____

5. Because Granny-Liz could not understand Becky's wish, she considered it foolish.
   Subject_____   Verb_____

6. Unless she got a bike, Becky would be very unhappy.
   Subject_____   Verb_____

7. When she asked them to teach her to ride, the boys ignored Becky.
   Subject_____   Verb_____

8. Things certainly changed for Becky after she got her own bicycle.
   Subject_____   Verb_____

B. Writing Application: The following sentences are about "Becky and the Wheels-and-Brake Boys." Complete each sentence with an independent clause. Add commas where necessary.

1. _____ whenever Becky came to watch them.

2. If Becky could only have a bike of her own _____.

3. When Becky asked her mother for a bike _____.

4. _____ when she tried to do her homework.

5. When Becky and Shirnette asked the boys to teach them to ride

   _____.

Name _____ Date _____

Reading Strategy: Predicting

As you read a story, you probably find yourself predicting what characters will do or what events will occur next. The predictions you make are logical guesses based on information and details in the story, or on your own experience. For example, at the beginning of "Becky and the Wheels-and-Brake Boys," you might wonder if Becky will get the bike she wants. Based on clues in the story, such as the words of Becky's mother, "Becky, d'you think you're a boy?" you might predict that she won't get the bike. However, based on your own experience with asking for things you want very much, you might predict that Becky will get her bike in the end.

DIRECTIONS: As you read "Becky and the Wheels-and-Brake Boys," use the chart below to help you to predict the events in the story. Fill in the chart with details the author includes, logical predictions you can make based upon these details, and your reasons for making these predictions. The first row in the chart has been filled in as an example.

Detail	Prediction	Reason for Prediction
Becky wants a bike very much.	Becky will find some way to get her bike.	Becky is a strong-minded and persistent character.

Name _____ Date _____

"**Becky and the Wheels-and-Brake Boys**" by James Berry

Literary Analysis: Conflict

In most short stories there is a **conflict**, a struggle between two forces, that will be resolved in the end. In "Becky and the Wheels-and-Brake Boys," the two opposing forces are Becky's fierce desire for a bicycle and her mother's belief that the family's small income should not be wasted on what she considers a boy's possession. This conflict determines the **action**, or series of events in the story. Some events contribute to the conflict; others occur as a result of the conflict. For example, in "Becky and the Wheels-and-Brake Boys," Becky's grandmother's opinion about girls riding bikes contributes to the conflict. Becky and her mother make friends with Mr. Dean as a result of the conflict.

DIRECTIONS: Look through "Becky and the Wheels-and-Brake Boys." Note the forces that are either for or against Becky's side of the conflict. List the forces you note on the organizer below. An example of each has been filled in for you.

Forces for Becky's Side of Conflict	Forces Against Becky's Side of Conflict
Becky's determined personality	Mother's and grandmother's feeling that bikes are only for boys

"Overdoing It" by Anton Chekhov
"Eleven" by Sandra Cisneros

Build Vocabulary

Using Foreign Terms in English

The Word Bank word *prolonged* came into the English language from French a long time ago. There are many modern foreign words and expressions, however, that English-speakers sometimes use. Here are some examples.

siesta: (Spanish) a nap taken in the afternoon
chic: (French) stylish or fashionable
du jour: (French) available on this day
fiesta: (Spanish) a celebration
nonchalant: (French) unworried or indifferent
hacienda: (Spanish) a large estate

A. DIRECTIONS: Write sentences by following each instruction below.

1. Write a sentence about a cranky baby. (Use *siesta*)

_____

2. Write a sentence about a special meal at a restaurant. (Use *du jour*)

_____

3. Write a sentence about a girl's birthday. (Use *fiesta*)

_____

4. Write a sentence about a new outfit. (Use *chic*)

_____

Using the Word Bank

prolonged	emaciated	wry	foresee	emerged	meditated

B. DIRECTIONS: Use a word from the Word Bank to replace the italicized word or words in each sentence below.

1. The horse looked so *thin and sickly* _____ that I couldn't believe it would be able to pull the wagon.

2. She sat at her desk and *thought seriously and carefully* _____ for hours about how she could help her friend.

3. We *know beforehand* _____ that we are going to have a great school year.

4. After the talks were *extended for days* _____, the two nations reached an agreement.

5. The lady made a *twisted and distorted* _____ face by wrinkling her brow and turning down her mouth in disgust.

6. The animal *came out of and into view* _____ slowly from the forest.

Name _____ Date _____

"**Overdoing It**" by Anton Chekhov
"**Eleven**" by Sandra Cisneros

Build Spelling Skills: Homophones with *r* and *wr*

Spelling Strategy The **sound *r*** at the beginning of words can be spelled *r* as in *right* or *wr* as in *write*. The words *right* and *write* are **homophones**—words have the same sound, but different spellings and meanings. The meaning of a sentence lets you know which homophone is the correct one to use.

Here are some examples of other homophones with the sound *r*.

rap to tap; a kind of music
ring bell sound; jewelry for the finger
rest to relax
write to form letters
rye a type of grain

wrap to enclose in a covering
wring to twist
wrest to take forcefully
right correct, opposite of left
wry bent, twisted

A. Practice: In each sentence below, replace the italicized word or words with one of the homophones in parentheses. Write the correct homophone on the line next to each sentence.

1. Please *place a covering around* this birthday gift. (rap/wrap) _____

2. I hear a *quick, sharp tap* on the door. (rap/wrap) _____

3. We heard the telephone *make a sound like a bell*. (ring/wring) _____

4. You need to *twist* the clothes before hanging them out to dry. (ring/wring) _____

5. He wants to *form letters or words on a surface, as with a pen or pencil* a story about his experience. (right/write) _____

6. This is not the *correct* answer. (right/write) _____

7. The baker wants to use *a special kind of grain* to make a tasty party bread. (rye/wry) _____

8. The actor's face showed a *twisted and distorted* smile to show disapproval. (rye/wry) _____

9. The police officer tried to *take forcefully* the money from the thief. (rest/wrest) _____

10. After such a long trip, we need to *relax* for a while. (rest/wrest) _____

B. Practice: Complete the following short passage with the correct homophones from the list above. Remember to use sentence meaning to help you know which homophone to write.

To _____ a story as good as those of Anton Chekhov is not easy. You have to find just the _____ blend of narration and dialogue, and you need to create believable characters. Chekhov doesn't _____ his characters in any kind of wordy descriptions; he portrays them directly through their words and actions. In "Overdoing It," for example, the _____ face that Klim makes after listening to the land surveyor lets readers know he is not happy with his passenger, while the passenger's words show that he is afraid that Klim wants to _____ his possessions from him. I think that the way Chekhov had both characters react to being scared was brilliant.

"Overdoing It" by Anton Chekhov
"Eleven" by Sandra Cisneros

Build Grammar Skills: Subordinate Clauses

A **subordinate clause**, or dependent clause, is a group of words that has its own subject and verb but cannot stand as a complete sentence by itself. It is dependent on the rest of the sentence to complete its meaning. A subordinate clause usually begins with a **subordinating conjunction**. Here are some of the most common subordinating conjunctions: *as, before, after, during, if, because, wherever, when, whenever, while,* and *until.*

In the following examples, the subordinate clauses are underlined, and the subordinating conjunction is in italics. Notice that when a subordinate clause appears first in a sentence, the clause is usually followed by a comma.

The land surveyor was worried *because* his field of vision was completely obstructed.

Rachel cried *until* there weren't any more tears left in her eyes.

When Rachel's papa comes home from work, they will eat the cake.

A. Practice: Underline the subordinate clause in each sentence.

1. Because there was no one in sight, the surveyor felt nervous.

2. After he heard the surveyor's words, Klim ran away.

3. The surveyor was surprised when Klim ran off.

4. The surveyor couldn't find his way unless he got Klim to come out of the forest.

5. It sometimes takes months to say eleven when they ask you.

6. You don't feel smart until you're almost twelve.

7. Rachel has to wear the sweater if Mrs. Price insists.

8. When Rachel tried to speak, nothing came out of her mouth.

B. Writing Application: Join the independent clause with the subordinate clause to form a sentence. Write each complete sentence on the line, using correct punctuation.

1. he bragged about his guns   because he wanted to hide his fear

   _____

2. Klim emerged from the forest   after a period of time had passed

   _____

3. everyone stared   as Mrs. Price gave Rachel the sweater

   _____

4. Phyllis Lopez claimed the sweater   just before the lunch bell rang

   _____

"Overdoing It" by Anton Chekhov
"Eleven" by Sandra Cisneros

Reading Strategy: Recognizing Word Origins

You may not know it, but seventy percent of the English language is made up of words that have been borrowed from other languages. The borrowing of these words is one of the reasons that English is such a rich language. Words like *peasant* and *ruffian*, from "Overdoing It" and "Eleven," came into the English language a very long time ago. Now they are no longer recognizable as having been borrowed from French. Today, the English language is still borrowing words from other languages; for example, *pizza* from Italian, and *déjà vu* and *cul de sac* from French. When you encounter a foreign word while reading, you should try to determine the meaning using the context or by looking the word up in a dictionary.

A. DIRECTIONS: Read the following sentence from "Overdoing It." The underlined words are all words that were borrowed from other languages many years ago. Use the context to try to determine the meanings. Check your answers using a dictionary.

Klim, having perhaps decided that a real cutthroat would have long since got away with his horse and wagon, emerged from the thicket and approached his passenger.

1. wagon _____

2. emerged _____

3. thicket _____

4. approached _____

5. passenger _____

B. DIRECTIONS: Each word listed below is commonly used in English, but is borrowed from another language. Write sentences using each word listed. If you do not know the meaning, look it up in the dictionary.

1. bon appétit _____

2. hors d'oeuvre _____

3. chic _____

4. entreé _____

5. amigo _____

"Overdoing It" by Anton Chekhov
"Eleven" by Sandra Cisneros

Literary Analysis: Characterization

The ways in which an author reveals what a character is like is called **characterization**. An author might use **direct characterization** by making direct statements about a character's personality and appearance. For example, an author might say, "The man was frightened." More often, however, an author uses **indirect characterization** by revealing a character's traits through the character's own words and actions, through what other characters say and think about her or him, and through the other characters' reactions to what she or he does and says. For example, in "Overdoing It," Anton Chekov uses Smirnov's own words and actions to let you know Smirnov is lying to hide his fear. In "Eleven," Sandra Cisneros indirectly characterizes Mrs. Price as an unsympathetic character by having her say, "You put that sweater on right now and no more nonsense."

DIRECTIONS: In each part of the pyramid below, jot down words, thoughts, actions, and direct statements to either tell about Gleb Smirnov or Rachel.

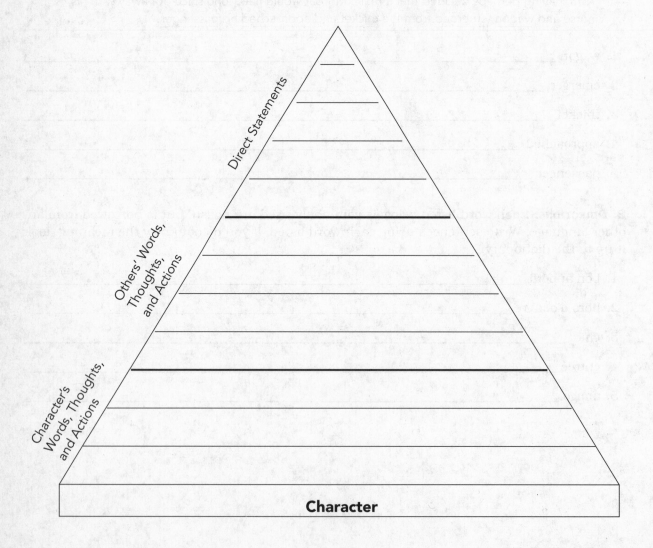

Name _____ Date _____

"The Lawyer and the Ghost" by Charles Dickens
"The Wounded Wolf" by Jean Craighead George

Build Vocabulary

Using the Prefix *in-*

If you did not know the meaning of the Word Bank word *inconsistent*, you could probably figure it out by looking at its two parts. The prefix *in-* means "no," "not," "without," "the lack of," or "the opposite of." The word *consistent* means "staying the same" or "making sense." Therefore, *inconsistent* means "not always the same" or "not making sense."

A. DIRECTIONS: Complete each sentence by combining the word in parentheses with the prefix *in-*. Write the new word in the blank.

1. It was very _____ of Jim to watch television while we talked to our guests. (considerate)

2. Laura felt _____ and nervous on the high diving board. (secure)

3. The story was so strange, it was _____ . (credible)

Using the Word Bank

sufficient	inconsistent	stoic
expend	massive	gnashes

B. DIRECTIONS: Use one word from the Word Bank to complete each of the following sentences.

1. We entered the _____ building through the huge, heavy doors.

2. The dog _____ and grinds his teeth as he chews up a bone.

3. I will _____ every ounce of energy I have to win the race.

4. Margarite was _____ and did not cry when the doctor gave her an injection.

5. The dinner was _____ and satisfied my appetite.

6. Joseph is _____ in his schoolwork, doing well in some subjects but not in others.

Recognizing Antonyms

C. DIRECTIONS: Circle the letter of the word that is most nearly *opposite* to the word in CAPITAL LETTERS.

1. INADEQUATE
   a. sufficient
   b. expend
   c. inconsistent
   d. massive

2. FRUITFUL
   a. inconsistent
   b. massive
   c. stoic
   d. barren

"The Lawyer and the Ghost" by Charles Dickens
"The Wounded Wolf" by Jean Craighead George

Build Spelling Skills: The Sound *shent* Spelled *cient*

Spelling Strategy Many words that end in the sound *shent* are spelled *cient*, such as the Word Bank word *sufficient*. Other examples are *efficient*, *proficient*, and *deficient*.

A. Practice: Write the word from the list that best completes each sentence below.

proficient: skilled, accomplished

sufficient: enough

inefficient: wasteful, not productive

deficient: lacking

efficient: productive, orderly

prescient: foresighted, able to make predictions

1. The assembly line is _____ and needs to be redesigned to work better.

2. Viewers believe that the accurate weather forecaster must be _____ .

3. José is _____ in both Spanish and English.

4. To stay healthy, you should get _____ exercise daily.

5. The car has a very _____ engine and goes far on one tank of gas.

6. The man took vitamins because his diet was _____ in many ways.

B. Practice: Complete the following advertisement. Using the context clues, choose four words from the list above to fill in the blanks.

Have you always wanted to be _____ in another language? Have you visited a foreign land and felt _____ because you couldn't communicate with the people? Your worries are over! Our new Learn-a-Language program will have you talking confidently in the language of your choice in just seven days or your money back. In just one short week, you will have _____ vocabulary to speak like a native! Other language programs are _____ and take far too long for results. Learn-A-Language is the most effective language program on the market today. Won't you give it a try?

Challenge: The Word Bank word *gnashes* begins with the two letters *gn*. When this combination begins a word, the *g* is almost always silent. Other similar words are: *gnarled*, *gnat*, *gnaws*, and *gnome*.

On the lines below, write a short paragraph using all five of these words beginning with *gn*. If you are unfamiliar with the meaning of a word, look it up in a dictionary.

_____

_____

_____

_____

"The Lawyer and the Ghost" by Charles Dickens
"The Wounded Wolf" by Jean Craighead George

Build Grammar Skills: Simple Sentences With Compound Subjects and Verbs

A **simple sentence** is a sentence containing just one independent clause, and no dependent clauses. Some simple sentences have a **compound** subject, or more than one subject. Some simple sentences have a **compound verb**, or more than one verb. In the following three examples, the subjects are underlined once and the verbs twice.

<u>Weakness</u> <u>overcomes</u> him. (one subject, one verb)

The <u>ravens</u> and the <u>fox</u> <u>move</u> in on Roko. (compound subjects: *ravens* and *fox*)

The <u>raven</u> <u>flies</u> and <u>circles</u> back. (compound verbs: *flies* and *circles*)

The following sentences are not simple sentences because they contain more than one clause. In each, one clause is in italics and the other is underlined.

Roko stops and <u>his breath comes hard</u>.

It penetrates the rocky cracks <u>where the Toklat ravens nest</u>.

A. Practice: Write SS for each simple sentence. Underline all compound subjects once. Underline all compound verbs twice. Put an X next to each sentence that is not a simple sentence. The first sentence has been done for you.

1. They <u>plunge</u> and <u>turn</u>. __SS__

2. The ravens and the owl stare at Roko. _____

3. Young Roko glances down the valley. _____

4. He gnashes, gorges, and shatters bits upon the snow. _____

5. The ravens fly overhead, and the white fox waits in the snow. _____

B. Writing Application: Rewrite each pair of sentences as one simple sentence. Follow the directions in parentheses. The first pair of sentences has been rewritten for you.

1. The ghost appeared. The ghost spoke to the lawyer. (Simple sentence with one subject and a compound verb) The ghost appeared and spoke to the lawyer.

2. The ghost had a conversation. The lawyer had a conversation. (Simple sentence with a compound subject and one verb) _____

3. The ghost left. He left the lawyer alone. (Simple sentence with one subject and one verb)

_____

4. The ravens alight upon the snow. They follow the wolf. (Simple sentence with one subject and a compound verb) _____

5. The wolf answers. He answers the call of the pack. (Simple sentence with one subject and one verb) _____

6. Roko ran down the Ridge. Kiglo ran down the Ridge. (Simple sentence with a compound subject and one verb) _____

Name _____ Date _____

Reading Strategy: Picturing the Action and Setting

When you read, you see more than words on a page. The words create images, or pictures that you "see" in your head like a movie. Good writers use clear, colorful words to make you **picture** what is happening. They use words that appeal to your senses of sight, hearing, smell, touch, and taste.

Here is an example from "The Lawyer and the Ghost":

> He had hardly spoken the words, when a sound resembling a faint groan, appeared to issue from the interior of the case.

The passage above appeals to your sense of sound. As you read it, you can almost hear the sound the ghost makes from inside the case.

Look for passages in your reading that make the action and setting real to you by appealing to your senses of sight, sound, touch, taste, and smell.

DIRECTIONS: Read each passage below. The first is from "The Wounded Wolf," and the second is from "The Lawyer and the Ghost." In the first column of the organizer, fill in the details that appeal to your senses. Then write in the second column how you picture the action or the setting.

1. "Young Roko glances down the valley. He droops his head and stiffens his tail to signal to his pack that he is badly hurt. Winds wail. A frigid blast picks up long shawls of snow and drapes them between young Roko and his pack. And so his message is not read."

2. "At that moment, the sound was repeated: and one of the glass doors slowly opening, disclosed a pale and emaciated figure in soiled and worn apparel, standing erect in the press. The figure was tall and thin, and the countenance expressive of care and anxiety; but there was something in the hue of the skin, and gaunt and unearthly appearance of the whole form, which no being of this world was ever seen to wear."

Passage 1—Details	Passage 2—Details
Hearing:	**Sight:**
Sight:	
How I Pictured the Action:	**How I Pictured the Action:**
How I Pictured the Setting:	**How I Pictured the Setting:**

Name _____ Date _____

"The Lawyer and the Ghost" by Charles Dickens
"The Wounded Wolf" by Jean Craighead George

Literary Analysis: Setting

Every story has a **setting**—the place and time in which it takes place. The place can be a kind of environment, such as Toklat Ridge in "The Wounded Wolf" or the tattered room where the story "The Lawyer and the Ghost" takes place. The time of the setting can be a historical era, like 19th-century England, or a time of year or season.

Sometimes the author will state the setting directly. Other times you will have to be a literary detective and look for clues that tell you what the place and time are. As you read, look for these clues provided by the author.

Read the following passage from "The Wounded Wolf."

> A wounded wolf climbs Toklat Ridge, a massive spine of rock and ice. As he limps, dawn strikes the ridge and lights it up with sparks and stars. Roko, the wounded wolf, blinks in the ice fire, then stops to rest and watch his pack run the thawing Arctic valley.

Details about place include: Details about time include:

1. Toklat Ridge is made of rock and ice   1. dawn strikes the ridge
2. It is an Arctic valley   2. the thawing Arctic valley

From these details, you can determine that the setting is Toklat Ridge in the frozen Arctic regions. You can also determine that it is dawn and that the valley is starting to thaw, indicating that spring is coming.

A. DIRECTIONS: On the lines below each excerpt, write the details that are clues to the setting of place and time. Then write what the setting is.

1. The hours pass. The wind slams snow on Toklat Ridge. Massive clouds blot out the sun. In their gloom Roko sees the deathwatch move in closer.

Details about place setting   Details about time setting

1. _____   1. _____

2. _____   2. _____

Conclusion: _____

_____

2. "I knew [a] man—let me see—it's forty years ago now—who took an old, damp, rotten set of chambers, in one of the most ancient Inns, that had been shut up and empty for years and years before. There were lots of old women's stories about the place, and it certainly was very far from being a cheerful one; but he was poor, and the rooms were cheap.

Details about place setting   Details about time setting

1. _____   1. _____

2. _____   2. _____

Conclusion: _____

_____

"The All-American Slurp" by Lensey Namioka
"The Stone" by Lloyd Alexander

Build Vocabulary

Using Related Words: Forms of *migrate*

The Word Bank word *migrate* is a verb that means "to travel." *Migrate* is related to the verbs *emigrate* and *immigrate*. When a person *emigrates*, he or she moves *away from* one place to settle somewhere else. The person *leaving* the place is an *emigrant*. When a person *immigrates*, he or she moves *to* another country in order to live there. That person arriving in the new country is known as an *immigrant*. Notice the way each of these words is used in the sentence below.

migrate: Each year in late autumn, many birds *migrate* to warmer climates.

emigrate: Though the Lins chose to *emigrate* from China, they still missed their old life there.

immigrate: When people *immigrate* to a new country, they must get used to new customs.

emigrant: Saying good-bye to loved ones at home is often a sad experience for an *emigrant*.

immigrant: For the *immigrant* entering a new country, a new language can be a challenge.

A. DIRECTIONS: Use the correct word to complete each sentence. Write your answers on the lines.

1. Some species of birds (migrate, immigrate) _____ for the winter.

2. The Lins (immigrated, emigrated) _____ from China.

3. At the airport, the Lins' relatives kissed the (immigrants, emigrants) _____ good-bye.

4. A U.S. customs inspector checked the passport of each (emigrant, immigrant) _____ .

Using the Word Bank

B. DIRECTIONS: Choose the word from the Word Bank that has the same meaning as the underlined word or words in the following sentences. Write the new sentence on the lines provided.

emigrated	etiquette	plight	rue
consumption	jubilation	fallow	

1. When our great-grandparents <u>left one country to settle in another</u>, they did not forget their old habits and customs _____.

2. Sometimes, they had trouble with <u>acceptable social manners</u> . _____

3. The <u>eating and drinking</u> of strange foods can be difficult at first. _____

4. At times, a person may <u>regret</u> an embarrassing action. _____

5. Mastering a new language can lead to a feeling of <u>triumph</u>. _____

6. When a person is in a difficult <u>situation</u>, it's best to ask for help. _____

7. The main character's fields are <u>unproductive</u> as a result of a foolish wish. _____

"The All-American Slurp" by Lensey Namioka
"The Stone" by Lloyd Alexander

Build Spelling Skills: The *k* Sound Spelled *qu*

Spelling Strategy In some words, such as the Word Bank word *etiquette*, the k sound is spelled *qu*. Other words that use *qu* to spell the k sound are *racquet*, *physique*, and *plaque*. Notice that the *u* in these words is silent. Some other ways the k sound can be spelled are c as in *cat*, k as in *fake*, and ck as in *back*.

Since there is no rule to let you know when to use *qu* to spell the *k* sound, look up a word in the dictionary if you are not sure how the *k* sound should be spelled.

A. Practice: Look at the following words. They all have the *k* sound. In the chart, sort the words according to the way the *k* sound is spelled.

plaque   stack   steak   racquet   castle   antique   slick
etiquette   quake   tackle   crumb   physique   blank

k sound spelled *qu*	k sound spelled *k*	k sound spelled *c*	k sound spelled *ck*

B. Practice: Revise the following sentences to correct the errors in the spelling of words that have the *k* sound. Write any misspelled words correctly on the lines. If there are no misspelled words in a sentence, write OK.

1. The plack on the wall said the gymnasium had been built one year before. _____

2. The new Chinese gazed around in confusion. _____

3. She had a strong, athletic physike and loved sports. _____

4. However, she did not fully understand the etikette in her new school. _____

5. She was good at rackit sports and hoped to make the tennis team. _____

Challenge: The Word Bank word *rue* dates back to Old English, or English as it was spoken before the year A.D. 1150, more than 850 years ago. In Old English, *rue* was spelled *hreow*. *Rue*, meaning "regret," can be a noun or a verb. Compare these two sentences:

Poor Maibon felt *rue* for his hasty wish. (used as noun)

The miserable man *rued* the moment he set eyes on the magic stone. (used as verb)

Rue is also related to *rueful*, which means *sorry* or *regretful*.

On the lines below, write a sentence for each of the following words: *rue*, *rued*, and *rueful*.

1. _____

2. _____

3. _____

"The All-American Slurp" by Lensey Namioka
"The Stone" by Lloyd Alexander

Build Grammar Skills: Compound Sentences

A compound sentence is two or more **independent clauses** joined by a coordinating conjunction or a semicolon (;). The **coordinating conjunctions** are *and, but, or, nor, yet,* and *for.* In the following sentences, each independent clause is underlined. The coordinating conjunctions are italicized. Notice that each independent clause could stand on its own as a complete sentence.

> Mother didn't tell me how the rest of the dinner went, *and* I didn't want to know.

> Those eggs should have hatched by now, *but* the hen is still brooding on her nest.

Notice that a comma is used before the coordinating conjunction in a compound sentence.

A. Practice: Write a C on the line for each compound sentence. If a sentence is compound, underline each independent clause once. Underline the coordinating conjunction twice. For sentences that are not compound, write NC on the line.

_____ 1. My mother also puts everything on the table and hopes for the best.

_____ 2. I got acquainted with a few other kids, but Meg was still my only real friend.

_____ 3. Mrs. Gleason announced that dinner was served and invited us to the table.

_____ 4. Then I picked up a stalk, and my brother did too.

_____ 5. The dwarf squeezed shut his bright red eyes and began holding his breath.

_____ 6. You'll stay as you are, but I'll turn old and gray.

_____ 7. The weeds aren't growing, but neither is the wheat.

_____ 8. Never again did Maibon meet any of the Fair Folk, and he was just as glad of it.

B. Writing Application: Rewrite each pair of sentences below as a compound sentence. Use the coordinating conjunction in parentheses to join the two independent clauses in each compound sentence that you write. Remember to use a comma before the coordinating conjunction.

1. Maibon could have chosen a practical wish. Instead, he chose a foolish one. (but)

_____

2. Maibon's wife wanted him to get rid of the stone. It caused nothing but trouble. (for)

_____

3. The eggs weren't hatching. The wheat wasn't growing. (and)

_____

4. Maibon had to get rid of the stone. Nothing would grow. (or)

_____

5. Maibon tried to get rid of the stone. It kept coming back. (yet)

_____

Name _____ Date _____

"The All-American Slurp" by Lensey Namioka
"The Stone" by Lloyd Alexander

Reading Strategy: Drawing Inferences

Authors do not always come right out and state simply and directly what they mean. You often have to figure out the meaning of what you are reading by drawing **inferences**, or judgments, based on the details and information the author does give you.

Read this passage from "The All-American Slurp." What can you infer from the details the author provides?

> My brother didn't have any problems making friends. He spent all his time with some boys who were teaching him baseball, and in no time he could speak English much faster than I could—not better, but faster.

The author doesn't come right out and explain the personality differences between the narrator and her brother. From this passage, however, you can make the inference that the brother is outgoing and athletic but the sister is probably more shy and reserved. As you continue reading, you gather further details and information that support your understanding of the characters.

DIRECTIONS: As you read each of the stories, complete one of the flowcharts below. Each chart should contain two details and one logical inference that can be drawn from these details.

"The All-American Slurp"

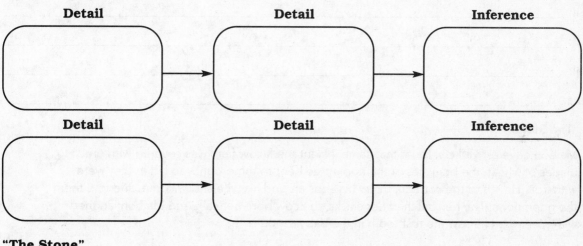

"The Stone"

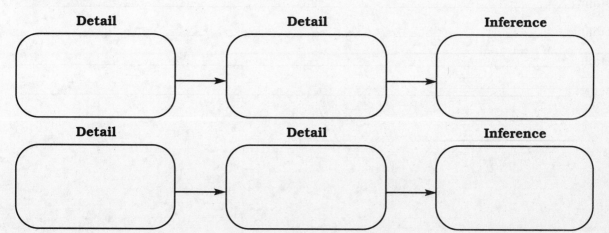

"The All-American Slurp" by Lensey Namioka
"The Stone" by Lloyd Alexander

Literary Analysis: Theme

A **theme** is the message or main insight about life that an author wishes to communicate to readers. In a story, the author usually does not state the theme directly, but implies or suggests it by showing how characters react to the events, people, and places in their lives.

For example, as you read "The All-American Slurp," by Lensey Namioka, you will notice events and details that suggest the story's main theme—the challenges of adjusting to a new country and culture.

DIRECTIONS: Read the following passages from "The All-American Slurp" and "The Stone." Make a list of three events or details that suggest each story's theme. On the last line provided, write a sentence stating the theme.

1. **"The All-American Slurp"**

All of us, our family and the Chinese guests, stopped eating to watch the activities of the Gleasons. I wanted to giggle. Then I caught my mother's eyes on me. She frowned and shook her head slightly, and I understood the message: the Gleasons were not used to Chinese ways, and they were just coping the best they could. For some reason I thought of celery strings.

Detail: _____

Detail: _____

Detail: _____

Theme: _____

2. **"The Stone"**

Maibon gave a joyful cry, for at that same instant the fallow field was covered with green blades of wheat, the branches of the apple tree bent to the ground, so laden they were with fruit. He ran to the cottage, threw his arms around his wife and children, and told them the good news. The hen hatched her chicks, the cow bore her calf. And Maibon laughed with glee when he saw the first tooth in the baby's mouth.

Detail: _____

Detail: _____

Detail: _____

Theme: _____

"**The Shutout**" by Patricia C. McKissack and Frederick McKissack, Jr.

Build Vocabulary

Using the prefix *ir-*

The prefix *ir-*, like the prefixes *un-* and *in-*, means "not." It is attached only to words beginning with *r*.

> **Examples:**   *ir-* + rational = <u>ir</u>rational; *ir-* + relevant = <u>ir</u>relevant
> • Not all words beginning with *r* use *ir-* as a negative-forming prefix. Many use *un-*.
>
> **Exceptions:**   *un-* + reasonable = <u>un</u>reasonable; *un-* + related = <u>un</u>related
>   *un-* + reliable = <u>un</u>reliable; *un-* + responsive = <u>un</u>responsive
> • Whenever you're not sure of a spelling, look in a dictionary.

A. DIRECTIONS: Make a new word by adding the prefix *ir-* to each word in the chart below. Then write the meaning of the new word. The first row has been filled in for you.

Word	Meaning	New word with *ir-*	Meaning of new word
regular	normal	irregular	not normal
responsible	trustworthy		
replaceable	able to be replaced		
resolvable	able to be resolved		
retrievable	able to be gotten back		

Using the Word Bank

anecdotes	evolved	irrational	diverse	composed

B. DIRECTIONS: Complete each sentence with a word from the Word Bank.

1. A winning baseball team is often _____ of the best players.

2. Many people prefer _____ to long, serious stories.

3. If you were sad after hitting a home run, your reaction would be _____.

4. American baseball _____ over a period of time.

5. I'm tired of pizza and would like to see a more _____ menu.

Recognizing Synonyms

C. DIRECTIONS: Circle the letter of the word that is closest in meaning to the word in CAPITAL LETTERS.

1. IRRATIONAL: a. soggy   b. insane   c. reasonable   d. nervous

2. EVOLVED: a. rotated   b. concerned   c. judged   d. changed

3. DIVERSE: a. different   b. alike   c. careful   d. rhyming

Unit 7: Nonfiction

"**The Shutout**" by Patricia C. McKissack and Frederick McKissack, Jr.

Build Spelling Skills:
Using the prefix *ir-* with words that begin with *r*

Spelling Strategy The prefix *ir-*, meaning "not," is used only with words that begin with the letter *r*. When you add *ir-* to a word, remember to keep both *r*'s. In the examples below, notice how both *r*'s are kept when the prefix *ir-* is added.

Examples: *ir + replaceable = irreplaceable* (not able to be replaced)

ir + revocable = irrevocable (not able to be revoked or taken back)

ir + responsible = irresponsible (not responsible, not trustworthy)

A. DIRECTIONS: On the line following each sentence, rewrite the italicized word as a negative by adding *ir-* or *un.*

1. The *responsible* player was often late for practice. _____

2. The game was one of the most *exciting* ones I've seen. _____

3. The excellent coach was *replaceable.* _____

4. The fans found the long wait *interesting.* _____

5. The disagreement between them was *reconcilable.* _____

B. DIRECTIONS: Proofread the following paragraph. Cross out each misspelled word that begins with *ir-.* Then write the correctly spelled word above it.

The people who began organizing professional baseball leagues irationally excluded non-

white athletes. However, at the time, the decision to segregate teams was irevokable. For

talented African American players, life without baseball was an ireconcilable notion. They

decided to organize a league of their own.

Challenge: In the essay, the word *shutout* describes the way African American athletes were excluded from professional baseball. In sports, the word is more commonly used to describe a game in which one side doesn't score at all. Baseball is filled with words that are used uniquely in the game. The word *strike* for instance, ordinarily means "to hit." In baseball, however, a strike is a pitch a batter swings at and misses. The word *fly*, usually a verb, becomes a noun in baseball and refers to a ball that is hit high in the air. Similarly, the word *run*, usually used as a verb, is a noun referring to a point scored when a player crosses home plate.

On the lines below, write three sentences using the following words as they are used in baseball: *strike, fly, run.* Use a different word in each sentence.

_____

_____

_____

"The Shutout" by Patricia C. McKissack and Frederick McKissack, Jr.

Build Grammar Skills: Compound and Complex Sentences

A **compound sentence** is made up of two or more independent clauses. These clauses may be joined by a coordinating conjunction: *and, but, for, or, yet,* or *so.* In the following example, the independent clauses are underlined, and the coordinating conjunction appears in italics:

In 1857–1858, the newly organized National Association of Baseball Players was formed, *and* baseball became a business.

A **complex sentence** consists of one independent clause and one or more subordinate clauses. Subordinate clauses usually begin with such words as *who, which, that, although, after, because, before, when,* and *until.* In these examples, the subordinate clauses are underlined. Notice that they cannot stand alone.

After the Civil War ended, returning soldiers helped to inspire a new interest in baseball all over the country.
A number of records and documents show that people were playing stick-and-ball games long before the 1839 date.

A. DIRECTIONS: Identify each sentence below. Write *CP* if the sentence is compound; write *CX* if it is complex. For compound sentences, underline the coordinating conjunction. For complex sentences, underline the subordinate clause.

_____ 1. When the rules became established, the pitcher had to stand forty-five feet from home plate.

_____ 2. A professional baseball player was someone who played for money.

_____ 3. Individual sports were preferred by slave owners because their slaves could enter into competitions.

_____ 4. A few African Americans made it to the majors, but they mostly were kept out of major leagues.

_____ 5. Did Abner Doubleday really invent baseball while he was a West Point cadet?

B. Writing Application: Use the coordinating and subordinating conjunctions shown below to combine each pair of sentences into a single sentence.

1. a) There are many myths about the origins of baseball.
   b) Research states that most of them are untrue. (although)

   _____

   _____

2. a) Baseball's growth began to dwindle during the Civil War.
   b) Teams continued to play. (but)

   _____

   _____

3. a) Teams began to develop in the North and Midwest.
   b) African Americans became interested in joining these new clubs. (when)

   _____

   _____

Unit 7: Nonfiction

"**The Shutout**" by Patricia C. McKissack and Frederick McKissack, Jr.

Reading Strategy: Clarify Author's Meaning

The author's meaning in a selection is closely linked to his or her purpose, tone, and main ideas. While you are reading a work, pause every so often to **clarify the author's meaning.** This three-part strategy will help you clarify the author's meaning when you are reading nonfiction.

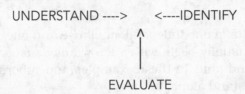

- **Understand the author's purpose and tone**. Authors of nonfiction have a reason, or a purpose, for writing. They also have a tone, or attitude, toward their topic and their reader. Consider the purpose and tone to determine the author's message.
- **Identify the author's main ideas.** Ask yourself what the author wants you to learn or think as a result of reading his or her work.
- **Evaluate the author's message.** Are the author's main points logical? Do you agree or disagree with them?

DIRECTIONS: Read the following passage from "The Shutout," and use the three-part strategy, Understand—Identify—Evaluate to answer the questions below.

The history of baseball is difficult to trace because it is embroidered with wonderful anecdotes that are fun but not necessarily supported by fact. There are a lot of myths that persist about baseball—the games, the players, the owners, and the fans—in spite of contemporary research that disproves most of them. For example, the story that West Point cadet Abner Doubleday "invented" baseball in 1839 while at Cooperstown, New York, continues to be widely accepted, even though, according to his diaries, Doubleday never visited Cooperstown. A number of records and documents show that people were playing stick-and-ball games long before the 1839 date.

1. What is the author's purpose in this passage? How would you describe their tone?

   _____

   _____

2. What main idea about the history of baseball do the authors stress in this passage?

   _____

   _____

3. Consider whether or not the authors support their main idea. How would you evaluate their message?

   _____

   _____

"The Shutout" by Patricia C. McKissack and Frederick McKissack, Jr.

Literary Analysis: Historical Essay

A **historical essay** is a short piece of nonfiction about events that happened in the past. The author of a historical essay includes **facts**, such as the date when an event occurred, names of people who were involved, and the place where the event occurred. The author usually includes **evidence** to show that the facts are true. A historical essay also includes **explanations**, such as the reason that something happened or how one event was the cause of another. In addition, the author usually includes personal **insights**—the meaning that he or she finds in the event. Following are examples of these kinds of information included in "The Shutout."

Facts:
Date: National Association of Base Ball Players formed 1857–1858
Name: Samuel Hopkins Adams, who stated that his grandfather was playing base-
                   ball in the 1820s
Place: New York, where the New York Knickerbocker Club was organized.

Evidence: Report of baseball being played in the 1820s is evidence that it was
                   founded before 1839.

Explanation: Exclusion from major-league teams was the reason that African Americans
                   organized their own teams.

Insight: Irrational, racist thinking was behind the December 1867 vote to exclude
                   African Americans from major-league baseball.

DIRECTIONS: On the lines below, write additional examples of facts (dates, names, or places), evidence for facts, explanations, and insights found in "The Shutout."

Facts

  1. _____

  2. _____

Evidence

  3. _____

  4. _____

Explanation

  5. _____

Insight

  6. _____

"Letter to Scottie" by F. Scott Fitzgerald
"Olympic Diary" by Amanda Borden

Build Vocabulary

Using Forms of *document*

The word *document* is a noun that means "something that is printed or written," often something that can be used to prove a fact or identity—a library card, a birth certificate, or a passport, for example. Here are several other forms of the word *document*, along with their meanings and examples of their use:

- **document** (*verb*) A person can *document* (prove) the fact that he or she graduated from high school by showing a diploma.
- **documented** (*adjective*) When you write a report, make sure your facts are *documented* (backed up with proof).
- **documentation** (*noun*) I proved my identity by showing the proper *documentation* (written evidence).
- **documentary** (*noun*) I saw a *documentary* (film or TV show that shows a visual record of an event or time period) about dog shows.
- **undocumented** (*adjective*) Too many facts in the students' reports were *undocumented* (not backed up with proof or documentation).

A. DIRECTIONS: Complete each of the following sentences by filling in the blank with the correct form of *document* from the list above. *Hint: Document* may be used as a noun or a verb.

1. His birth certificate served as _____ that he was twelve years old.

2. The class watched a _____ about desert animals.

3. A driver's license is a _____ that all drivers should carry with them.

4. Many of the statements the reporter made were _____ .

5. She showed her passport to _____ her citizenship.

6. My report card would serve as _____ that I had taken a science class.

Using the Word Bank

documentation	compulsory	intrigued

Sentence Completions

B. DIRECTIONS: Complete each sentence with a word from the Word Bank.

1. In gymnastics competitions, some exercises are _____ .

2. At airports, travelers must produce _____ to prove their identity.

3. We were _____ by the rhythms of the electronic keyboard.

"Letter to Scottie" by F. Scott Fitzgerald
"Olympic Diary" by Amanda Borden

Build Spelling Skills: *ie/ei* rule

Spelling Strategy Remember this rule: *i* before *e* except after *c* and when sounded like *ay*, as in *neighbor* and *weigh*.

When a word has a long *e* sound, use *ie*. Examples: *niece, field*

When a word has a long *a* sound, use *ei*. Examples: *weigh, reign*

When a word has a long *e* sound preceded by the letter *c*, use *ei*.

Examples: *perceive, receipt, ceiling*

A. Practice: Fill in the blanks below with either *ie* or *ei*. Write the words in the blanks next to their definitions below.

ch _ _ f   ach _ _ ve   n _ _ ce   c _ _ ling   dec _ _ ve

w _ _ ght   n _ _ ghbors   rec _ _ ved   fr _ _ nds

1. to succeed or accomplish _____

2. overhead surface of a room _____

3. to lie or mislead _____

4. daughter of a person's sister or brother _____

5. leader of a group or people _____

6. people who live nearby _____

7. people who are fond of each other _____

8. got something sent _____

9. heaviness _____

B. Practice: In each sentence below, find a word or words with the letter *ie* or *ei*. If a word is misspelled, cross it out and write it correctly. If the word is spelled correctly, write a *C* above it. The first one has been done for you.

             neighbor

1. Together with her ~~nieghbor~~ Amanda practiced ballet.

2. When she broke her elbow, her friends encouraged her.

3. In 1996, Amanda received an invitation to compete at the Budget Gymnastics Invitational.

4. Gymnasts have to be light on their feet and watch their wieght.

5. In the Georgia Dome at the Olympics, the applause for the gymnasts thundered from the floor all the way up to the ceiling.

"Letter to Scottie" by F. Scott Fitzgerald
"Olympic Diary" by Amanda Borden

Build Grammar Skills: Subject and Object Pronouns

A **subject pronoun** is always used as the *subject* in a sentence or as a *subject complement* following a *linking verb*, often a form of the verb *to be*. The subject pronouns are *I, you, he, she, it, we, you* (plural), and *they*. In the following sentences, subject pronouns are used as subjects and as subject complements.

Subject: He was a famous writer. (The subject pronoun *he* is the subject.)

Subject complement: The only gymnast to score over 9.7 was she . (The subject pronoun *she* is a subject complement. The linking verb is *was*.)

An **object pronoun** is used as a *direct object* (receiving the action of the verb) or an *indirect object* (showing to whom or for whom an action is done). The object pronouns are *me, you, him, her, it, us,* and *them*. Object pronouns can also be used after prepositions.

Direct Objects: I watched her in the 1984 Olympics.

Am I making my body useful or am I neglecting it?

Indirect Object: When the doctor gave me the OK, I started training again.

Tell them your story.

Object of a Preposition: The teacher recommended several stories by Fitzgerald to us.
Between you and me, I like gymnastics best.

A. Practice: Underline the subject and object pronouns in each sentence below. On the lines, write *S* if the pronoun is a subject pronoun and *O* if it is an object pronoun.

____ 1. In the letter to Scottie, Fitzgerald gives her some advice.

____ 2. Fitzgerald does not like Scottie to call him "Pappy."

____ 3. We had 22,000 fans cheering loudly.

____ 4. The gymnast with the highest score was she.

____ 5. These diary entries were written by her.

B. Fill in the blanks in the following sentences with the correct direct object and indirect object pronouns.

1. If you read carefully, Fitzgerald's letter will give_____ insights into the writer's mind.

2. Fitzgerald missed his daughter and wrote _____ a long letter.

3. When gymnasts must deal with problems, it helps make _____ better people.

4. Borden is grateful to the people who helped _____ become a world-class athlete.

5. To compete in the Olympics would give _____ the biggest thrill of my life.

"Letter to Scottie" by F. Scott Fitzgerald
"Olympic Diary" by Amanda Borden

Reading Strategy: Understand the Author's Purpose

F. Scott Fitzgerald devotes much of his "Letter to Scottie" to stressing the importance of effort and responsibility. Fitzgerald's main **purpose** in writing the letter is to encourage Scottie to develop goals and values in life. Authors may have different purposes in mind when they write. Sometimes they write to share information, and sometimes they may want to entertain readers. Writers often have a mixture of purposes in mind. For example, although Fitzgerald's letter is mostly serious, he includes some good-natured joking about nicknames.

DIRECTIONS: Two of Amanda Borden's purposes in writing her "Olympic Diary" were to make readers understand the challenges she faced as a gymnast, and to give readers an idea of the emotions she felt. Fill out the graphic organizer below by writing, under the appropriate heading, some details from the selection that serve to accomplish either of these purposes. One detail has been given under each heading as an example. Add three additional details under the one that is given.

"OLYMPIC DIARY"

Challenges	Feelings
Breaking elbow before U.S. Championship.	Unhappy at not making 1992 team.

"**Letter to Scottie**" by F. Scott Fitzgerald
"**Olympic Diary**" by Amanda Borden

Literary Analysis: Letters and Journals

Unlike stories, essays, and poems, **letters and journals** are "private" writing, usually meant to be read by no more than one person other than the writer. Several characteristics distinguish the writing in letters and journals from public writing: the expression of personal feelings, the inclusion of details that are meaningful only to the writer and the person addressed, and a more informal tone than would be used in "public" writing.

DIRECTIONS: In the left column of the chart below, write two details from each selection in this group that is more typical of a letter or journal than of "public writing." In the right column, explain why you chose these details. One has been done for each piece as an example.

Detail	Reason for Choosing
"Letter to Scottie"	
Author dislikes the name "Pappy."	Only the writer's daughter would know about this.
"Olympic Diary"	
"Wow! Did my life change!"	Use of informal language is appropriate to private writing.

"My Papa, Mark Twain" by Susy Clemens
"The Drive-In Movies" by Gary Soto
"Space Shuttle *Challenger*" by William Harwood

Build Vocabulary

Unit 7: Nonfiction

Using the Word Root -sequi-

The Word Bank word *consequently*, which comes from the Latin root *sequi*, means "to follow." *Consequently* is an adverb meaning "following as a result."

Example: Jen practiced more often; *consequently*, her guitar playing improved.

In the sentence above, Jen's improved guitar playing *followed as a result* of her increased practice. Other words formed from the word root -*sequi*- also show the order of events. *Sequence*, for example, is a noun that means "a series in which one thing follows another."

A. DIRECTIONS: Complete each sentence with one of the following words.

consequently   sequel   sequence

1. Did Gary Soto write a _____ to his book *Crazy Weekend*?

2. I slept too late this morning; _____ I missed the school bus.

3. I alphabetized my CDs so that they are all in correct _____.

Using the Word Bank

incessantly	consequently	consumed	prelude	crescent
pulsating	vigorously	monitoring	occasionally	accumulations
moot	peripheral	catastrophic		

B. DIRECTIONS: In the following paragraph, cross out each underlined word or phrase and write an appropriate Word Bank word above the line. Be sure to choose the word that makes the most sense.

When Eleanor babysat for her baby brother Jake, he cried <u>without ceasing</u>. As the <u>introduction</u>, he screamed when he saw his parents going out the door. He yelled even more <u>forcefully</u> when Eleanor tried to amuse him with toys. He hurled his <u>moon-shaped</u> teething ring across the room. <u>Following as a result</u>, Eleanor started to get a headache. After an hour, her head was <u>throbbing</u>. Jake finally fell asleep about five minutes before Eleanor's parents came home. By that time, every bit of her energy had been <u>used up</u>, and she needed a nap herself.

C. DIRECTIONS: Circle the letter of the word that is most opposite in meaning to the word in CAPITAL LETTERS.

1. OCCASIONALLY: a. immediately   b. always   c. suddenly   d. weakly

2. MOOT: a. unresolved   b. silly   c. important   d. seldom

3. PERIPHERAL: a. rapid   b. central   c. slow   d. incomplete

4. CATASTROPHIC: a. superficial   b. chilly   c. decisive   d. magnificent

"My Papa, Mark Twain" by Susy Clemens
"The Drive-In Movies" by Gary Soto
"Space Shuttle *Challenger*" by William Harwood

Build Spelling Skills: Words with *cess*

Spelling Strategy Remember that the letter sequence *cess* is spelled with one c and two s's. For example:

That squirrel outside my window chatters in<u>cess</u>antly.

Our class always goes to the park during re<u>cess</u>.

There is an ex<u>cess</u> of clothing in this suitcase.

A warm coat is a ne<u>cess</u>ity for a winter in the Northeast.

A. Practice: Read the definition of each word below, then fill in the missing letters.

1. something that is needed and essential: ne___ ___ ___ ___ity

2. the time when children leave their classroom to play outdoors: re___ ___ ___ ___.

3. without stopping: in___ ___ ___ ___antly

4. too much of something: ex___ ___ ___ ___.

B. Practice: Cross out each misspelled word in the following paragraph, and write it correctly above the line.

At a very early age, biographers often begin the writing prosess by making notes about

people. A child who becomes such a writer may be more interested in listening to people's

conversations than in playing kickball during recces. For a sucsessful writer, the ability to

observe is a nesesity. Some writers admit that they watch and listen to others inseccantly.

Perhaps an exccess of curiosity is a gift to anyone who wants to write about a person's life.

Challenge: The word *vigorously*, meaning "forcefully" or "powerfully," contains the noun *vigor* and the adjective *vigorous*, which come from the Latin word for "liveliness" or "energy." The words *invigorate* and *invigorated* also come from the same Latin root. Use a dictionary to find the definitions of these two words; then write a sentence using each one.

1. _____

_____

2. _____

_____

"My Papa, Mark Twain" by Susy Clemens
"The Drive-In Movies" by Gary Soto
"Space Shuttle *Challenger*" by William Harwood

Build Grammar Skills: Writing Titles

Below are some helpful rules for writing titles of written works and works of art.

- **Capitalize** the first word and all other important words in the titles of books, periodicals, poems, stories, plays, paintings, and other works of art. Articles and short prepositions or conjunctions should be capitalized only when they are used as the first or last word in a title.

- **Use underlining or italics** for the titles of longer works, such as books, plays, long poems, movies, television series, magazines, newspapers, and book-length collections of stories or poems.

- **Use quotation marks** for the titles of shorter works, such as short stories, short poems, articles, songs, and episodes of television series.

A. Practice: Rewrite each title given below, using capitalization, underlining, and quotation marks correctly.

1. the adventures of huckleberry finn (one of Mark Twain's most famous novels)

   _____

2. oranges (a short poem by Gary Soto)

   _____

3. astronomy now (the title of a magazine)

   _____

4. baseball in april (a collection of short stories by Gary Soto)

   _____

5. a connecticut yankee in king arthur's court (a book by Mark Twain)

   _____

B. Writing Application: Rewrite the sentences below, correcting any errors you find in the capitalization and punctuation of titles.

1. Didn't William Harwood publish a number of articles in the Washington Post?

   _____

2. In "the elements of San Joaquin," Gary Soto explores the lives of migrant farm workers.

   _____

3. Have you read Mark Twain's short story *The Celebrated Jumping Frog Of Calaveras County?*

   _____

4. Twain published his novel "The Prince and the Pauper" in 1882.

   _____

Unit 7: Nonfiction

"My Papa, Mark Twain" by Susy Clemens
"The Drive-In Movies" by Gary Soto
"Space Shuttle *Challenger*" by William Harwood

Reading Strategy: Author's Evidence

When authors tell stories of their own lives or the lives of other people, they often make statements about their subjects' appearance or personalities. For example, Susy Clemens says of Mark Twain that he is "a very striking character." She then goes on to give details about his hair, nose, eyes, mustache, head, and profile. Without the **evidence**, the story of her father's life would not be very believable or interesting. It would just be a string of statements with no interesting details to back them up.

DIRECTIONS: Read the following passage from "My Papa, Mark Twain." Then find the evidence the author uses to support the statement she makes about her father. Record your findings on the chart provided.

Papa is very fond of animals particularly of cats, we had a dear little gray kitten once that he named "Lazy". . . and he would carry him around on his shoulder, it was a mighty pretty sight! the gray cat sound asleep against papa's gray coat and hair. The names that he has give our different cats are really remarkably funny, they are named Stray Kit, Abner, Motley, Fraeulein, Lazy, Buffalo Bill, Soapy Sall, Cleveland, Sour Mash, and Pestilence and Famine.

STATEMENT:	Evidence:
	Evidence:
	Evidence:
STATEMENT:	Evidence:
	Evidence:
	Evidence:

"**My Papa, Mark Twain**" by Susy Clemens
"**The Drive-In Movies**" by Gary Soto
"**Space Shuttle** *Challenger*" by William Harwood

Literary Analysis: Biography and Autobiography

Biography and **autobiography** are two kinds of literature that tell the story of a person's life. In a biography, readers see the subject and the events and people in the subject's life through the eyes of the author. In an autobiography, the subject is the author, so readers share the author's thoughts and feelings about his or her own life.

In "My Papa, Mark Twain," Twain's daughter Susy Clemens writes from the point of view of a thirteen-year-old who deeply loved and admired her father. We see the famous author, Mark Twain, through her eyes. In "The Drive-In Movies," author Gary Soto recalls a day from his childhood. We learn what he was thinking and feeling that day through his own memories, which other people would not know unless he had told them himself.

DIRECTIONS: Read the following passages from "The Drive-In Movies." After each one, write the letter AO (for *author only*) if the passage provides information that only the author would know about himself; write SE (for *someone else*) if the passage provides information that someone else could have written.

_____ 1. For our family, moviegoing was rare.

_____ 2. So on Saturday we tried to be good.

_____ 3. One Saturday I decided to be extra good.

_____ 4 . . . my brain was dull from making the trowel go up and down . . .

_____ 5. I made a face at them when they asked how come I was working.

_____ 6. I . . . was ready to cry when Mother showed her face at the window.

_____ 7. My arms ached from buffing, which though less boring than weeding, was harder.

_____ 8. After lunch, we returned outside with tasty sandwiches.

_____ 9. I promised myself I would remember that scene with the golf tees and promised myself not to work so hard the coming Saturday.

_____ 10. Twenty minutes into the movie, I fell asleep with one hand in the popcorn.

"Restoring the Circle" by Joseph Bruchac
"How the Internet Works" by Kerry Cochrane
"Turkeys" by Bailey White

Build Vocabulary

Using Forms of *tolerate*

The word *tolerate* means "to put up with" or "endure."

Example: I can usually tolerate (put up with) barking dogs , but not at night.

Forms of *tolerate* include the past-tense verb *tolerated*, the noun *tolerance*, the adjectives *tolerant*, *intolerant*, *tolerable*, and *intolerable*, and the adverb *tolerably*.

A. DIRECTIONS: Write the correct word to complete each sentence.

1. According to Joseph Bruchac, many portrayals of Native Americans have been stereotyped and reflect _____ (intolerant, intolerance).

2. One problem with Internet routers is that they do not _____ (tolerate, tolerant) the slighest spelling mistakes in addresses.

3. When the ornithologists arrived, the turkey exhibitied _____ (intolerant, tolerable) behavior.

4. She found the scientists _____ (intolerant, intolerable) and wished they'd go.

5. I hate waiting and have little _____ (tolerate, tolerance) for crowds.

Using the Word Bank

tolerance	detrimental
dilution	vigilance

B. DIRECTIONS: Fill in each blank with an appropriate word from the Word Bank.

1. I had to use _____ to keep the puppy from getting out of the yard.

2. Eating too much candy can be _____ to your teeth.

3. When you add water to lemonade, you cause _____.

4. When you are patient with a younger child, you show _____.

"Restoring the Circle" by Joseph Bruchac
"How the Internet Works" by Kerry Cochrane
"Turkeys" by Bailey White

Build Spelling Skills: Changing -*ent* and -*ant* to -*ence* and -*ance*

When words that end in -*ent* and -*ant* are changed to related words that end in -*ence* and -*ance*, they keep the same vowel.

Examples: vigil**a**nt, vigil**a**nce   correspond**e**nt, correspond**e**nce

A. Practice: In each of the following sentences, change the word in parentheses from a word ending in -*ant* or -*ent* to a word ending in -*ance* or -*ence*.

1. (correspondent) Mom uses e-mail for her business _____correspondence_____.

2. (assistant) They asked their older brother for his _____.

3. (resident) Another word for the place where you live is your _____.

4. (tolerant) Her mother had _____ for noise, but not for rudeness.

5. (insistent) Our teacher's _____ that we do our homework on time keeps us on schedule.

B. Practice: In the following paragraph, change each word ending in -*ant* or -*ent* to the related word ending in -*ance* or -*ence* to correctly complete the sentences.

Pure wild turkeys have become rare; so it is unusual to find a wild-turkey nest filled with

eggs. In "Turkeys," however, this is just what a group of ornithologists find, in (defiant)

_____ of the odds. Unfortunately, the mother turkey soon abandons the

nest, which has been her (resident) _____. The ornithologists worry about

the eggs, which, having little (resistant) _____ to cold, must be kept at a

warm and even temperature. Due to the kindliness and (tolerant) _____

of the author's mother, the eggs are saved in the end. With the (assistant)

_____ of the author, the eggs hatch overnight safely tucked next to her

feverish body.

Name _____ Date _____

"Restoring the Circle" by Joseph Bruchac
"How the Internet Works" by Kerry Cochrane
"Turkeys" by Bailey White

Build Grammar Skills: Punctuating and Capitalizing Dialogue

Quotation marks are used to enclose the exact words of a speaker. In "Turkeys," for example, the author uses quotation marks to record the ornithologists' conversation:

"Feels just right, I'd say."
"A hundred and two—can't miss if we tuck them up close and she lies still."

The first word of a direct quotation is capitalized, even if the quotation begins in the middle of a sentence.

In the story, the narrator whispers to herself, "The ornithologists have been here.

A comma, question mark, or exclamation point always separates the speaker's words from the words that tell who said them. The punctuation appears inside the closing quotation marks.

"Does your little girl still have measles?" he asked.
"One hundred percent wild turkey!" they said.

If the sentence includes introductory words before the opening quotation marks, those introductory words are followed by a comma.

The ornithologist said to the girl's mother, "I'll be right over."

A. Practice: Rewrite each of the following sentences, using quotation marks and capitalization correctly.

1. Wild turkeys are very rare, the ornithologist told my mother.

_____

2. They asked, would you allow us to put the eggs in your daughter's bed?

_____

3. Will they hatch overnight? my mother asked.

_____

4. The ornithologist answered, yes, with any luck.

_____

B. Writing Application: The following sentences could be from an interview with the author of "Turkeys." Rewrite each sentence adding any necessary punctuation or capitalization. Be sure to place the quotation marks correctly.

1. The interviewer asked isn't there a vaccine for measles now?

_____

2. Yes, but there wasn't at that time the author answered.

_____

3. How did you feel when you woke up asked the interviewer.

_____

4. The author answered Well, I was rather surprised at first!

_____

"Restoring the Circle" by Joseph Bruchac
"How the Internet Works" by Kerry Cochrane
"Turkeys" by Bailey White

Reading Strategy: Using Context Clues

Unit 7: Nonfiction

When you encounter an unfamiliar or confusing word, one strategy you can use to uncover its meaning is to look for **context clues**—information provided in the words and phrases around it. For example, in this sentence you will find a clue to the meaning of *detrimental*:

> When you have respect for another culture, then you are much less likely to do things that will be *detrimental* to that culture and the people of that culture.

Because the sentence states that respectful people are not likely to do *detrimental* things, you can guess that *detrimental* means *harmful*.

DIRECTIONS: For each of the following items, context clues could be used to figure out the meaning of the italicized word. Write the word's meaning and your explanation on the lines provided.

1. As portrayed by Native American authors, Indians are sometimes good, sometimes not so good, but no longer one-dimensional *stereotypes*.

   _____

   _____

2. If you read a book about another culture, you may be more likely to have understanding and *tolerance* for that culture.

   _____

   _____

3. There are local post offices in small towns, *regional* postal systems in big cities, and national postal services for countries.

   _____

   _____

4. TCP breaks each message into *manageable* chunks and numbers each chunk in order. Then, the numbered groups of information are marked with the IP address of the other computer and are sent out to it.

   _____

   _____

5. They were rare, and the pure-strain wild turkeys had begun to interbreed with farmers' domestic stock. The species was being degraded. It was extinction by *dilution*.

   _____

   _____

6. It seems that the turkey hen had been so disturbed by the elaborate *protective* measures that had been undertaken on her behalf that she had abandoned her nest on the night the eggs were due to hatch.

   _____

   _____

"**Restoring the Circle**" by Joseph Bruchac
"**How the Internet Works**" by Kerry Cochrane
"**Turkeys**" by Bailey White

Literary Analysis: Types of Essays

An essay is a short nonfiction work written about a particular subject. There are several different types of essays, each written for a different purpose.

Type of Essay	*Purpose*
Persuasive	To persuade, or convince, readers to act or think in a certain way
Informational	To explain or inform
Narrative	To tell a story about a true experience or event

"Restoring the Circle" is an example of a **persuasive essay**: The author tries to persuade readers to see the importance of cultural traditions. "How the Internet Works" is an **informational essay**; it informs readers about a subject they might not understand. "Turkeys" is a **narrative essay**; it is based on a memorable event in the author's life.

DIRECTIONS: For each question below, circle the letter of the choice that best identifies the type of essay named.

1. Which of the following details from "Restoring the Circle" lets you know that the essay is persuasive?

   a. Native Americans envision life as a circle.
   b. The author explains damage caused by Native American stereotypes.
   c. More than 400 languages are spoken by Native Americans in North America.

2. Choose the statement that indicates "How the Internet Works" is an informational essay.

   a. The author uses the pronoun "I" in his writing.
   b. The author provides detailed facts and explanations about the Internet.
   c. The author has an Internet address of his own.

3. Choose the statement that indicates that "Turkeys" is a narrative essay.

   a. The author describes an event from her childhood.
   b. The auther uses vivid language.
   c. The author includes dialogue in the essay.

The Phantom Tollbooth, Act I
based on the book by Norton Juster, by Susan Nanus

Build Vocabulary

Using the Prefix *pre-*

The prefix *pre-* means "before." When it is added to the beginning of a word, it adds the meaning of "before" or "in advance" to the word. In the Word Bank word *precautionary*, for example, cautionary means "with caution"; *precautionary* means "with caution beforehand," or "caution in advance."

Examples:

It's good to take *cautionary* measures in a dangerous situation, but it's even better to take *precautionary* measures beforehand.

You can *cook* a meal at the last minute, or you can *precook* some of the dishes and heat them up later.

We took *prefilled* bottles of milk along for the baby. When they were used up, we *filled* up some more.

Exception: Not all words that begin with the letters pre have the prefix *pre-*. For example, words such as *precious* and *pretty* do not have meaning *before*.

A. Directions: Keeping in mind the meaning of the prefix *pre-*, write your definition for each underlined word in the sentences below.

1. Let's <u>prearrange</u> our plans for vacation. _____

2. We had a chance to <u>preview</u> the new hit movie. _____

3. Eleven- and twelve-year-olds are sometimes called <u>preteens</u>. _____

4. Don't <u>prejudge</u> a person before you get to know her. _____

5. I like to read about <u>prehistoric</u> times. _____

Using the Word Bank

ignorance	precautionary	misapprehension

B. Directions: Complete each sentence with the Word Bank Word that makes the most sense.

1. A little _____ advice is always helpful when beginning a new experience.

2. Some say that experience is the best teacher, but reading can also put an end to

   _____.

3. If you think you may have a _____ about something a friend said or did, it's best to clear it up right away.

The Phantom Tollbooth, Act I
based on the book by Norton Juster, by Susan Nanus

Build Spelling Skills: Spelling Words With *tion* and *sion*

Spelling Strategy The letters *tion* and *sion* can both be used to spell the sound *shun*.

- In the Word Bank word *precau**tion**ary* , the *shun* sound is spelled *tion*. Some other words that spell the *shun* sound *tion* are *predic**tion**s, expecta**tion**s, atten**tion***, and *ques**tion***.

- In the Word Bank word *misapprehen**sion***, the *shun* sound is spelled *sion*. Other words that spell the *shun* sound *sion* include *comprehen**sion**, exten**sion**, expan**sion***, and *suspen**sion***.

A. Practice: Read the following sentences, looking for errors in words spelled with the *shun* sound. Cross out the misspelled words, and write them correctly above the line. Write **C** next to any sentences that contain no errors. Use a dictionary if you are not sure whether to spell the shun sound *tion* or *sion*.

_____ 1. I am a globe has three. I have three dimenshuns.

_____ 2. If you have me, you have a misunderstanding. I am a misapprehention.

_____ 3. You can also make me about the end of a story you're reading. I am a predicshun.

_____ 4. word for me is *care*. I am causion.

_____ 5. If you're not sure of something, you ask me. I am a question.

_____ 6. I am something you should "pay" to your teacher. I am attension.

_____ 7. On a reading test, it's important to have me. I am comprehention.

_____ 8. I'm whatever you want to be when you grow up, I am your ambition.

B. Practice: In the following paragraph, you will find that some words are incomplete. Complete each word by adding the ending *-tion* or *-sion* to spell the *shun* sound. If you are not sure which spelling to use, check the words in the box below.

dimension   misapprehension   prediction   caution   question   attention

   Milo found it difficult to pay _____ to anything for more than a little while.

He had the _____ that there was nothing interesting to do with his time. One

day a talking clock and a mysterious package started him on a journey into another

_____, where he met all sorts of strange beings. Along the way, Milo had to use

_____ to avoid danger. When Milo met the Whether Man, he asked him a

_____ about the land of Expectations. The odd man made no

_____ about the adventures Milo would have in the future but said "Whether or

not you find your own way, you're bound to find some way."

The Phantom Tollbooth, Act I
based on the book by Norton Juster, by Susan Nanus

Build Grammar Skills: Subject and Verb Agreement

In a sentence, the verb and subject must **agree** in number. A **singular** subject refers to one person, place, or thing. A **plural** subject refers to more than one. If the subject of a verb in the present tense is *he, she, it,* or a singular noun or proper noun such a "the boy," or "Milo," the verb usually end in *s*. If the subject of a verb in the present tense is *they* or a plural noun or proper noun such as "people" or "the Smiths," or "Milo and Tock," the verb does not end in *s*.

Singular Subject	Singular Verb	
He	goe**s**	on a journey.
The boy	goe**s**	on a journey
Milo	goe**s**	on a journey

Plural Subject	Verb	
They	go	together.
The characters	go	together.
Milo and Tock	go	together.

A. Practice: In the blank following each sentence below, write **S** if the subject and verb are singular. Write **P** if the subject and verb are plural.

_____ 1. The boy begins the journey to strange lands. _____

_____ 2. The rule book and map prepare Milo for an unusual adventure. _____

_____ 3. The traveller soon arrives at his first destination. _____

_____ 4. The Whether Man speaks in a confusing manner. _____

_____ 5. The Lethargarians want to rest all day. _____

_____ 6. They wonder why anyone would want to be active. _____

_____ 7. Milo dislikes the sleepy land called the Doldrums. _____

_____ 8. The sleepy people annoy Milo with their incredible laziness. _____

B. Writing Application: Revise the following paragraph so that all subjects and verbs agree in number.

In *The Phantom Tollbooth*, a boy named Milo goes on a fantastic journey in which he learn some important lessons about life. His companion on his journey is a dog named Tock. Milo and Tock first goes to the land of Expectations, where they meets the Whether Man. He tells them that some people never goes beyond Expectations. Milo and Tock, however, do arrive at their first destination, Dictionopolis, where a king named Aziz rule over the land.

_____

_____

_____

_____

_____

Unit 8: Drama

The Phantom Tollbooth, Act I
based on the book by Norton Juster, by Susan Nanus

Reading Strategy: Summarizing

When you **summarize**, you retell what has happened in your own words. A summary of a piece of literature should include details of important characters and review the important events in the order in which they occur in the original work. When you summarize, you should show how certain ideas and events are related, or belong together. For example, you should tell if one character is another's friend or enemy, or if one event is the cause of another.

DIRECTIONS: Use the roadmap below to note events and details that you find in Act I of *The Phantom Tollbooth*. Include the important information in the space provided on each signpost. You can choose any events and details that you find significant and interesting.

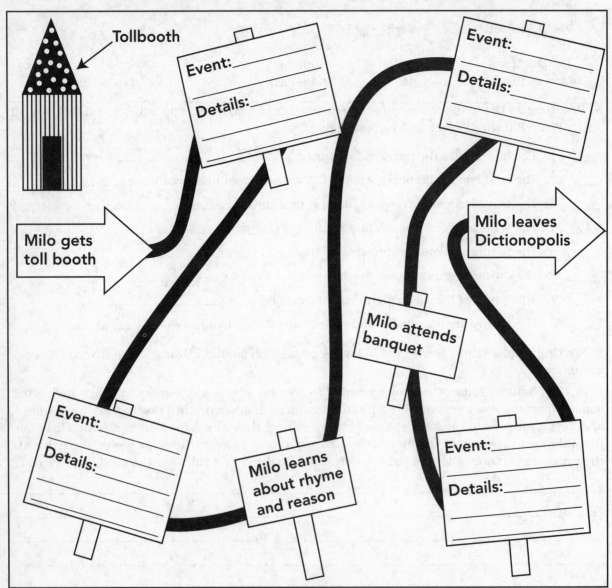

The Phantom Tollbooth, Act I
based on the book by Norton Juster, by Susan Nanus

Literary Analysis: Elements of Drama

Drama is a special literary form because unlike a story or poem, it is meant to be staged rather than read. An audience watches the **plot** unfold as actors "become" the **characters,** speaking lines of **dialogue** and expressing thoughts and emotions so that viewers can understand what is happening in the play. Like any story, a drama has a **setting,** or place where the action occurs. Unlike an ordinary story, much information about the characters, setting, and action is given in **stage directions,** and, in order to give a clear structure and sequence to a drama, the author may divide it into **acts** and **scenes,** rather than chapters.

A. DIRECTIONS: On the lines provided, answer the following questions about *The Phantom Tollbooth,* Act I.

1. Read the opening stage directions for **Scene i** and write the first sound the audience hears as the play begins.

_____

2. What is the name of the main character in the play?

_____

3. What is Milo's first line of dialogue in **Scene ii**?

_____

4. What is the setting for the end of **Act I**?

_____

5. What plot event prevents King Azaz and the Mathemagician from solving their arguments?

_____

6. Read the stage directions that describe King Azaz of Dictionopolis, and describe what he looks like.

_____

7. Read the stage directions that describe the Mathemagician, and describe what he looks like.

_____

B. DIRECTIONS: Read the following passage from *The Phantom Tollbooth,* Act I. On the lines, write words from the passage that refer to plot, setting, and characters.

> The two princesses. They used to settle all the arguments between their two brothers who rule over the Land of Wisdom. You see, Azaz is the king of Dictionopolis and the Mathemagician is the king of Digitopolis and they almost never see eye to eye on anything. . . . But then one day, the kings had an argument to end all arguments . . .

Plot _____

Setting _____

Characters _____

Unit 8: Drama

The Phantom Tollbooth, Act II
based on the book by Norton Juster, by Susan Nanus

Build Vocabulary

Using the Word Root *-son-*

The word root *-son-* comes from the Latin verb *sonare*, which means "to sound." Words formed from the word root *-son-* include the idea of sound in their meanings. For example, the word *dissonance* means "unpleasant sound." Other words built from the word root *-son-* are *resonate* ("make an echoing sound"), *supersonic* (faster than the speed of sound), *sonorous* (rich and full in sound), and *sonata* (musical composition for one instrument). Here are other examples:

sonar: "an instrument that uses sound waves to detect underwater objects and to determine their location." (Short for *sound navigation ranging*) The scientists used *sonar* to follow the whale.

sonic boom: "a loud, explosive noise caused by an aircraft traveling at or above the speed of sound." When the jet hit the speed of sound, you could hear the *sonic boom*.

A. Directions: Complete each sentence below by writing one of the following words. Use the meaning of the root *-son-* and sentence context to help you select the correct word.

sonar	resonate	consonant	dissonant	sonnet	sonata

1. I could no longer listen to the awful _____ sounds coming from the band room.

2. The letter *t* is a _____, while the letter *a* is a vowel.

3. When stretched tightly and then plucked, a rubber band will _____.

4. The poet wrote a beautiful _____.

5. The scientists are testing new _____ equipment for a deep-diving submarine.

6. The pianist played a very difficult _____ by Beethoven.

Using the Word Bank

dissonance	admonishing	iridescent	malicious

B. Directions: Use one word from the Word Bank to replace the italicized word or words in each sentence below. Rewrite your new sentences on the lines provided.

1. The doctor in *The Phantom Tollbooth*, Act II, specialized in creating *a harsh or disagreeable combination of sounds.*

   _____

2. The stars in the sky were so bright they looked *shimmering.*

   _____

3. We couldn't believe that our friend could say anything so nasty and *spiteful.*

   _____

4. The teacher gave the noisy class a look, *warning* them to quiet down.

   _____

Name _____ Date _____

The Phantom Tollbooth, Act II
based on the book by Norton Juster, by Susan Nanus

Build Spelling Skills: The Sound *sh∂s* Spelled *cious*

Spelling Strategy The sound *sh∂s** at the end of a word can be spelled *cious* as in mali**cious**, pre**cious**, and gra**cious**. The *cious* spelling is always preceded by a vowel. This ending is used often used to form adjectives from nouns. Sometimes the *cious* ending is added to a word part such as *deli* to form an adjective, as in *deli**cious***. In the examples below, notice the spelling changes when *cious* is added.

noun or word part	adjective with *cious*	meaning
mali-	malicious	showing evil intentions
grace	gracious	well-mannered
space	spacious	roomy
suspicion	suspicious	believing someone is guilty
deli-	delicious	good tasting

A. Practice: In each sentence below, fill in the blank with an adjective formed by adding *cious* to the word in parentheses.

1. The stew tasted _____ (deli-)

2. That dog has a _____ streak, so don't get too near it. (mali-)

3. Our new apartment has _____ rooms. (space)

4. His face had a guilty expression that made me _____. (suspicion)

5. Our hosts were _____ and friendly to every guest in the room. (grace)

B. Practice: Complete the following short passage with the correct adjectives. Choose the adjectives from the ones that you wrote on the lines above. Use sentence context to help you know which adjective to write.

Milo has some interesting adventures in *The Phantom Tollbooth*, Act II. He visits the huge and

_____ numbers mine. He wonders why the _____ stew he eats

makes him more and more hungry. Before he leaves to rescue the princesses, he is

_____ when the Mathemagician tells him he will have to overcome obstacles.

Later, he finds out that the obstacles are_____ demons who chase him. When

he finally succeeds in rescuing the princesses Rhyme and Reason, they are kind and

_____ to him.

*The character *∂* is called *schwa* and represents the sound <u>uh</u>.

Unit 8: Drama

Name _____ Date _____

***The Phantom Tollbooth,* Act II** based on the book by Norton Juster, by Susan Nanus

Build Grammar Skills: Indefinite Pronouns

An **indefinite pronoun** refers to a person, place, or thing that is not specifically named. Indefinite pronouns are singular or plural.

- **Singular:** *another, anyone, anything, each, either, everyone, everything, much, neither, no one, nothing, one, someone, something*

- **Plural:** *both, few, many, several*

- **Singular or Plural:** *all, any, more, most, none, some*

The context will often help you to decide whether an indefinite pronoun is singular or plural.
All of the journey is difficult and dangerous. (singular)
All of the heroes run fast. (plural)

A. DIRECTIONS: Choose the correct verb given in parentheses and write the verb in the blank.

1. All of Doctor Dischord's noises _____ (was, were) unpleasant.

2. Almost everyone _____ (enjoy, enjoys) the sound of laughter.

3. Of these two roads, neither _____ (are, is) shorter.

4. All you need to build Beaver Dam _____ (are, is) a beaver 68 feet long!

5. Some of these numbers _____ (are, is) used for fractions.

6. Since Rhyme and Reason left, both of the kings _____ (has, have) not agreed on anything.

7. Several of the Mathemagician's statements _____ (was, were) mysterious.

8. Many of Rhyme's speeches _____ (are, is) in couplets.

B. Writing Application: Revise the following sentences so that subjects and verbs agree in number.

1. According to Dodecahedron, everything in Digitopolis are quite precise.

_____

2. Anyone who are in a hurry to travel should leave immediately!

_____

3. Nobody understand the number problems.

_____

4. Somebody need to talk to Mathemagician.

_____

5. Each of the travelers try to solve the problem.

_____

6. None of the Subtraction Stew were satisfying.

_____

7. All of these problems has been caused by the departure of Rhyme and Reason.

_____

8. Each of you agree that he will disagree with whatever each of you agree with.

_____

The Phantom Tollbooth, **Act II** based on the book by Norton Juster, by Susan Nanus

Reading Strategy: Recognizing Word Play

The Phantom Tollbooth is full of word play, which often confuses the characters but amuses the audience. For example, a **pun** is the use of a word or words that are formed or sounded alike in order to connect or bring out two or more meanings, usually in a humorous way. For example, when Milo first sees the numbers mine, the Mathemagician puns on the word *mine:*

> **MILO.** [*Awed.*] Whose mine is it?
>
> **VOICE OF MATHEMAGICIAN.** By the four million eight hundred and twenty-seven thousand six hundred and fifty-nine hairs on my head, it's mine, of course!

This pun depends on two different uses of the word *mine*: a) as a noun meaning "a deep excavation in the earth," and b) as a pronoun meaning "the one(s) belonging to me."

DIRECTIONS: On the lines provided, explain the pun in each passage below.

1. **MILO.** Well, in that case, I think we ought to have a square meal . . .

   AZAZ. [*Claps his hands.*] A square meal it is! [*Waiters serve several trays of Colored Squares of all sizes.*]

   _____

   _____

2. **MATHEMAGICIAN.** Most of the time I take the shortest distance between two points. And of course, when I have to be in several places at once . . .

   [*He writes 3 x 1 = 3 on the notepad with his staff.*] I simply multiply.

   [THREE FIGURES *looking like the* MATHEMAGICIAN *appear on a platform above.*]

   _____

   _____

3. **MILO.** So this is the Land of Ignorance. It's so dark. I can hardly see a thing. Maybe we should wait until morning.

   VOICE. There'll be mourning for you soon enough! [*They look up and see a large, soiled, ugly* BIRD.]

   _____

   _____

4. **MILO.** But I don't mean . . .

   BIRD. Of course you're mean. Anyone who'd spend a night that doesn't belong to him is very mean.

   _____

   _____

5. **SENSES TAKER.** Oh, this won't take long. I'm the official Senses Taker and I must have some information before I take your sense. Now if you'll just tell me: [*Handing them a form to fill. Speaking slowly and deliberately.*] When you were born, where you were born . . .

   _____

   _____

Unit 8: Drama

Name _____ Date _____

The Phantom Tollbooth, Act II
based on the book by Norton Juster, by Susan Nanus

Literary Analysis: Theme

The **theme** of a story or play is its central underlying message, usually about life or human nature. A theme is sometimes stated directly, but more often it is suggested through the title, the words and experiences of the characters, the events and conflict in the story, and other details. For example, if a person in a story overcomes great obstacles to win a race, the theme might be the importance of determination in accomplishing goals.

DIRECTIONS: Complete this diagram for *The Phantom Tollbooth,* Act II. In the center circle, write what you see as the theme of the play's second act. In the boxes, write details that led you to this conclusion.

Grandpa and the Statue by Arthur Miller

Build Vocabulary

Using the Word Root *-scrib-*

You can see the word root *-scrib-* in the Word Bank word *subscribe*. The word root, which may also be spelled *-scrip-*, as in *subscription*, comes from the Latin word *scribere*, meaning "to write." In the play, a neighbor asks Grandpa to *subscribe* to the fund to pay for a base for the Statue of Liberty. In other words, he wants Grandpa to sign or *write* his name on a list of people who promise to contribute money to the fund. Other useful words are also based on this root. Read the definitions and examples with the root in mind.

> **scribe:** in ancient times, a person paid to copy books or documents
>
> Before the invention of the printing press, books were copied by *scribes*.
>
> **scripture:** writings important to a religion
>
> Carrie went to the library to do research on ancient *scriptures*.
>
> **subscription:** a signed agreement to pay for something in advance
>
> We paid a year in advance for our newspaper *subscription*.

A. DIRECTIONS: Use the correct word to complete each sentence. Write your answer on the line.

scribe   scripture   subscription

1. Because they have a _____ to that magazine, my cousins get it every week.

2. In ancient times, a _____ wrote letters for people who did not know how to write.

3. The scholar had spent many years studying _____ of ancient religions.

Using the Word Bank

subscribed	peeved	uncomprehending	tempest

B. DIRECTIONS: In the space following each of these sentences, write the Word Bank word that could replace the underlined word or words in each sentence.

1. Monaghan was <u>annoyed</u> with Sheean. _____

2. Monaghan expected that, in a <u>strong wind storm</u>, the Statue of Liberty would fall. _____

3. August was <u>not understanding</u> about why Young Monaghan liked to spend hours looking at the Statue of Liberty. _____

4. At the end of the radio play, Monaghan wishes that he had <u>signed up to give money</u> to the fund for the base of the Statue of Liberty. _____

Grandpa and the Statue by Arthur Miller

Build Spelling Skills: Adding -er or -est

Spelling Strategy When you add the ending -er or -est to an adjective that ends in y, change the y to i before adding the ending.

   Example: Although the comedian's jokes were **funny**, I've heard **funnier** jokes, and the jokes in this book are the **funniest** I've ever heard.

When the adjective ends in y, change the y to i before adding the ending.

Exception: When you add -er or -est to a word ending in y preceded by a vowel, do not change the y to i.

   Example: The sky looked **gray** yesterday, but it looked even **grayer** today.

A. Practice: Add -er and -est to each adjective.

1. grouchy _____, _____

2. gray _____, _____

3. sturdy _____, _____

4. pretty _____, _____

5. grand _____, _____

6. likely _____, _____

7. manly _____, _____

8. young _____, _____

9. crummy _____, _____

B. Practice: In each sentence below, add the ending in parentheses to the underlined adjective. Write the adjective with its ending on the line.

1. Grandpa was <u>testy</u> when Sheean asked him for a donation, but he was even _____ when Sheean asked again. (-er)

2. The weather had been <u>windy</u> all week, but the day they went to see the Statue up close was the _____ day in a long time. (-est)

3. Buying peanuts made the boy <u>happy</u>, but he was even _____ to see his grandfather leave a coin on the base of the statue. (-er)

4. It's getting <u>sunny</u>, and later it will be even _____. (-er)

5. That is so <u>silly</u>, it's the _____ thing I've ever heard. (-est)

6. Before the storm, the <u>gray</u> sky turned even _____. (-er)

7. The teacher was <u>happier</u> with us this morning, and she was the _____ we've ever seen her this afternoon. (-est)

Name _____ Date _____

Grandpa and the Statue by Arthur Miller

Build Grammar Skills: Pronoun and Antecedent Agreement

A pronoun doesn't make sense by itself. It needs an **antecedent**, which is the noun or proper noun to which the pronoun refers. For a pronoun to make sense, it must **agree** with its antecedent in gender (masculine or feminine) and number (singular or plural). For example, in the following sentences from *Grandpa and the Statue*, each pronoun is underlined twice, and its antecedent is underlined once.

> I didn't think there was a <u>statue</u> but there is. <u>She's</u> all broke, it's true . . .

The pronoun *she* refers to the noun *statue*. Because the noun *statue* is singular (there is only one) and feminine (this statue represents a woman), the pronoun is also singular and feminine (she).

> "I don't really think your <u>grampa</u> knows what <u>he's</u> talkin' about."

The pronoun *he* refers to the noun *grampa*. Because the noun *grampa* is singular (he is just one person), and masculine (*grampa* means "grand**father**"), the pronouns is also singular and masculine (he). If the above sentence were written, "I don't really think your grampa knows what <u>they're</u> talkin' about," it would lose its intended meaning.

A. Practice: On the line following each sentence, write *A* if the pronoun and antecedent agree in gender and number. Write *X* if the pronoun does not agree with the antecedent. For each *X*, write the correct pronoun.

1. Young Monaghan tells a story about his grandfather. _____

2. All the people gave money because they wanted to be proud of Butler Street.

   _____

3. The statue needed a base, and the money would go to pay for them. _____

4. Each boy enjoyed their visit to the statue. _____

5. Finally, the grandfather admits that it was wrong about the statue. _____

B. Writing Application: Rewrite each sentence, filling in the blank with a pronoun that agrees in gender and number with the underlined antecedent.

1. When <u>people</u> listen to the play, _____ imagine being in Brooklyn long ago.

2. <u>Sheean</u> paid Grandpa's streetcar fare to the warehouse, but _____ wouldn't pay the return fare.

3. Everyone in my family except my youngest <u>sister</u> has been to the Statue of Liberty, but _____ hopes to go soon.

4. When <u>my friend</u> and I saw a film about the Statue of Liberty, _____ learned a lot.

5. By carefully reading what the <u>characters</u> said, I figured out the meaning of _____ words.

6. <u>Each boy</u> is eager to see the statue, and each hopes for _____ turn to go.

Unit 8: Drama

Grandpa and the Statue by Arthur Miller

Reading Strategy: Distinguishing Fact and Fantasy

Historical fiction combines elements of reality and fantasy to make the fantastic more believable. When you are reading, it is important to **distinguish fact and fantasy**, or determine which details are true and which are fictitious.

- **Facts** are true details that can be proven.

- **Fantasy** is made up in the imagination of the author.

DIRECTIONS: To practice distinguishing between fact and fantasy, complete the chart below as you read. Write factual elements in the "Fact" column and elements of fantasy in the "Fantastic" column.

Fact	Fantastic
Example: The French gave the Statue of Liberty to the United States.	Jack Sheean collected money for the Statue of Liberty fund on behalf of the residents of Butler Street.
1.	2.
3.	4.
5.	6.
7.	8.
9.	10.

Grandpa and the Statue by Arthur Miller

Literary Analysis: Dialogue

In a story, the author has many ways of giving you important information about the setting and action and the characters' thoughts and feelings. For example, an author might write, "Jerry was terrified, but he tried to look brave." In a play, the author has only one way of letting you know a character's feelings, and that is through **dialogue**, the conversation that takes place among characters in a play. By reading or listening to the dialogue, you find out where the characters are, how they feel about one another, what they are thinking and feeling, and other important information.

For example, in "Grandpa and the Statue," you know where the boy and his grandpa are when the boy says,

> "Gee, it's nice ridin' on a boat, ain't it, Grandpa?"

Grandpa's answer lets you know that he is worried that the neighbors will find out about his trip to see the Statue of Liberty.

> "Never said there was anything wrong with the boat. Boat's all right. You're sure now that Georgie's father is takin' the kids in the afternoon."

DIRECTIONS: Using the chart below, select a short piece of dialogue for each of the three characters on the chart. Write the dialogue you have selected in the first column. Write the information the dialogue provides in the second column.

Character's Dialogue	Information
Sheean:	
Grandpa Monaghan:	
Child Monaghan:	

Unit 8: Drama

"The Walrus and the Carpenter" by Lewis Carroll
"The Geese" by Richard Peck
"Jimmy Jet and His TV Set" by Shel Silverstein

Build Vocabulary

Multiple Meanings

The Word Bank word *antennae* from "Jimmy Jet and His TV Set" can mean "metal rods that receive TV or radio signals" or "sense organs on the heads of insects." From the context of the poem, you can tell that the meaning being used is the first one.

Here are some other words from the selections with multiple meanings along with two definitions of each word.

> **odd:** strange / not even, not evenly divisible by two
> **watch:** to look at / a timepiece worn on the wrist
> **lean:** thin, with little or no fat / to bend or to stand at a slant
> **lure:** a powerful attraction / artificial fishing bait

A. DIRECTIONS: In each sentence, write the correct meaning of the italicized word from the definitions above.

1. Will you *watch* the movie with me? _____

2. The magician asked a member of the audience to pick an *odd* number.

   _____

3. Mr. Sanchez tied the *lure* to the end of his fishing rod.

   _____

4. To stay *lean*, we follow a diet that includes many fruits and vegetables.

   _____

Using the Word Bank

beseech	lean	antennae

B. DIRECTIONS: Use a Word Bank word to replace the italicized word or words in the following sentences. Write your words on the lines provided.

1. Don't overfeed your pet if you want to keep it *thin*. _____

2. "I *beg* of you to spare my life," the prisoner said to the king. _____

3. When dad raised the *metal rod*, the stations came in clearer on our car radio. _____

Analogies

C. DIRECTIONS: Circle the letter that best completes each analogy.

1. Tall is to short as fat is to _____.

   a. beseech   b. lean   c. antennae   d. odd

2. Sounds are to ears as signals are to _____.

   a. beseech   b. lean   c. antennae   d. watch

Name _____ Date _____

"The Walrus and the Carpenter" by Lewis Carroll
"The Geese" by Richard Peck
"Jimmy Jet and His TV Set" by Shel Silverstein

Building Spelling Skills: long e sound (ee, ea)

Spelling Strategy The long e sound can be spelled in several ways. One way is
ee, as in the Word Bank word be**see**ch, and the words k**ee**n and betw**ee**n. Another
way is ea as in the Word Bank word l**ea**n and the words m**ea**n and cl**ea**n.

A. Practice: Complete the sentences below, using the following words.

        mean   keen   between   clean   beseech   lean

1. The cottage stood on a hill _____ the lake and the woods.

2. I _____ you not to go out tonight.

3. Most dogs have a _____ sense of smell.

4. The runners in the race were all _____ and fit.

5. It was _____ of you not to invite Sally to the party.

6. Once a week I completely _____ my room.

B. Practice: Complete the following dialogue. Using the clues in parentheses for help, choose
five words from your chart to fill in the blanks.

Walrus: My dear fellow, just (ee word) _____ you and me, I miss the poor oysters.

Carpenter: Yes, it was (ea word) _____ of us to eat them.

Walrus: I (ee word) _____ you, let us find some new little friends to walk with.

Carpenter: Let me ask the lobsters to join us.

Walrus: We can (ea word) _____ up our kitchen and have them to lunch.

Carpenter: Oh, dear. We won't stay very (ea word) _____ that way!

Challenge: The plural form of the Word Bank word *antenna* is *antennae* (pronounced an TEN
ee). Words that end in *a* and form the plural by adding *e* come from the ancient language Latin.
Other Latin words ending in *a* form the plural in the same way. For example, the plural of *formula* is *formulae* (pronounced FOR mew lee), and the plural of *alumna*, which means female
graduate, is *alumnae* (pronounced uh LUM nee). On the lines below, write three sentences
using the plural form of *antenna*, *formula*, and *alumna*.

_____

_____

_____

Unit 9: Poetry

"The Walrus and the Carpenter" by Lewis Carroll
"The Geese" by Richard Peck
"Jimmy Jet and His TV Set" by Shel Silverstein

Building Grammar Skills: Regular Comparisons

Adjectives and adverbs have different forms when they are used to compare two items and when they are used to compare three or more items. The **comparative** form is used to compare two items. The **superlative** form is used to compare three or more items.

Short adjectives and adverbs usually form the comparative by adding *-er* to the positive or base form. For example, the comparative form of the adjective *strong* is *stronger*. Short adjectives and adverbs usually form the superlative by adding *-est* to the positive. The superlative form of the adjective *strong* is *strongest*. Longer adjectives and most adverbs add the word *more* to form the comparative, as in *more graceful* and *more quickly*. Longer adjectives and most adverbs add the word *most* to form the superlative, as in *most graceful* amd *most quickly*.

> **Comparative:** Those oysters are *tastier* than these. (adjective)
> Butter spreads *more easily* than marmalade. (adverb)
> **Superlative:** These oysters are the *tastiest* of all. (adjective)
> Of all the problems, this one can be solved *most easily*. (adverb)

Exceptions: There are a few adjectives that cannot take comparative and superlative forms. The adjective *unique* means "one of a kind" or "without equal." Something that is *unique* cannot be compared to anything else. The sentence, "Of all the jewels, the diamond was the *most unique*" is incorrect. The sentence should read, "Of all the jewels, the diamond was *unique*." Other adjectives that cannot be used in the comparative or superlative forms include *original, complete*, and *perfect*.

A. Practice: In each of the following sentences, underline the comparative or superlative form of the adjective or adverb. Write **C** on the line if the sentence contains a comparative, and **S** if it contains a superlative. The first sentence has been done for you.

_C_ 1. The walrus is <u>funnier</u> than the Carpenter.

_____ 2. Jimmy Jet was the laziest boy in school.

_____ 3. The author has a closer acquaintance with geese than I do.

_____ 4. Lewis Carroll's rhymes are the cleverest of any I know.

_____ 5. This poem uses wittier words than that one.

_____ 6. Of all these waterfowl, geese honk the most loudly.

B. Writing Application: Complete the following sentences by choosing the correct word in parentheses.

1. My father heard the passage of the geese (earlier, earliest) _____ than I did.

2. The leader in the V formation flew (higher, highest) the _____ of all the birds.

3. Winter's wind comes (sooner, soonest) _____ than you might expect.

4. Of all the people in our family, Father lay awake the (longer, longest) _____ .

5. Whose report on geese was (more accurate, most accurate) _____, Jenna's or Kim's?

"The Walrus and the Carpenter" by Lewis Carroll
"The Geese" by Richard Peck
"Jimmy Jet and His TV Set" by Shel Silverstein

Reading Strategy: Identifying the Speaker in a Poem

Sometimes a poem is in the first person, using words such as *I*, *we*, and *my*.
"Jimmy Jet and His TV Set": *"I'll tell you the story of Jimmy Jet"*
　　　　　　　　　　　 "We all sit around and watch him."
"Geese": *"My father was the first to hear"*

The person referred to by pronouns such as *I* and *my* in a poem is not necessarily the poet, but an imaginary character, or **speaker**, who says the words made up by the poet. For example, in "Jimmy Jet and His TV Set," the speaker tells a story about someone he or she knew. Usually, a poem contains clues about the speaker. For example, in "The Geese," you can tell that the speaker is a person who misses his or her father. Sometimes, however, there is very little evidence to the identity of the speaker. In "The Walrus and the Carpenter," you can only guess that the speaker is a person who likes to entertain other with clever nonsensical stories.

DIRECTIONS: Fill in the chart below to identify the speaker in the poems. Include the clues that helped you write your answers. The first box in the chart has been filled in for you. (You may not have something to fill in under every heading for each poem.)

	What relationships does the speaker have with others?	Can you tell if the speaker is male or female?	In what kind of place does the speaker probably live?	Do you think the speaker is an older person or a younger person?
"The Geese"	The speaker has a relationship with his or her father, because the poem tells how the speaker remembers the father.			
"Jimmy Jet and His TV Set"				
"The Walrus and the Carpenter"				

Unit 9: Poetry

"The Walrus and the Carpenter" by Lewis Carroll
"The Geese" by Richard Peck
"Jimmy Jet and His TV Set" by Shel Silverstein

Literary Analysis: Narrative and Lyric Poetry

There are two main kinds of poetry—narrative poetry and lyric poetry. Narrative poetry tells a story with a setting, characters, a plot, and an outcome. Some **narrative** poems, such as "The Walrus and the Carpenter," contain dialogue between the characters. **Lyric** poetry puts less emphasis on actions and more on the speaker's feelings and thoughts. For example, the main idea of the poem "The Geese" is the speaker's remembrance of his or her father listening to the passage of the geese, not a sequence of events that may have occurred on that occasion.

DIRECTIONS: Fill in the graphic organizer below for each of the poems.

Title of Poem	Narrative or Lyric?	How Can You Tell?
"The Walrus and the Carpenter"		
"Jimmy Jet and His TV Set"		
"The Geese"		

"**The Sidewalk Racer**" by Lillian Morrison
Haiku by Matsuo Bashō
Limerick Anonymous

Build Vocabulary

Using Homophones

Homophones are words that sound exactly the same but have different meanings. The words are often spelled differently, as in the words *flea* and *flee*. The noun *flea* refers to a tiny insect. The verb *flee* means "to run away."

Occasionally homophones are spelled the same. For example, the word *can* may mean "a metal cylinder-shaped container," as in "Please open the can of peas." Can may also mean "able to," as in "I can do that math problem." The following words are homophones:

be / bee   flea / flee   flue / flew   through / threw

A. DIRECTIONS: Complete the following sentences with the correct homophone from the list above.

1. The skateboard _____ up in the air.

2. He skated _____ the tunnel.

3. I want to _____ a professional athlete.

4. It is wise to _____ from danger.

5. Sam _____ a rock into the pond.

6. Smoke drifted from the _____.

7. A _____ hummed over the fragrant flower.

8. The _____ bite was itchy and painful.

Using the Word Bank

skimming	flue	flee	flaw

B. DIRECTIONS: In the limerick below, fill in the blanks with the correct words from the Word Bank.

A crow on a _____ belching smoke

Said, "Something's amiss, that's no joke.

What a _____ in the day.

I'll go _____ away

And _____ this flue, else I will choke."

C. DIRECTIONS: Choose the lettered pair of words that best expresses a relationship similar to that expressed by the words in CAPITAL LETTERS.

1. SMOKE : FLUE ::   a. water : spout   b. house : chimney   c. bird : flight

2. SKIMMING : LIGHTLY ::   a. skating : running   b. skiing : jumping   c. tramping : heavily

3. FLEE : DANGER ::   a. avoid : attraction   b. escape : harm   c. run : walk

4. FLAW : CORRECTED ::   a. mistake : fault   b. stain : cleaned   c. perfect : sentence

Unit 9: Poetry

"The Sidewalk Racer" by Lillian Morrison
Haiku by Matsuo Bashō
Limerick Anonymous

Build Spelling Skills: Spelling Homophones

Homophones are words that sound the same but have different meanings. Homophones also may have different spellings.

Spelling Strategy: Use a dictionary to clarify the spellings and meanings of homophones that present a problem for you. Here are some commonly confused homophones:

hear/here: *hear* is a verb meaning "to perceive sounds"; *here* is an adverb meaning "in this place"

peace/piece: *peace* means "quiet order"; *piece* is "a part of something"

principal/principle: *principal* means "main or most important" as an adjective, and as a noun it means "the head of a school"; *principle* means "a main fact or law" or "a rule of conduct"

right/write: *right* is usually an adjective meaning "correct"; *write* is a verb meaning "to communicate using printed words"

their/there/they're: *their* is the possessive form of the pronoun *they*; *there* is an adverb meaning "in that place"; *they're* is the contracted form of *they are*

your/you're: *your* is generally a possessive adjective; *you're* is the contracted form of *you are*

A. Practice: Complete the sentences with the correct word from each pair in parentheses.

1. (Their, There) _____ skateboard is newer than ours.

2. How long do you think it would take you to (right, write) _____ a haiku?

3. "I laughed a lot when I read (your, you're) _____ limerick, Sue," said Tim.

4. An appeal to nature's beauty is one of the (principal, principle) _____ features of haiku.

5. Reading that haiku gave me a wonderful feeling of (peace, piece) _____.

B. Practice: Write a sentence for each word below. Check a dictionary to make sure you are using and spelling each word correctly.

1. a) meet _____

   b) meat _____

2. a) sight _____

   b) site _____

3. a) plane _____

   b) plain _____

4. a) tail _____

   b) tale _____

Name _____ Date _____

"**The Sidewalk Racer**" by Lillian Morrison
Haiku by Matsuo Bashō
Limerick Anonymous

Build Grammar Skills: Irregular Comparisons

Most adjectives and adverbs have three forms: positive, comparative, and superlative. Usually, the comparative is formed by adding the ending -*er* or the word *more;* the superlative is usually formed by adding the ending -*est* or the word *most*. Some adjectives, however, change completely in the comparative and superlative forms. These are called **irregular comparisons.** Here is an example:

Positive: The apples tasted <u>good</u>.
Comparative: The apples tasted <u>better</u> than the pears.
Superlative: The oranges tasted the <u>best</u> of all the fruit we tried.

Because each irregular comparison is different, you should learn each one. Here are some others:

Positive	Comparative	Superlative
good / well	better	best
bad	worse	worst
many / much	more	most
little	less	least
far	farther	farthest

A. Practice: Replace the positive form of the modifier with the comparative or superlative form.

1. That frog jumped (far) _____ into the pond than this one did. (comparative)

2. Your limerick gave me the (bad) _____ case of the giggles I had ever had.

   (superlative)

3. That skateboarder would be (well) _____ off if he were more careful. (comparative)

4. Of all the students, Stan spent the (little) _____ time writing his haiku. (superlative)

5. "The Sidewalk Racer" is the (good) _____ concrete poem I have ever read. (superlative)

B. Writing Application: Rewrite each sentence below changing the underlined word as indicated in parentheses. The first sentence has been done for you.

1. I think that Bashō is a <u>better</u> writer than Lillian Morrison. (superlative)

   I think Bashō is the best writer in this selection

2. My house is <u>far</u> from our school. (comparative)

   _____

3. My sister's cough is <u>worse</u> today than yesterday. (superlative)

   _____

4. <u>Many</u> people arrived at the end of the bake sale. (superlative)

   _____

© Prentice-Hall, Inc.

Selection Support **193**

"**The Sidewalk Racer**" by Lillian Morrison
Haiku by Matsuo Bashō
Limerick Anonymous

Reading Strategy: Using Your Senses

You will experience a poem more fully if you **use your senses** when you read it. The first sense you use when you read a poem is your sense of *sight*, as you look at the way the words are arranged on the page. As you continue to read, you can use all your senses to almost *see, hear, touch, smell,* and *taste* the images the poem describes. Look for words that appeal to your five senses. The passages below are examples of how words in poems can appeal to your senses:

Sight: "an asphalt sea" ("The Sidewalk Racer")
Hearing: "A frog jumps into the pond,/Splash!" ("Haiku" by Bashō)

Then use your senses to *experience* the poem rather than simply read the words.

A. DIRECTIONS: Use the chart below to help you **use your senses** as you read the poems. The limerick line "A flea and a fly in a flue" has been charted as an example.

Sight	Hearing	Smell	Touch	Taste
darkness bricks covered with soot	sound of fly buzzing	the smell of soot	hardness of brick	

B. DIRECTIONS: Match the poems, numbered on the left, with one of the senses you might use to experience them, lettered on the right.

____ 1. "Haiku" by Bashō

a. hearing the sound of wheels on concrete

____ 2. "A flea and a fly " limerick

b. sight of a man as he stumbles and falls

____ 3. "The Sidewalk Racer"

c. hearing the splash of water

____ 4. "There was a young fellow—" limerick

d. feeling the closeness of being inside a chimney

Name _____ Date _____

Literary Analysis: Special Forms of Poetry

Poets sometimes use **special forms** of poetry that put words into action in specific, and sometimes new and inventive ways. Here are three examples of special forms of poetry:

Concrete poems: Words are arranged in a shape on paper to reflect the subject of the poem.

Haiku: This unrhymed and deeply expressive Japanese form of poetry has only three lines, with a pattern of five syllables in the first line, seven in the second, and five in the third.

Limerick: In this short, humorous form of poetry, the first, second, and fifth lines rhyme, as do the third and fourth lines. The lines that rhyme have the same rhythm. Limericks are named for the county of Limerick in Ireland.

A. DIRECTIONS: Answer the question about each form of poetry below by circling the letter of the most important fact about that poem's special form.

1. Why is the concrete form important to "The Sidewalk Racer?"
   a. The skateboard shape of the poem catches the reader's eye and intensifies interest in the poem's subject.
   b. Skateboards are used on concrete.
   c. The concrete form is a unique way to write poetry.

2. Why is the haiku form important for the poem by Bashō?
   a. The haiku form uses five, seven, and five syllables in its three lines.
   b. The form's few words create deeply expressive images.
   c. Haiku is a Japanese verse form.

3. Why is the special form of the two limericks important to these two poems?
   a. In order to be funny, a poem has to have rhyming lines.
   b. The rhythm and rhyme of the words add to the silliness and fun of the poem's subjects.
   c. Language serves many purposes in limericks.

B. DIRECTIONS: Decide whether the statements below about special forms of poetry are true or false. In the line following each statement write **T** if the statement is true and **F** if it is false.

1. In a concrete poem, words are arranged so that the lines rhyme. _____

2. A haiku poem has three lines and does not have to rhyme. _____

3. Limericks are often sad or serious. _____

4. A concrete poem uses words arranged in a special shape that reflects the subject of the poem. _____

5. Haiku is a form of Irish verse. _____

6. The limerick form uses a specific pattern of rhythm and rhyme. _____

"Wind and water and stone" by Octavio Paz
"February Twilight" by Sara Teasdale
"The Fairies' Lullaby" by William Shakespeare
"Cynthia in the Snow" by Gwendolyn Brooks
"Parade" by Rachel Field

Build Vocabulary

Using the Suffix *-ly*

The suffix *-ly* is an ending for many adverbs, words that describe verbs, adjectives, and other adverbs by answering the questions *when, how,* or *in what way.* In many cases, when added to an adjective, the suffix *-ly* turns the adjective into an adverb.

Examples:

Adjectives	*bright*	*tender*	*foolish*	*sad*
Adverbs	*brightly*	*tenderly*	*foolishly*	*sadly*

A. DIRECTIONS: Change each adjective in the following list to an adverb by adding the suffix *-ly.* Then fill in the blank in each sentence below with the adverb that best completes the following sentence.

slow   brisk   handsome   wild   loudly

1. The horses trotted _____ and soon passed the lumbering elephants.

2. Their riders were dressed _____ in red or blue costumes.

3. The crowd cheered _____ as the parade went by.

4. Several camels at the end of the parade strolled _____ by us.

5. The parade master had to shout _____ above the noise of the crowds.

Using the Word Bank

gilded	leisurely	nigh	hence	offense

B. DIRECTIONS: Use your understanding of the Word Bank words to complete this exercise. Circle the letter of the choice that best completes each sentence.

_____1. leisurely   a. go away from this place

_____2. offense   b. coated with a thin layer of gold

_____3. gilded   c. near

_____4. hence   d. in an unhurried way

_____5. nigh   e. harmful act

Name _____ Date _____

"Wind and water and stone" by Octavio Paz
"February Twilight" by Sara Teasdale
"The Fairies' Lullaby" by William Shakespeare
"Cynthia in the Snow" by Gwendolyn Brooks
"Parade" by Rachel Field

Build Spelling Skills: Exceptions to the *ie/ei* rule

Spelling Strategy: Remember these rules to spell words with the letter combination *i* and *e*.

- The letter *i* usually goes first when *i* and *e* come together.

   Examples: niece, piece, chief, achieve

- Write *e* before *i* if the letter combination comes after *c*.

   Examples: receive, ceiling, perceive

- Write *e* before *i* when the letter combination spells the long *a* sound

   Examples: neighbor, weigh, veil, reign

- **Exceptions:** There are also certain words that do not follow the above rules. These words must be learned and memorized in order to be spelled correctly.

   Examples: height, neither, seize, weird, leisurely, foreign

A. Practice: The following words are missing the letters *i* and *e*. Write the words, with the missing letters in the correct order, in the blanks next to their definitions below.

   l___ ___surely   c___ ___ling   w___ ___rd   p___ ___ce   retr___ ___ve

1. overhead surface of a room _____

2. strange _____

3. part of a whole _____

4. in an unhurried way _____

5. to bring back _____

B. Practice: The following words are missing the letters *i* and *e*. Write the words, with the missing letters in the correct order, in the blanks; then complete the sentences below.

   n___ ___ther   s___ ___ze   for___ ___gn   re___ ___gn   w___ ___gh

1. (period of a monarch's rule) The Queen's _____ was peaceful and prosperous.

2. (outside one's own country) No invasions from _____ lands disturbed the people.

3. (grab) The clashing cymbals at the parade would certainly _____ the spectators' attention.

4. (not one or the other) The fairies made sure that _____ the spiders nor the beetles dared to disturb the fairy Queen.

5. (be heavy as) I can only imagine what one of those circus elephants might _____.

Unit 9: Poetry

"Wind and water and stone" by Octavio Paz
"February Twilight" by Sara Teasdale
"The Fairies' Lullaby" by William Shakespeare
"Cynthia in the Snow" by Gwendolyn Brooks
"Parade" by Rachel Field

Build Grammar Skills: Commas and Semicolons

One major use of a **comma** is to separate two simple sentences that are joined in a compound sentence. The two parts of a compound sentence are usually joined by a coordinating conjunction, such as *but, and, for, or, so,* or *yet.*

Example: The circus arrived on time, and the people cheered loudly.

A **semicolon** may also be used to separate the two parts of a compound sentence. When a semicolon is used, no coordinating conjunction is necessary. Use a semicolon to show a strong connection between ideas or a direct contrast between the two parts of the compound sentence.

Example: The floats were in dragon shapes; the clowns were on stilts.

A. Practice: Combine each pair of simple sentences to form a compound sentence. Follow the directions in parentheses.

1. The musicians played brass instruments. The drummers beat their drums. (Use the coordinating conjunction *and*)

_____

2. The sky was cloudy. Showers did not interrupt the parade. (Use the coordinating conjunction *but*)

_____

3. Ed and Roscoe had arrived early to set up the chairs. We all had a good view. (Use the coordinating conjunction *so*).

_____

4. The camels strutted with their heads held high. The trunks of the elephants swept the grass. (Use a semicolon)

_____

5. Some riders were dressed in blue. Others wore red. (Use a semicolon)

_____

B. Writing Application: Write a compound sentence about each topic below, following the directions given in parentheses.

1. Write a sentence in which you identify your favorite color and your favorite food. (Use a semicolon.)

_____

2. Write a sentence about one of your likes and one of your dislikes. (Use the conjunction *but.*)

_____

3. Write a sentence about what you might do with your family and friends this weekend. (Use the conjunction *or.*)

_____

4. Write a sentence in which you compare or contrast scary movies with comedies. (Use a semicolon.)

_____

"Wind and water and stone" by Octavio Paz
"February Twilight" by Sara Teasdale
"The Fairies' Lullaby" by William Shakespeare
"Cynthia in the Snow" by Gwendolyn Brooks
"Parade" by Rachel Field

Reading Strategy: Read According to Punctuation

Sometimes, when people read poetry aloud, they stop or pause at the end of every line. This makes the poem difficult for listeners to understand. Poetry makes more sense and is more enjoyable to listen to if the reader avoids these pauses, pausing instead at punctuation marks only, as if he or she were reading a prose passage. For example, try reading the following lines from the poem "Parade" in two different ways. First pause at the end of each line. Then read the lines again, with no pause after lines 1, 3, or 4, and only a slight pause after the comma following "drums" at the end of line 2.

> Line 1: This is the day the circus comes
> Line 2: With blare of brass, with beating drums,
> Line 3: And clashing cymbals, and with roar
> Line 4: Of wild beasts never heard before
> Line 5: Within town limits.

Even when you read poetry silently to yourself, it will make better sense and sound better if you follow these rules:

- **Slight pause** after a comma

- **Longer pause** after a colon, semicolon, or dash

- **Stop longest** for end marks such as periods, question marks, or exclamation points.

- **Don't stop** at all at the ends of lines where there is no punctuation.

A. DIRECTIONS: Below is the poem, "Cynthia in the Snow." At the end of each line, write SP for *slight pause*, SL for *stop longest*, or DS *for don't stop*.

It SUSHES. _____

It hushes _____

The loudness in the road. _____

It flitter-twitters, _____

5 And laughs away from me. _____

It laughs a lovely whiteness, _____

And whitely whirs away, _____

To be _____

Some otherwhere, _____

10 Still white as milk or shirts. _____

So beautiful it hurts.

B. DIRECTIONS: Explain briefly why you should not pause between lines 8 and 9 ("To be" and "Some otherwhere"). Tell why a good reader would not pause at this point.

_____

_____

"Wind and water and stone" by Octavio Paz
"February Twilight" by Sara Teasdale
"The Fairies' Lullaby" by William Shakespeare
"Cynthia in the Snow" by Gwendolyn Brooks
"Parade" by Rachel Field

Literary Analysis: Sound Devices

Onomatopoeia (ah nuh mah tuh PEE uh) and alliteration are two **sound devices** used in poetry and other types of writing. **Onomatopoeia** is a way of using words to imitate sounds.

Examples from "Parade":   clashing   roar

Examples from "Cynthia in the Snow":   sushes   hushes

Examples from "The Fairies' Lullaby":   lulla, lulla, lullaby

Notice that *sushes* is a word made up by the poet to imitate the sound of falling snow.

Alliteration is a way of giving words a musical sound by repeating sounds at the beginnings of words.

Example from "Parade":   blare of brass

Examples from "Cynthia in the Snow":   laughs a lovely whiteness whitely whirs

Examples from "The Fairies' Lullaby":   lovely lady, beetles black

A. DIRECTIONS: Underline the examples of onomatopoeia and alliteration in the following sentences. On the line following each sentence, write O for onomatopoeia or A for alliteration. (For the one sentence that uses both, write both O and A on the line.) The first sentence has been done for you.

1. The <u>big, brown bear</u> stood on its hind legs. __A__

2. The sound of bells jingling in the distance let us know the parade was approaching. _____

3. The drip, drip, drip of the rain on the roof finally put me to sleep. _____

4. His long, graceful fingers made the piano keys tinkle. _____

5. I was startled when the car behind me honked loudly. _____

6. As she rode, her long, lovely hair streamed out behind her. _____

B. DIRECTIONS: Find one example of onomatopoeia and one example of alliteration in the following lines. Write the examples on the lines below.

When our cat had her first litter, the kittens were so tiny, you could hold them in the palm of your hand. But as tiny as they were, when their mother licked them to give them a bath, their purring sounded like a motor boat. As the kittens grew older, they became more playful. They looked like little balls of fluff chasing each other around in circles and pouncing on one another. I loved watching our funny, fluffy kittens as they grew.

1. Example of onomatopoeia: _____

2. Example of alliteration: _____

"Simile: Willow and Ginkgo" by Eve Merriam
"Fame Is a Bee" by Emily Dickinson
"April Rain Song" by Langston Hughes

Build Vocabulary

Using Musical Words

As in other fields, music has its own special words and terms. Read the following examples of **musical words**:

soprano: high in pitch   The *soprano* voices are the highest.

chorus: a large group of people singing together; a piece of music sung by a *chorus*

I hope I will be chosen to sing in the school *chorus*.

orchestra: a large group of musicians who play together

Our school *orchestra* gave a concert.

crescendo: a gradual increase in loudness in a musical composition

The symphony ended in an exciting *crescendo*.

fanfare: a short, loud piece of music, usually played by trumpets to introduce an important person or event

The trumpets announced the entrance of the queen with a loud *fanfare*.

Some musical terms are used to describe things that are not musical. For example, notice how the italicized musical words are used in the following sentences:

When mom asked if we wanted popcorn, we answered 'Yes!' in *chorus*.

Everyone turned around as my brothers' argument came to a *crescendo*.

A. DIRECTIONS: Complete each sentence below, using one of the words above.

1. The band greeted the winning team with a loud _____ .

2. I heard the high _____ voice of the child calling her mother.

3. The music rose to a _____ , then became very quiet and peaceful.

4. Before the concert, the audience sang the national anthem along with the _____ .

5. There were so many birds singing in the tree, they sounded like an _____ .

Using the Word Bank

soprano	chorus

B. DIRECTIONS: Circle the letter of the pair of words that expresses a relationship most similar to that expressed by the pair in CAPITAL LETTERS.

1. SOPRANO: HIGHEST :: a. bass: lowest   b. tenor: mellow   c. voice: opera

2. CHORUS: MANY :: a. song: group   b. solo: one   c. refrain: singers

"**Simile: Willow and Ginkgo**" by Eve Merriam
"**Fame Is a Bee**" by Emily Dickinson
"**April Rain Song**" by Langston Hughes

Build Spelling Skills: Forming the Plural of Words that End in *o*

Words that end in an *o* preceded by a consonant usually form the plural by adding *s*. Most musical words that end in *o* follow this rule. For example, the plural of *alto* is *altos*. The plural of *soprano* is *sopranos*. All of the following words form the plural by adding *s*: *pistachios, photos, radios, portfolios, pianos, solos, videos, zeros*.

Exceptions: Some words that end in *o* preceded by a consonant form the plural by adding *es*. For instance, the plural of *tomato* is *tomatoes*. Other exceptions include *potatoes, echoes,* and *heroes*.

A. Practice: The words in parentheses following each of the sentences below end in *o*. For each sentence, change the word in parentheses to its plural form.

1. We took _____ of all the relatives at the family reunion. (photo)

2. We could hear the _____ of our voices in the canyon. (echo)

3. The _____ were tuned to different stations. (radio)

4. We kept eating _____ until all that was left was a pile of shells. (pistachio)

5. The two students who helped the firefighters were treated like _____ . (hero)

B. Practice: Proofread the paragraph below. Watch for misspelled plurals of words that end in *o*. Cross out each incorrectly spelled word and write the correctly spelled word above it.

Everyone was eager to hear which team would win the game. Radioes were turned on in

every home. Some people watched on TV and recorded videoes for friends who couldn't be home

to watch. When the game was over, the players on the winning team were cheered like heroes.

It still seems that I can hear the echoes of the cheering crowds. Newspaper photographers took

photoes of the star players.

"Simile: Willow and Ginkgo" by Eve Merriam
"Fame Is a Bee" by Emily Dickinson
"April Rain Song" by Langston Hughes

Build Grammar Skills: Colons

Use a **colon** to introduce a list of items following an independent clause.

Example: We identified four species of tree: willow, gingko, elm, and maple.

Colons are also used in the following special situations:

Usage	Example
to show time with numerals	12:29 P.M.
after a salutation in a business letter	Dear Ms. Ramos:
on labels for important ideas	**Caution:** High voltage

A. Practice: Rewrite each sentence below, inserting a colon where it is needed.

1. We discussed three figures of speech simile, metaphor, and personification.

   _____

2. According to Emily Dickinson, fame and bees have the following features in common a song, a sting, and a wing.

   _____

3. Langston Hughes imagines the rain as participating in a variety of activities singing a lullaby, making still pools on the sidewalk, and playing a sleep-song on the roof.

   _____

4. Which of these three poets do you prefer Eve Merriam, Emily Dickinson, or Langston Hughes?

   _____

5. The subjects of these poems are as follows trees, bees, and rain.

   _____

B. Writing Application: Copy these items, adding the colon missing from each.

1. I finished writing my paraphrase of "April Rain Song" around 700 P.M.

   _____

2. Dear Governor Wright

   _____

3. People respond to nature in different ways through art, through music, and through poetry.

   _____

4. A simile is usually introduced by one of the following words *like, as, than*, or *resembles*.

   _____

5. **Warning** Trespassers will be prosecuted!

   _____

Unit 9: Poetry

"Simile: Willow and Ginkgo" by Eve Merriam
"Fame Is a Bee" by Emily Dickinson
"April Rain Song" by Langston Hughes

Reading Strategy: Paraphrasing

When you **paraphrase** a piece of writing, you restate it in your own words, keeping the meaning but not the style of what the author wrote. You may find paraphrasing especially helpful when you read poetry because the language and images in poems can sometimes make the author's meaning hard to understand. When you find such a passage, paraphrase it, using clear language to summarize the sense of the poet's words. Reread the poem, keeping your paraphrase in mind. You will find that the poem is now easier to follow. A chart such as the one below can be useful in helping you paraphrase.

DIRECTIONS: In the left column of the following chart are some passages from the poems in this grouping. Paraphrase each passage in the column on the right. The first one has been done as an example.

Poem	Paraphrase
1. The gingko is like a crude sketch Hardly worthy to be signed	The gingko tree looks messy and not at all artistic.
2. *My eyes feast upon the willow,* *But my heart goes to the gingko.*	

3. Fame is a bee.
   It has a song—
   It has a sting—
   Ah, too, it has a wing.	

4. Let the rain kiss you.
   Let the rain beat upon your head
      with silver liquid drops.	

Name _____ Date _____

"**Simile: Willow and Ginkgo**" by Eve Merriam
"**Fame Is a Bee**" by Emily Dickinson
"**April Rain Song**" by Langston Hughes

Literary Analysis: Figurative Language

Poems often express thoughts and feelings by using **figurative language**. The use of *simile*, *metaphor*, and *personification* help you to see and feel things in a new way. Figurative language can also make complicated subjects and emotions easier to understand or imagine.

- **Simile** uses the words *like* or *as* to compare two things that, at first, do not seem alike. "The willow is **like** a nymph with streaming hair."

- **Metaphor** directly compares seemingly unlike things by describing one as if it were the other, without using the words *like* or *as*. "Fame **is** a bee."

- **Personification** gives human qualities to non-human things. "Let the rain **sing** you a lullaby."

A. DIRECTIONS: Circle the letter of the sentence that correctly answers each question below.

1. Which of the following sentences contains a simile?

   a. The willow branches embraced me.

   b. The poem was a ripe apple.

   c. Anna was as frisky as a colt.

2. Which of the following sentences contains an example of metaphor?

   a. The rain was as soft as silken threads.

   b. The halfback was a charging bull.

   c. The wind wrestled with the trees.

3. Which of the following sentences contains an example of personification?

   a. The sun embraced the sea.

   b. She uses words as a sculptor uses clay.

   c. Her greeting was a bouquet of wildflowers.

B. DIRECTIONS: In the following paragraph, identify the figurative language. Circle each example of figurative language and decide whether it is simile, metaphor, or personification. Write **S** for simile, **M** for metaphor and **P** for personification above the circled word or words. The first use of figurative language has been identified for you as an example.

                                            P

It began to drizzle as we walked home. The rain (tapped me on the shoulder.) Gentle raindrops fell like flower petals upon our heads and shoulders. The soft downfall was a surprising gift. We had been working like machines, trying to finish our homework, and now, the little shower was a kindly messenger telling us to forget our worries and cares.

Unit 9: Poetry

"The Ant and the Dove" by Leo Tolstoy
"He Lion, Bruh Bear, and Bruh Rabbit" by Virginia Hamilton
"Señor Coyote and the Tricked Trickster" by I. G. Edmonds

Build Vocabulary

Using Forms of *dignity*

The word *dignity* means "the quality of being worthy." Words that are related to dignity include the idea of worthiness. For example, the Word Bank word *indignantly* means "angrily; as if not worth a response." A *dignitary* is a person worthy of respect. An *indignity* is something that insults one's worth.

A. DIRECTIONS: Choose the correct word to complete each sentence. Write your answers on the lines.

1. He Lion thought of himself as a (dignitary, dignity) _____ among animals.

2. When Bruh Rabbit politely asked him if he could try being more quiet, he Lion considered the question an (indignity, indignantly) _____.

3. He (indignity, indignantly) _____ reminded Bruh Rabbit of his high rank.

4. He lion expressed his belief in his own (dignitary, dignity) _____.

Using the Word Bank

startled	lair	cordial	ungrateful	reproachfully	indignantly

B. DIRECTIONS: Answer each of the following questions to demonstrate your understanding of the Word Bank words. Circle the letter of your choice.

1. Which of the following would be considered a *lair*?

   a. a fox's den   b. a fox's cub

2. In which of the following situations does someone answer *indignantly*?

   a. Bill asked Mary how much money she made, and Mary answered "None of your business."

   b. Susan asked Tom if he would like half of her sandwich, and Tom answered, "Yes. Thank you very much."

3. Which of the following statements would someone make *reproachfully*?

   a. "I think you are very kind."   b. "I think you are very inconsiderate."

4. Which of the following statements would sound *ungrateful*?

   a. "Thank you for the gift."   b. "That's not the gift I wanted."

5. Which of the following might you describe as *cordial*?

   a. a smile   b. an insult

6. Which of the following is more likely to have *startled* someone?

   a. the sound of a soft rainfall   b. the sound of a car alarm

"The Ant and the Dove" by Leo Tolstoy
"He Lion, Bruh Bear, and Bruh Rabbit" by Virginia Hamilton
"Señor Coyote and the Tricked Trickster" by I. G. Edmonds

Build Spelling Skills: Spelling the *j* Sound With *di*

Spelling Strategy Sometimes the *j* sound is spelled with *di*, as it is in the Word Bank word *cordial*. Another word in which the *j* sound is spelled in this way is *soldier*. In certain other words, the *j* sound is spelled with a *d* followed by a *u*. Say the following words to yourself. Notice the *j* sound in each one.

educate   gradual   graduate   individual   schedule

A. Practice: Use one or more of the words listed above to answer each question. Write your answers on the lines.

1. Which word could be used to describe the movement of a glacier? _____

2. Which two words have to do with school? _____

3. Which word names something you might make if you were planning a large project?

   _____

4. Which word means "a single person"? _____

B. Practice: Proofread the following sentences, looking for the errors in the spellings of words that contain the *j* sound. When you find a misspelled word, cross it out, and write it correctly above the line. Write **C** next to the sentence if there are no errors.

____ 1. After Leo Tolstoy gradjuated from law school, he served in the army.

____ 2. His experiences as a soljier taught him a great deal about life.

____ 3. Tolstoy wrote books and essays about religion, philosophy, and education.

____ 4. Many Russians wanted to meet this fascinating and influential indivijual.

____ 5. Although Tolstoy was extremely busy, he received his visitors cordially.

Challenge: In "Señor Coyote and the Tricked Trickster," the mouse *gnaws*, or chews, a piece of leather to free Coyote from a trap. In the word *gnaw* and several other words, the *n* sound at the beginning is spelled *gn*.

   Match each meaning in the left column with the correct word in the right column. Write the letter of your choice on the line next to each meaning. Use a dictionary if you are not sure of any of the words.

____ 1. to grind one's teeth together   a. gnarl

____ 2. an imaginary troll-like creature   b. gnash

____ 3. a large animal from the antelope family   c. gnat

____ 4. a tiny insect   d. gnome

____ 5. to snarl; to growl   e. gnu

Selection Support **207**

Unit 10: The Oral Tradition

"The Ant and the Dove" by Leo Tolstoy
"He Lion, Bruh Bear, and Bruh Rabbit" by Virginia Hamilton
"Señor Coyote and the Tricked Trickster" by I. G. Edmonds

Build Grammar Skills: Capitalize People's Titles

The title of a person is capitalized when it is followed by the person's name or when it is used in place of the person's name.

Examples: Señor Coyote   King Lion   Bruh Bear
               Excuse me, Señor, could you please help me?

Titles showing family relationships are also capitalized when the title is used with the person's name or in place of the person's name. However, when a title comes after a possessive noun or pronoun, it is not capitalized.

Examples: I don't think Father will be able to trick Señor Snake.
               My father has a serious problem.

A. Practice: Rewrite each of the sentences, adding capital letters for titles where necessary.

1. One day señor Coyote and señor Mouse had a quarrel.

   _____

2. Excuse me, señor, my father has been caught by señor Snake.

   _____

3. He Lion thinks he should be call king Lion.

   _____

4. Mouse told the snake about mamacita and her stories.

   _____

5. Bruh Bear sought the advice of bruh Rabbit.

   _____

6. Bruh Bear asked, "Why, lion, do you always roar during the day?"

   _____

B. Writing Application: Write a sentence for each word in parentheses. Make sure to pay close attention to capitalization

1. (señor) _____

   (Señor) _____

2. (bruh) _____

   (Bruh) _____

3. (father) _____

   (Father) _____

4. (king) _____

   (King) _____

"The Ant and the Dove" by Leo Tolstoy
"He Lion, Bruh Bear, and Bruh Rabbit" by Virginia Hamilton
"Señor Coyote and the Tricked Trickster" by I. G. Edmonds

Reading Strategy: Recognizing the Storyteller's Purpose

You will increase you understanding and enjoyment of folk tales if you **recognize the storyteller's purpose**—that is, if you understand the storyteller's reason for sharing the tale.

Many folk tales have more than one purpose. For example, in "He Lion, Bruh Bear, and Bruh Rabbit," certain descriptions, events, and details are included to amuse and entertain readers. Other details are included to teach a lesson in life.

DIRECTIONS: Use the chart below to help you recognize the storyteller's purpose as you read these tales. First, jot down details from the tale. Then, note whether each detail teaches, entertains or both. One example is given.

	Detail	Entertains	Teaches
"The Ant and the Dove"	Humorous description of the quarrel between Coyote and Mouse		
"He Lion. . ."			
"Señor Coyote and the Tricked Trickster"			

"The Ant and the Dove" by Leo Tolstoy
"He Lion, Bruh Bear, and Bruh Rabbit" by Virginia Hamilton
"Señor Coyote and the Tricked Trickster" by I. G. Edmonds

Literary Analysis: Folk Tales

Folk tales are the stories that the people, or "folk," of a country or culture have passed down from generation to generation. These tales may entertain, teach a lesson, or explain something in nature. Through their details and their messages, these stories also reflect the cultures in which they originated.

DIRECTIONS: Read each of the following passages. Then write your answers to the questions.

"The Ant and the Dove"
   A thirsty ant went to the stream to drink. Suddenly it got caught in a whirlpool and was almost carried away.
   At that moment, a dove was passing by with a twig in its beak. The dove dropped the twig for the tiny insect to grab hold of. So it was that the ant was saved.
   A few days later a hunter was about to catch the dove in his net. When the ant saw what was happening, it walked right up to the man and bit him on the foot. Startled, the man dropped the net. And the dove, thinking that you never can tell how or when a kindness may be repaid, flew away.

1. Do you think the purpose of "The Ant and the Dove" is to teach a lesson in life or to explain something in nature? Why?

   _____

   _____

2. Do you think that the people who passed the story along through the years thought that kindness toward others is important? Why?

   _____

   _____

"Señor Coyote and the Tricked Trickster"
   One day long ago in Mexico's land of sand and giant cactus, Señor Coyote and Señor Mouse had a quarrel.
   None now alive can remember why, but recalling what spirited caballeros these two were, I suspect that it was that some small thing that meant little.
   Be that as it may, these two took their quarrels seriously and for a long time would not speak to each other.

3. Identify three details that are related to Mexican culture.

   _____

   _____

4. Which of these details do you think adds a humorous and entertaining touch to the story? Why?

   _____

   _____

"Why Monkeys Live in Trees" by Julius Lester
"Arachne" by Olivia E. Coolidge
"A Crippled Boy" by Tran My-Van
"The Three Wishes" by Ricardo E. Alegría

Build Vocabulary

Using the Word Root *-mort-*

The Word Bank word *mortal* contains the word root *-mort-*, meaning "death." Here is a list of words with the word root *-mort-*:

mortal: able to die, or a person who will not live forever

immortal: able to live forever, or a being (such as a god) who will live forever

mortician: person who prepares the dead for burial

mortify: make feel humble and ashamed

mortuary: building where the dead are kept until buried

A. DIRECTIONS: Use one of the words above to complete each of the sentences below.

1. The captain will _____ me if she yells at me in front of the whole team.

2. The god granted three wishes to the worthy _____.

3. The _____ helped to plan my great-grandmother's funeral.

4. The body was laid in the _____ until the funeral.

5. The ancient Greeks believed their gods were all-powerful and _____.

Using the Word Bank

obscure	mortal	obstinacy
embraced	covetousness	

B. DIRECTIONS: Match each word in the left column with its definition in the right column. Write the letter of the definition on the line next to the word it defines.

____ 1. obscure   a. stubbornness

____ 2. mortal   b. wanting what another person has

____ 3. obstinacy   c. not well known

____ 4. embraced   d. clasped in the arms

____ 5. covetousness   e. referring to humans who will die

El Sereno Middle School
2839 North Eastern Avenue
Los Angeles, California 90032

"Why Monkeys Live in Trees" by Julius Lester
"Arachne" by Olivia E. Coolidge
"A Crippled Boy" by Tran My-Van
"The Three Wishes" by Ricardo E. Alegría

Build Spelling Skills: -cy and -sy

Spelling Strategy Many words end in the letters -cy or -sy. The two word endings are spelled differently and have different meanings but the same pronunciation. It might help to remember that the suffix -cy often means "the quality or state of." Here are several examples:

obstina<u>cy</u> the state of being obstinate or stubborn

accura<u>cy</u> the quality of being accurate

courtesy politeness

controversy argument

prophecy prediction of the future

A. Practice: Write the word from the list that above that best completes each of the following sentences.

1. In my family _____ is expected of everyone.

2. Often in myths, a character makes a _____ about the future.

3. We questioned the _____ of the news report.

4. Our class had a _____ over where to go on our class trip.

5. Because of his _____, he would not change his mind, no matter what.

B. Practice: Complete the following letter. Using the context clues, choose four words from the list above to fill in the blanks.

Dear Helen,

   I went to visit our old friend Arachne the other day. I was worried, because I'd heard that she has gotten into a _____ with the goddess Athene about who is the better weaver. I've always thought Arachne could use a lesson in _____, especially when talking to goddesses. Although she weaves with amazing _____, I would make a _____ that her rudeness will get her into trouble some day. She wasn't at home when I got there, but in the place where she usually sits and weaves, I saw a large spider spinning a web. What do you think happened to Arachne?

                                        Your friend,
                                        Iris

Challenge: The Word Bank word *bellowed* contains several smaller words not related to its meaning. One example is owe. Can you find at least five other small words in *bellowed*? Write your answers on the lines provided.

_____ _____ _____ _____ _____

"Why Monkeys Live in Trees" by Julius Lester
"Arachne" by Olivia E. Coolidge
"A Crippled Boy" by Tran My-Van
"The Three Wishes" by Ricardo E. Alegría

Building Grammar Skills: Variety in Sentence Structure and Style

Variety is the spice of life. It's also the spice of good writing. If every sentence began with the subject, a story would sound monotonous, and the reader would become bored. You can keep your writing fresh and interesting by varying the structure and style of your sentences.

One way to vary a sentence is to begin it with an adverb, a prepositional phrase, or a subordinate clause rather than with the subject.

Adverb: Never had Arachne been matched against anyone whose skill was equal to her own.

Prepositional phrase: At that exact moment , one of Leopard's children ran up to him.

Subordinate clause: When the goddess saw this insult , she did not wait until the cloth was judged.

Another way to vary your writing is to use different kinds of sentences, not just declarative sentences that make a statement.

Interrogative: How did Arachne dare to challenge the immortals?

Imperative: Rest content with your fame of being the best spinner.

Exclamatory: What a clever trick the moneys played on King Gorilla!

A. Practice: Write *S* if the sentence begins with the subject, *A* if it begins with an adverb, *P* if it begins with a prepositional phrase, and *C* if it begins with a subordinate clause.

_____ 1. After that the king always treasured Theo's presence.

_____ 2. No sooner had he said these words than the donkey ears vanished.

_____ 3. Another mandarin opened his mouth to speak.

_____ 4. When she heard the people murmur, she would stop her work and turn around angrily.

_____ 5. Finally, Leopard discovered Monkey's trick.

B. Writing Application: Use the directions in parentheses to revise each declarative sentence below so that it is interrogative, imperative, or exclamatory. Feel free to change some of the words around to form your new sentences.

1. Leopard admired his beautiful coat and whiskers. (interrogative)

_____

2. Athene stepped forward angrily. (exclamatory)

_____

3. Athene told the wicked girl to live on. (imperative)

_____

4. Arachne became a little dusty brown spider. (exclamatory)

_____

Unit 10: The Oral Tradition

"Why Monkeys Live in Trees" by Julius Lester
"Arachne" by Olivia E. Coolidge
"A Crippled Boy" by Tran My-Van
"The Three Wishes" by Ricardo E. Alegría

Reading Strategy: Predicting

When you read a story or book it is fun to **predict** what is going to happen next. Many times the author will give you clues as to what will happen. For example, when you read in "Why Monkeys Live in Trees" that the mound of black dust is a mound of black pepper, you might predict that the other animals won't have any easier time eating it than Hippopotamus did.

You can base your predictions on what you have already read. Often, folk tales are more predictable than other kinds of stories because they usually follow a pattern. You can be fairly certain that kind and generous characters will be rewarded, whereas wicked or greedy characters will most likely be punished.

DIRECTIONS: Read each passage below. Then, on the lines provided, write a prediction about what will happen and your reasons for making the prediction.

1. "Why Monkeys Live in Trees"
From his limb high in the tree Leopard could see into the tall grasses when Monkey went to rest. Wait a minute! Leopard thought something was suddenly wrong with his eyes because he thought he saw a hundred monkeys hiding in the tall grass.

Prediction:_____

Reason for Prediction:_____

2. "Arachne"
Thus as Athene stepped back a pace to watch Arachne finishing her work, she saw that the maiden had taken for her design a pattern of scenes which showed evil or unworthy actions of the gods, how they had deceived fair maidens, resorted to trickery, and appeared on earth from time to time in the form of poor and humble people.

Prediction:_____

Reason for Prediction:_____

3. "The Three Wishes"
"It doesn't seem possible that you could be so stupid! You've wasted one of our wishes, and now we have only two left! May you grow ears of a donkey!"
He [the woodsman] had no sooner said the words than his wife's ears began to grow, and they continued to grow until they changed into the pointed, furry ears of a donkey.

Prediction:_____

Reason for Prediction:_____

"Why Monkeys Live in Trees" by Julius Lester
"Arachne" by Olivia E. Coolidge
"A Crippled Boy" by Tran My-Van
"The Three Wishes" by Ricardo E. Alegría

Literary Analysis: Oral Tradition

Myths and folk tales are stories that people have told other over and over again down through generations. They are created from what is called the **oral tradition**. These stories often reflect the traditions, beliefs, and values of the people who created them. Many myths and folk tales are told for the purpose of teaching an important lesson about life.

DIRECTIONS: Read the following passages from the selection. Then fill in the blanks by answering the questions, basing your answers on details in the passage.

1. "Why Monkeys Live in Trees"
The monkeys ran in all directions. When the other animals saw monkeys running from the grasses, they realized that the monkeys had tricked them and started chasing them. Even King Gorilla joined in the chase. He wanted his gold back.
The only way the monkeys could escape was to climb to the very tops of the tallest trees where no one else, not even Leopard, could climb.
And that's why monkeys live in trees to this very day.

What lesson about life does this tale teach? _____

2. "Arachne"
At that the body of Arachne shriveled up, and her legs grew tiny, spindly, and distorted. There before the eyes of the spectators hung a little dusty brown spider on a slender thread.
All spiders descend from Arachne, and as the Greeks watched them spinning their thread wonderfully fine, they remembered the contest with Athene and thought that it was not right for even the best of men to claim equality with the gods.

What lesson about life does this tale teach? _____

3. "A Crippled Boy"
For once the king could speak as much as he wanted without being interrupted. The King was extremely pleased with his success and the help that Theo had given him.

What lesson about life does this tale teach? _____

4. "The Three Wishes"
The old man left, but before going, he told them that they had undergone this test in order to learn that there can be happiness in poverty just as there can be unhappiness in riches.

What lesson about life does this tale teach? _____